THE SMOKE AND THE FIRE

By the same author:

MONS: THE RETREAT TO VICTORY (1960; 1991)

DOUGLAS HAIG: THE EDUCATED SOLDIER (1963)

THE WESTERN FRONT (1964)

GENERAL JACK'S DIARY (1964)

THE GREAT WAR: AN ILLUSTRATED HISTORY (1965)

THE LIFE AND TIMES OF LORD MOUNTBATTEN (1968; 1980)

IMPACTS OF WAR 1914 AND 1918 (1970)

THE MIGHTY CONTINENT (1974)

TRAFALGAR (1976)

THE ROAD TO PASSCHENDAELE (1977)

TO WIN A WAR: 1918 THE YEAR OF VICTORY (1978)

WHITE HEAT: THE NEW WARFARE 1914-18 (1982; 1992)

THE RIGHT OF THE LINE: THE ROYAL AIR FORCE
IN THE EUROPEAN WAR 1939-1945 (1985)

BUSINESS IN GREAT WATERS: THE U-BOAT WARS 1916-1945
(1989)

The Smoke and the Fire

Myths and Anti-Myths of War
1861–1945

JOHN TERRAINE

'No smoke without fire'
(OLD SAYING)

LEO COOPER
London

First published in 1980 by Sidgwick & Jackson Ltd
Republished in 1992 by
LEO COOPER
190 Shaftesbury Avenue, London WC2H 8JL
an imprint of
Pen & Sword Books Ltd,
47 Church Street, Barnsley, South Yorkshire S70 2AS

Copyright © John Terraine 1980, 1992

Picture research by Annie Horton

ISBN 0 85052 330 3

A CIP catalogue record for this book is available
from the British Library

Revisions typeset by Yorkshire Web, Barnsley, South Yorkshire
in Times Roman 11 point

Printed by Redwood Press Limited
Melksham, Wiltshire

To The Historian Thucydides
who taught me a lesson

'. . . I do not think that one will be far wrong in accepting the conclusions I have reached from the evidence which I have put forward. It is better evidence than that of the poets, who exaggerate the importance of their themes, or of the prose chroniclers, who are less interested in telling the truth than in catching the attention of their public, whose authorities cannot be checked, and whose subject-matter, owing to the passage of time, is mostly lost in the unreliable streams of mythology. We may claim instead to have used only the plainest evidence and to have reached conclusions which are reasonably accurate . . .'

Thucydides: *The Peloponnesian War,* Book 1, Chapter 1, translation by Rex Warner (Penguin Classic, 1954)

ACKNOWLEDGMENTS

The author and publishers would like to thank the following for permission to publish extracts from copyright material in their possession: Ernest Benn Ltd for *From Chauffeur to Brigadier* by Brigadier-General C. D. Baker-Carr (1930); Cassell Ltd for *Into Battle* by Sir John Glubb (1977) and *The Second World War* by Sir Winston Churchill (1950); J. M. Dent & Sons Ltd for *Sir Douglas Haig's Despatches* edited by Lieutenant-Colonel J. H. Boraston (1919); the Estate of Sir John Monash for *The Australian Victories in France in 1918* (1936) and *War Letters* (1925) by Sir John Monash; Eyre & Spottiswoode (Publishers) Ltd for *The Private Papers of Douglas Haig 1914–1919* edited by Robert Blake (1952) and *In London During the Great War* by Michael MacDonagh (1935); Faber and Faber Ltd for *In Parenthesis* by David Jones; John Farquharson Ltd for *The American Civil War* by Peter J. Parish (Eyre Methuen Ltd, 1975); Hamish Hamilton Ltd for *Lincoln and His Generals* by T. H. Williams (1952); David Higham Associates Ltd for *The Conduct of War 1789–1961* (Eyre & Spottiswoode [Publishers] Ltd, 1961), *The Decisive Battles of the Western World* (Eyre & Spottiswoode [Publishers] Ltd, 1956), and *The Generalship of Ulysses S. Grant* (John Murray [Publishers] Ltd, 1929) by Major-General J. F. C. Fuller, and *Defeat into Victory* by Field Marshal Lord Slim (Cassell Ltd, 1956); Houghton Mifflin Inc. for *The Second World War* by Sir Winston Churchill (1950); Alfred A. Knopf Inc. for *Lincoln and his Generals* by T. H. Williams (1952); Little, Brown and Company for *Grant Takes Command* by Bruce Catton (J. M. Dent & Sons Ltd, 1968); Macmillan, London and Basingstoke for *The Anvil of War* by F. S. Oliver (1936); Oxford University Press for *The Great War and Modern Memory* by Paul Fussell (1975); and George Sassoon for *Base Details* and *The General* by Siegfried Sassoon.

CONTENTS

LIST OF PLATES

INTRODUCTION

On the sixtieth anniversary of the Armistice which ended the First World War, 11 November 1978, *The Times* Saturday Review published an article of mine entitled 'A Comfortless Mythology'. This dealt, as best it could within the compass of a newspaper article, with some of the strange, discouraging mythology which has grown up during the last six decades on the subject of that war. I was surprised—perhaps foolishly—at the impact the article seemed to have. I had written it in a mood chiefly of impatience at the sheer persistence, despite their palpable silliness, of some of the myths— the machine-gun myth, the tank myth, the cavalry myth, and so on, all the way from the Angels of Mons to the 'Futility of War'. It was encouraging to see how interested people were in the demolition of some of these curiosities; 'debunking' does, of course, often have an entertainment value which I had failed to take into account.

In fairness to some of the originators of the First World War myths, it must be added that they, in their day, were also doing some debunking—trying to rid a too-credulous public of the 'death or glory' images, what one soldier-writer (Sidney Rogerson) called 'the grim-smiling-faces-of-undaunted-boys' war of the early correspondents with attacking battalions dribbling footballs across a sporting No-Man's-Land'.[1] He mentions other myths, too, among them 'the Generals' war, of the clean map-squares, in which there was never any muddle, no one was ever afraid, and the troops always advanced, by the right, in perfect formation, "as if on parade". Even when they came back again, as they not infrequently did, they retired reluctantly, in good order, dressed by the left.'

There was for a long time, I am afraid, a lot too much of that sort of thing. My first school prize (1933) was a book entitled *The Crown of Honour: Being stories of Heroism, Gallantry, Magnanimity, and Devotion from the Great War of 1914–18*,[2] selected and arranged by William Moodie, who was also author of *Tools for Teachers*— which gives one to think a little. Two brief quotations from my uplifting prize will amply suffice to indicate its message:

A wounded private of the Seaforths heard that a woman with a new-born baby was in a cottage in a village that was being shelled by the Germans. He left the Red Cross van and rushed in and saved both mother and child as a shell crashed through the roof. As he left, another shell demolished the cottage.

'You have been badly wounded, comrade,' said a Frenchman to a British officer, as he noticed a blood-stained gash on the left side of his khaki tunic. 'It is nothing,' was the quick response. 'The Germans sought my heart, but they have not found it. I have given it to France.'

Unfortunately, the act of sweeping away this sort of rubbish led to the opposite extravagances—what Sidney Rogerson called 'the war of the Sewers, in which no one ever laughed, those who were not melancholy mad were alcoholically hysterical, and most of the action took place in or near the crude latrines of the period'.

This was the first 'debunking'; its excesses were more mischievous than those that it replaced—as Sidney Rogerson said:

'In its distortion, the soldier looks in vain for the scenes he knew.'

Weaned on such soft diet as *The Crown of Honour,* then appetized afresh by the sharper-flavoured victuals of the Disenchanted, I spent a long time with myths. In due course, however, I came to see that the First World War, whatever else it may have been, was unquestionably a major watershed in history. I realized that, for that reason, it behoves us to make an attempt to understand it, and in order to do that it is necessary to push aside all the mythology, no matter how seemingly authoritative. (How powerful myth can be is shown by the fact that one learned writer whom I shall soon be quoting appears to think that the First World War does not belong to history at all, see P. Fussell, page 130). Prompted by friendly publishers, I perceived that apart from the various books on First World War themes that I have already written, most of what I have been writing in articles or lecturing about during the last, say, twenty years has been an attempt to clear out myth and discover countervailing truths about the watershed—to blow away the smoke and get at the fire. That is what this book is about; a substantial amount of it is fresh material, but parts have appeared in print before, in somewhat different forms, in *The Times,* in the *Journal* of the Royal United Services Institute for Defence Studies and in *History Today*.

It is impossible, in my opinion, to establish where the First World War stands in history, and what was really happening during the course of it, without reference to the experiences which are truly comparable to it; there are only two—the American Civil War of 1861–65, and the Second World War, 1939–45. These three are the great wars of the First Industrial Revolution. They throw light upon each other, they make each other comprehensible. Their technological bases are similar, their social and political backgrounds have important resemblances, their military problems and solutions also have strong resemblances, their consequences are profound. I would go so far as to say that to write sensibly about any of them, it is necessary always to have the other two in mind. Also, they constitute a chapter that has ended; after August 1945 war was never the same. Hanging over all the military proceedings of the great powers since that time has been the shadow of the bomb, the product of a new technology, the decisive element in a new Industrial Revolution.

Lincoln and Grant, von Schlieffen, Ludendorff, Foch and Haig, Hitler, Churchill, Roosevelt, Stalin, Zhukov and Eisenhower, whether they liked it or not, all operated in the period of the mass armies, and were accordingly subject to the same compelling logistical disciplines. Handling very large armies is *not* the same as handling small ones—as Napoleon discovered to his chagrin in 1812; the 'million-armies' of the First Industrial Revolution are a very particular phenomenon. Naturally, the introduction of the mass element profoundly affected generalship; the mass imposed its own strategic restraints; it also tended (as in all large organizations) towards administrative overweight and anonymity at the top. It was the middle part of the period (the First World War) which first experienced the full force of these maladies (and therefore produced the largest crop of myth); the sickness constituted, in the words of a general of the old school (Sir Ian Hamilton), 'a plague worse than those of Pharaoh: a General Staff war'. The beginnings of this condition, however, were already to be seen in 1864, and the fruits were apparent in the Second World War, in the great planning staffs of the Western Allies, the Combined Chiefs, the COSSAC organization, SHAEF and the rest. Paradoxically, it was the very largeness of these staffs which freed some leaders again to make a personal impact—but very few.

Ultimately, the war of masses made possible by one technology produced, as we might expect, a weapon of mass destruction, made possible by a new technology. I am not here concerned with that— beyond noting that what seemed about to dehumanize war completely has so far done nothing of the kind. Guerilla warfare and counter-insurgency—the main war-styles of our time—are highly personalized experiences depending greatly on personal human skills and human psychology. Also, they have long histories. Just as, contrary to much contemporary belief, military history did *not* come to a stop with the gas that stopped men breathing in 1915, thirty-five years of continuing military activity show that it did not come to a halt with atomic devastation in 1945 either. But certainly a remarkable phase did end in that year, and can now be studied in its entirety. I hope this book, by clearing away some of the myths which obscure the warfare of 1861–1945, and exposing some of its realities, may make a useful contribution to such studies.

JOHN TERRAINE

January 1980

1   Sidney Rogerson, *Twelve Days,* Arthur Barker, 1933, pp. xv–xvi.
2   James Clarke and Co.

I

MYTH AND LEGEND:

The Angels and the Hordes

'A cloud came out of a clear sky and stood between the two armies, and in the cloud men saw the chariots and horses of a heavenly host. Von Kluck turned back from pursuing, and the English went on unharmed.'

(*The Crown of Honour*, p. 126)

'. . . an immense force of Russian soldiers . . . passing through England on their way to France...'

(Michael MacDonagh, *In London During the Great War*)

War and legend are inseparable, which is scarcely surprising in view of the stresses to which the human imagination is subjected in war. Legend, unlike myth, is relatively innocent; according to the *Shorter Oxford English Dictionary* it is 'an unauthentic story handed down by tradition and popularly regarded as historical'. A myth, on the other hand, is 'a purely fictitious narrative . . . embodying some popular idea concerning natural or historical phenomena'. It is, says the Dictionary, 'often used vaguely to include any narrative having fictitious elements'—an attribute of which I propose to take full advantage. The key phrase, I suggest—revealing the real mischief of myth—is 'embodying some popular idea', because this is where doctrine and dogma enter the lists and usually inflict heavy defeats on truth.

Legend is often just naïve—none more so than the early legends of 1914. The Battle of Mons, the first action of the British

Expeditionary Force in the First World War, was fought on 23 August; it entered the realm of legend within a fortnight, and it remains firmly there. As early as 5 September Brigadier-General John Charteris recorded in a letter that the story of the 'Angel of Mons' was 'going strong through the 2nd Corps . . . how the angel of the Lord on the traditional white horse and clad all in white with flaming sword, faced the advancing Germans at Mons and forbade their further progress'.[1] Very soon similar stories were appearing in the British press, most notably one by Arthur Machen entitled 'The Bowmen' in the *Evening News* on 29 September. Machen substituted 'the bowmen of Agincourt' for the Heavenly Host as allies against the 'Prussian hordes', and claimed that his story was the unwitting origin of all the accounts of supernatural intervention in the Mons campaign.

It was no such thing; General Charteris's letter preceded Machen's story by over three weeks, and there were others. Private Frank Richards wrote of the retreat from Le Cateau (26 August): 'If any angels were seen on the Retirement, as the newspaper accounts said they were, they were seen that night. March, march, for hour after hour, without no halt: we were now breaking into the fifth day of continuous marching with practically no sleep in between . . . Stevens said: "There's a fine castle there, see?" pointing to one side of the road. But there was nothing there. Very nearly everyone were seeing things, we were all so dead beat.'[2] Non-existent buildings, mysterious beings—all these were commonplace. The *Evening News* itself had already printed (14 September—a fortnight earlier than Machen) a letter from 'a distinguished Lieutenant-Colonel' who said:

On the night of the 27th I was riding along in the column with two other officers. We had been talking and doing our best to keep from falling asleep on our horses.

As we rode along I became conscious of the fact that, in the fields on both sides of the road along which we were marching, I could see a very large body of horsemen.

These horsemen had the appearance of squadrons of cavalry, and they seemed to be riding across the fields and going in the same direction as we were going, and keeping level with us.

The night was not very dark, and I fancied that I could see squadron upon squadron of these cavalrymen quite distinctly.

I did not say a word about it at first, but I watched them for about twenty minutes. The other two officers had stopped talking.

At last one of them asked me if I saw anything in the fields. I then told him what I had seen. The third officer then confessed that he too had been watching these horsemen for the past twenty minutes.

So convinced were we that they were really cavalry that, at the next halt, one of the officers took a party of men out to reconnoitre, and found no one there.

The night then grew darker, and we saw no more.

The same phenomenon was seen by many men in our column. Of course, we were all dog tired and overtaxed, but it is an extraordinary thing that the same phenomenon should be witnessed by so many different people.

I myself am absolutely convinced that I saw these horsemen; and I feel sure that they did not exist only in my imagination. I do not attempt to explain the mystery – I only state facts.

It is obvious from the whole tone of this letter that the colonel did not consider these horsemen to be hostile. Nothing, in those days, was more dreaded than the sudden descent of enemy cavalry upon a retreating force, but there is no hint of alarm in the officer's narrative. The horsemen, like the bowmen and the angels, were protectors; these were kindly legends which no doubt helped to fortify the spirits of very weary men.

Later, however, Mons attracted less kindly legends (part, indeed, of the whole unkind myth of that War). The grim phrase was heard, 'hanging on the wire at Mons', and sometimes even 'gassed at Mons'. But there were no wire entanglements at Mons; it was an encounter battle, with half the British Expeditionary Force only arriving on the field at 3 a.m. on the day of the battle. If there had been any wire, it would, of course, have been British, with the attacking Germans hanging on it – but the B.E.F. possessed no such luxuries, and even if it had there would hardly have been time to use them because the first shots were fired at 6 a.m. As for gas, that did not enter the War's armoury until April 1915. Both these sayings were the products of sardonic soldiers' humour, intended to harrow gullible civilians. Later they were subsumed into the 'horror myth' lock, stock and barrel.

We find in 1978 in what purports to be a work of reference, 'The British fought a great battle at Mons . . . which did much to slow the German advance.' This is legend: the scale of the one-day Battle of Mons may be judged by its 1,600 British casualties. Set beside what was happening elsewhere along the front, and what the Army was to experience later, Mons scarcely rates as a battle at all; there is certainly no evidence that it slowed the Germans to any noticeable extent. The famous retreat, needless to say, has received similar inflationary treatment; thus a serious American writer could still say in 1956 that the B.E.F. was 'decimated in the terrible retreat from Mons'. 'Decimated' is a word that the military historian does well to shun; it means too many things to too many people. The B.E.F.'s actual casualties were about 15,000 (out of just over 100,000) in fourteen days, at the end of which it passed straight to counter-attack. French casualties during the same period were 210,000. But 'decimated' nicely fits the Great War casualty myth.

In the strain and over-excitement accompanying the opening of Britain's first great war for ninety-nine years, it was not only exhausted soldiers who suffered from hallucinations. Michael MacDonagh of *The Times* recorded the birth of another familiar legend in London on 8 September:

There is being circulated everywhere a story that an immense force of Russian soldiers – little short of a million, it is said – have passed, or are still passing, through England on their way to France. They are being brought from Archangel – just in time before that port was closed by ice – landed at Leith, and carried at night in hundreds of trains straight to ports on the south coast. This great news is vouched by people likely to be well informed, but it is being kept secret by the authorities – not a word about it is allowed in the newspapers – until all the Russians have arrived at the Western Front. It is said in confirmation that belated wayfarers at railway stations throughout the country saw long train after long train running through with blinds down, but still allowing glimpses of carriages packed with fierce-looking bearded fellows in fur hats.

What a surprise is in store for the Germans when they find themselves faced on the west with hordes of Russians, while other hordes are pressing on them from the east.[3]

Alas, there was no such surprise in store. One admires the ingenuity of the legend – especially the touch of the Russians leaving before Archangel became frozen, although this conflicts with the accounts of witnesses who asserted that they knew the horde was Russian because the men had snow on their boots. Yet, snow or no snow, it was nothing but legend, harmless and well-intentioned. Myth was another matter; Michael MacDonagh also reports the absurd spy myth which seized upon a large section of the public in the first weeks of war and inspired great hatred and harshness towards enemy aliens right to the very end. MacDonagh diagnosed in the most vociferous of the spy maniacs a bad attack of hysteria:

Their nerves are still jangling, and they seem to be enveloped in a mysterious darkness, haunted by goblins in the form of desperate German spies, and they can find no light or comfort afforded them by Press or Government. . . . The wildest stories are being circulated by

these people of outrages committed by Germans in our midst. Attempts
have been made to destroy the permanent ways of railways and wreck
trains! Signalmen in their boxes, armed sentries at bridges, have been
overpowered by bands of Germans who arrived speedily on the scene
and, their foul work done, as speedily vanished! Germans have been
caught red-handed on the East Coast, signalling with lights to German
submarines. Carrier pigeons have been found in German houses! More
damnable still, bombs have been discovered in the trunks of German
governesses in English county families![4]

These were cruel myths which caused much suffering, usually to
the innocent. The War itself, of course, was also cruel – very cruel
indeed, as they generally are; in one area of its cruelty myth and
truth mingled with confusing effect, the fire making the smoke and
the smoke hiding the fire. The word 'atrocities' was heard very
early in the war, on both sides.

----

1   Brigadier-General John Charteris, *At G.H.Q.*, Cassell, 1931, pp. 25–6.
2   Frank Richards, *Old Soldiers Never Die,* Faber Paperback, 1964, p. 19.
3   Michael MacDonagh, *In London During the Great War,* Eyre & Spottiswoode, 1935,
    pp. 21–2.
4   Ibid., pp. 32–3.

II

THE SMOKE AND THE FIRE:

Atrocities and Reprisals

'War is cruelty, and you cannot refine it.' (General W. T. Sherman, 1864)

'Brutes they were, and brutes they remain.' (Arthur Balfour, referring to the sinking of the *S.S. Leinster* by a German submarine on 16 October 1918)

In a moment of considerable insight, Goethe said of his fellow-countrymen: 'If there has to be a choice between injustice and disorder, the German prefers injustice.'[1] The German military mind, above all, abhorred disorder, and as the majestic opening measures of the Schlieffen Plan drew the German armies into Belgium on the morning of 4 August a horrid memory of disorder lurked in the minds of the German leaders. They remembered 1870, when in a few weeks the great von Moltke (the elder) had completely overthrown the regular forces of France. To the orderly German mind, these unquestioned victories (culminating in the surrender of Napoleon III and the French field army at Sedan) should have been the end of the matter. Instead, a French Government of National Defence declared war *à outrance* and proceeded to raise a 'National Army' while Paris endured a siege which tied down nearly a quarter of a million German soldiers. All this was distasteful enough, but far more revolting to the Germans was the guerilla warfare which they also encountered in the hour of victory in battle.

The *francs-tireurs* ('free-shooters') became a legend of the Franco-Prussian War whose echoes were loud and sinister. These were irregulars, loosely organized in bands of varying numbers *(corps francs)*, wearing any kind of uniform or none,[2] whose purpose was to harass the German lines of communication and attack their small detachments as the Spaniards had done very effectively to the French during the Peninsular War, and as the Germans liked to think they had also done in the 'War of Liberation' against Napoleon I in 1813.[3] Bloodthirsty proclamations and exhortations contributed powerfully to the *franc-tireur* legend; one public figure urged that they should 'harass the enemy and hang from trees all the enemies they can take well and truly by the neck, after having mutilated them'. The same amiable person also advocated bringing over from Algeria 20,000–30,000 Kabyle tribesmen 'and throwing them into Germany with leave to burn, pillage and rape all they find on the way'. He was ahead of his time, as those who had the misfortune to encounter the Moroccan *'goumiers'* of the Second World War will testify.[4] The actual performance of the *francs-tireurs* of 1870–71 was less lurid than the accompanying rhetoric. In all some 300 bands were formed, with a maximum strength of nearly 58,000 officers and men. Between them, they killed about 1,000 Germans, but far more important was the alarm they caused, which tied down about 120,000 German troops (nearly a quarter of their whole army in France) on the lines of communication.[5] They certainly made a profound impression on the German commanders; Bismarck told a French negotiator, 'We are hunting them down pitilessly. They are not soldiers: we are treating them as murderers.' So the pendulum rhythm established itself: ambush, reprisal, counter-reprisal, worse reprisal. In the end, 'each nation came to believe that it alone was upholding civilisation against a race of barbarians which could only be bullied into submission by brute force. Forty-four years later that belief was to be even more disastrously revived.'[6]

The unpleasant memory was still vivid after forty-four years. On the very first night of the First World War, 4 August, General Ludendorff ended a tiring day in the little Belgian town of Hervé; he tells us:

The whole town was intact and we went to bed with a quiet mind. During the night I was awakened by brisk firing, some of which was directed on our house. The *franc-tireur* warfare in Belgium had begun. It broke out everywhere the next day, and it was this sort of thing which aroused that intense bitterness that during those first years characterized the war on the Western front in contrast to the feeling prevailing in the East. The Belgian Government took a grave responsibility upon itself. It had systematically organized civilian warfare. . . . For my part, I had taken the field with chivalrous and humane conceptions of warfare. This *franctireur* warfare was bound to disgust any soldier. My soldierly spirit suffered bitter disillusion.[7]

Once more the rhythm of the pendulum began: Hervé, intact on 4 August, did not long remain so. A war correspondent of the *Berliner Tageblatt,* Heinrich Binder, on an official tour a few days later, inspected Hervé. It was 'razed to the ground', he reported. 'Of about five hundred houses at Hervé only nineteen remain. Corpses are lying all over the place; everywhere there is the smell of burning. The church is a broken heap of ruins . . .'[8]

Hervé was made an example; there were many others. And, as always when such deeds are committed, myths sprouted and multiplied. The Germans were accused of every kind of unspeakable atrocity; they retorted with variations of Ludendorff's words, 'the Belgian Government can alone be held responsible.' The Belgians, naturally, denied that they were conducting *franctireur* warfare; they denied civilian involvement, and insisted that shots fired at the Germans were fired by properly constituted forces – army detachments or stragglers and Civil Guards. I shall have more to say about the latter in a moment; just now it has to be said that two streams of propaganda here found themselves in conflict – the propaganda of Belgian innocence and the propaganda of Belgian patriotism. Thus in a contemporary narrative of the War we find;

The people of the Ardennes and of Belgian Luxemburg were not prepared to allow the enemy to invade them without resistance. They had prepared for the most troublesome of all campaigns for a regular army to meet – a peasant war. Every rustic had his weapon, and every man was anxious to use it. Not only in the Ardennes, but away up towards the Dutch frontier, the feeling of the people was everywhere the same. They hated the Germans . . . The countryside was made ready. Tracts of roadways were undermined, to be blown up as German soldiers went over them; barricades were piled up. The people meant to make their foe pay dearly for every yard.[9]

Making allowances for the over-excited language, there seems little reason to doubt that in essence this was true, certainly in the Walloon districts nearest to Germany. There was a spontaneous instinct towards what the Second World War generation would approvingly call a 'Resistance Movement'. The only 'fault' of the Belgian Government lay in not forbidding it – though as soon as the dreadful consequences were appreciated it did precisely that. Why, after all, should the Government have forbidden its citizens to resist the invaders? The position of neutrals in war had been defined in the Fifth Convention of the Hague Peace Conference in 1907, to which Germany was a signatory. Belligerents were forbidden to move troops or supplies across neutral territory; Article 5 of the Convention went further – it stated that neutrals *must not allow* such acts to occur. Article 10 stated that resistance to such acts by a neutral could not be regarded as itself a hostile act. The Belgian Government was merely conforming to what it took to be international law; its fault was simply being naïve – not for the last time. The Germans scorned neutrality; as long ago as 1900 the German Government had knowingly acquiesced in General von Schlieffen's decision to march through Belgium.[10]

There is only one word that may be added in mitigation (or, rather, explanation) of the German frame of mind. Ludendorff, accusing the Belgian Government of 'systematically organizing civilian warfare', adds: 'The *Garde Civique*, which in the days of peace had its own arms and special uniforms, were able to appear sometimes in one garb and sometimes in another.' He had a point – not a very strong one, but a point nevertheless. Of all military costumes in 1914, that of the Belgian Civil Guards must have been the least inspiring: a very plain overcoat, surmounted by what appears to be a cross between a top-hat and a bowler. In the heat of the early actions there was some excuse for mistaking these men for civilians; there was no excuse for continuing to do so. The Germans were on stronger ground in regard to Belgian reservists, called up too late and going into action without proper uniforms and equipment. But all these fine points of law fade into insignificance beside the overwhelming fact that the Germans had no business to be in Belgium at all.

There is, moreover, a distinct suggestion of orchestration in the immediate accusations of *franc-tireur* and other anti-German activity. It is, to say the least, remarkable that a seaman of the High Seas Fleet, far away in Wilhelmshaven, could write on 5 August, with the War only twenty-four hours old: 'Terrible reports of atrocities against German citizens arrived from Belgium. Our nation is not at all prepared for war, I thought as I read this.'[11] One cannot help feeling that the German Press was all too well prepared. It was only three days later (8 August) that Captain

Walter Bloem of the *12th Brandenburg Grenadiers* recorded on his way to the frontier:

We bought the morning papers at a wayside station and read, amazed, of the experiences of those of our troops already across the Belgian frontier – of priests, armed, at the head of marauding bands of Belgian civilians, committing every kind of atrocity, and putting the deeds of 1870 into the shade; of treacherous ambushes of patrols, and sentries found later with eyes pierced and tongues cut off, of poisoned wells and other horrors. Such was the first breath of war, full of venom, that, as it were, blew in our faces as we rolled on towards it.

The next day Bloem added: 'more and more stories of revolting cruelties on our troops by Belgian civilians filled the papers.'[12] Two days later Princess Blücher in Berlin was informed by a German officer that there were thirty officers lying in hospital in Aachen with their eyes put out by Belgian women and children.[13] A preconceived, systematic campaign of self-justification was clearly in operation from the very beginning of the War.

There was a lot to justify: the Germans were marching to a tight schedule; their advanced forces (whose function was to open the way for the massive right wing of Schlieffen's plan) were not strong enough to detach garrisons on their lines of communication; instead, they deliberately resorted to *Schrecklichkeit*. The literal meaning of this is 'terribleness', usually construed as 'frightfulness'. It was a policy designed to frighten the civil population into absolute submission and acquiescence with the least possible diversion of German military strength; never again would 25 per cent of the army be left on the lines of communication as in 1871. To defend deeds reminiscent of mediaeval barbarity, the Germans could cite in modern times such examples as General W. T. Sherman's march through Georgia and the Carolinas in 1864–65. Sherman was called the 'Attila of the West'; his army was accused of butchery and rape as well as wanton destruction. Many of these charges were untrue, but the reality needed little embellishment. 'A corridor, 250 miles long and up to 50 miles wide, from Atlanta to Savannah, was swept almost bare of provisions and livestock, and the systematic destruction of railroads, bridges, mills, workshops and many public buildings left a trail of twisted metal and smoke-blackened ruins behind the marching army.'[14] Sherman believed 'it was as important to break the civilian will to fight as the military capacity to fight'. He was a very modern soldier; Bomber Command Headquarters, 1942–45, would have understood him well. In their imperial wars on distant frontiers both the French and the British had adopted similar measures on a less dramatic scale. The Germans in 1914 improved substantially on Sherman's performance and chose a neutral as their first victim.

Schrecklichkeit was sometimes immediate, as at Hervé, sometimes delayed and performed not by the first wave of invaders in the heat of action but by the supports, acting with cold deliberation. The little town of Andenne, near Namur, was burned down on 20 August; the German proclamation of the deed said that 110 people were shot; according to Belgian accounts the figure was 211. At Seilles, it was fifty. At Tamines the cemetery contains 384 graves whose stones bear the inscription: '1914: Fusillé par les Allemands.' Visé, on the Dutch frontier, was destroyed on 23 August; people in Holland heard shooting during the night, and the next day 4,000 refugees crossed the frontier – the whole of the population left alive except for 700 men and boys taken to Germany for forced labour. This was another sign of things to come. So was the universal taking of hostages: ten from every street in Namur, elsewhere one from every house, as a guarantee of 'good behaviour'.

Two names illustrate *Schrecklichkeit* in all its odium: Dinant and Louvain. On 22 August the right wing of the French Fifth Army fell back from the line of the River Meuse below Namur, blowing the bridges behind it. Among them was the bridge at Dinant, a small, trim riverside town surmounted by a massive citadel at the top of steep cliffs on the right bank. The advancing Germans – General von Hausen's *Third (Saxon) Army* – naturally applied themselves to repairing the bridge as quickly as possible. The general claims to have witnessed personally 'perfidious' attempts by Belgian civilians to hamper the repair work – on the face of it a matter of some difficulty, short of bringing on a general battle. The German response was immediate and typical; hundreds of hostages were at once rounded up, fifty of them taken from church, the day (23 August) being a Sunday. They were apparently held under guard in the main square until evening, then lined up, men on one side, women on the other. Firing squads marched in, turned back to back, and began firing; 612 bodies were later identified and buried, among them an infant three weeks old. The Saxons then pillaged and burned the centre of the town. One of von Hausen's staff officers remarked that this deed would look bad in history. The general replied, 'We shall write the history ourselves.'[15] It is never a safe assumption.

The extreme tip of the German right wing was General von

Kluck's *First Army*; it passed through Louvain on its way to Brussels and Mons on 19 August. Louvain was a university city, renowned for its mediaeval buildings; its famous library, founded in 1426, contained some 230,000 volumes including 750 mediaeval manuscripts and over 1,000 very early printed books. The Gothic façade of the Hôtel de Ville (1448) occupied a high place among the architectural glories of northern Europe; the splendid church of St Pierre contained altar panels by early Flemish masters. The demeanour of the invaders in Louvain was at first correct, though stern; they requisitioned huge quantities of food, and demanded a cash indemnity, as they had done elsewhere. On the other hand, they paid for their purchases of postcards and souvenirs and even stood in line for haircuts among Belgian customers at the barbers' shops. The burgomaster posted up a proclamation to the citizens, telling them to remain calm and offer no resistance to the occupying army. The Germans nevertheless took a number of leading citizens as hostages, among them the burgomaster himself.

Days passed; the leading German troops swept on in their great encircling movement, and behind them came General von Boehn's *IX Reserve Corps*. One of its tasks was to guard the German line of communication against the Belgian Army, now concentrated in the fortress area of Antwerp, some thirty-five miles away to the north-west. On 25 August the Belgians made a sortie from Antwerp in considerable strength in the direction of Louvain. They drove back the German covering forces and evidently caused considerable confusion in the rear areas; it would appear that a riderless horse galloped into the town in the night, communicated its panic to others and caused a mild stampede. German sentries, in alarm, began shooting; there were shouts of 'The French are here!', 'The English are here!' – and, inevitably, 'The *francs-tireurs* are here!' The ingredients of *Schrecklichkeit* were conveniently to hand; the Germans determined to make a real example of Louvain.

General von Luttwitz, Military Governor of Brussels, pronounced the city's doom next day. He told the Spanish Ambassador and the American Ambassador, Mr Brand Whitlock, 'A dreadful thing has occurred at Louvain. Our general there has been shot by the son of the burgomaster. The population has fired on our troops – and now, of course, we have to destroy the city.' Mr Whitlock heard this story of German generals being shot by the sons and sometimes the daughters of burgomasters so often 'that it seemed to him the Belgians must have bred a special race of burgomasters' children like the Assassins of Syria'.[16] Burning and shooting had already begun, and continued for five days, which gave time for neutral correspondents and observers to witness it. An American journalist, Mr Gerald Morgan, wrote:

An hour before sunset we entered Louvain and found the city a smoking furnace. The railway station was crowded with troops, drunk with loot and liquor, and rapine as well. From house to house, acting under orders, groups of soldiers were carrying lighted straw, placing it in the basement, and then passing on to the next. It was not one's idea of a general conflagration, for each house burnt separately – hundreds of individual bonfires – while the sparks shot up like thousands of shooting stars into the still night air . . . Meanwhile, through the station arch we saw German justice being administered. In a square outside, where the cabs stand, an officer stood, and the soldiers drove the citizens of Louvain into his presence, like so many unwilling cattle on a market day. Some of the men, after a few words between the officer and the escorts, were marched off under fixed bayonets behind the railway station. Then we heard volleys, and the soldiers returned. Then the train moved out, and the last we saw of the doomed city was an immense red glare in the gathering dusk.[17]

The First Secretary of the American Legation, Mr Hugh Gibson, with Swedish and Mexican colleagues, went into the burning city on 28 August. They saw blackened buildings, the dead bodies of people and horses in the streets, wreckage of all kinds, and soldiers of *IX Reserve Corps,* often drunk, driving people out of their houses in order to complete the destruction. A German officer kept repeating to Gibson: 'We shall wipe it out, not one stone will stand upon another! *Kein stein auf einander!* Not one, I tell you. We will teach them to respect Germany. For generations people will come here to see what we have done!'[18]

The threat, for some reason now impossible to define, was not carried out. The precious library and many of the old university buildings were destroyed; the church of St Pierre was badly damaged by fire; about a fifth of the city's houses were gutted. But the Hôtel de Ville stood amid the surrounding ruins virtually unscathed – a miraculous survival. The toll of dead citizens is uncertain; the burgomaster was one of them, though the Rector of the University survived through American intervention.

That was the story of Louvain. The Germans were publicly quite unrepentant (though many no doubt harboured private misgivings); the chief of staff, the younger General von Moltke, discussed the episode with the ardently Germanophile Swedish explorer, Sven Hedin, who visited his headquarters in early September. After their conversation Sven Hedin roundly asserted:

'The wave of vandalism which passed over a part of Louvain was let
loose by the inhabitants themselves.'[19]

He repeated this charge, with embellishments, when he visited
Louvain some weeks later – [20]though he agreed that the loss of the
irreplaceable library was 'regrettable in the extreme' and said that
'the Germans themselves greatly regretted that they were
compelled against their will to adopt such measures'.

Schrecklichkeit – Louvain, Dinant, Visé, Tamines, Malines,
Termonde and many more unhappy place-names signifying
massacre and destruction – was the fire of truth from which
billowed the smoke of the evil myths which we call propaganda. It
goes without saying that no time was lost in perpetrating these
brutalizing tales. The *Daily News,* on 21 August, offered the
following:

'A woman was forced to undress amid the insults of the soldiers and was
then shot. The Mayor's wife was shot in her house and the body burned
with her home. An old man of 74, deaf and blind, received two volleys in
his body. Another was dragged on to the market place and tortured till he
died.'

And the same newspaper, on 26 August:

'An old man . . . had his arm sliced in three longitudinal cuts; he was then
hung head downwards and burned alive. Young girls have been raped
and little children outraged, and at Orsmeal several inhabitants suffered
mutilations too horrible to describe.'

The *Weekly Dispatch* proclaimed on 6 September, under the
headline 'GERMANS BURN BABIES':

'The truthful war picture would present Belgium as a slaughterhouse with
the peace-loving, unarmed inhabitants being killed in thousands by the
Germans. Rivers of blood, mountains of innocent dead, sacked towns
and villages – these have marked the advance of the Germans. The
civilised world stands aghast at the Kaiser's atrocities. Humanity cries
aloud for vengeance.'

One of the most celebrated atrocity stories, which gave rise to
repulsive illustration, did not appear until 13 May 1915; once again
it was The *Daily News* that gave it airing under the headline
'FOULEST CRIME OF THREE CENTURIES':

As the German soldiers came along a street . . . a small child . . . came out
of a house. The child was about two years of age. The child came into the

middle of the street so as to be in the way of the soldiers. The soldiers were walking in twos. The first line of two passed the child. One of the second line – the man on the left – stepped aside and drove his bayonet with both hands into the child's stomach. lifting the child into the air on his bayonet and carrying it away on his bayonet, he and his comrades still singing. The child screamed when the soldier struck it with his bayonet, but not afterwards.

Generally speaking, such effusions gain credibility with distance from the battle-front. Nevertheless it was a soldier who perpetrated one of the most blood-curdling stories of all; he is understandably vague about the exact location – a 'little town from which we had just been driven', retaken by counter-attack on 26 August, the day of the Battle of Le Cateau. I have myself written a book on the Battle of Mons and the retreat, which continued until 6 September; I know of no locality retaken by the B.E.F. on 26 August. But Major A. Corbett-Smith, Royal Field Artillery, in his book *The Retreat From Mons, By One Who Shared In It* (Cassell, 1916), gives a graphic account of the charge into this elusive town, 'the cavalry sweeping up on the flank':

Then it was that our men first saw a little of the hideous work of the invaders upon the civilian population. And if anything more were needed to brace them up to fight to the last man, they had it in that brief hour in the recaptured town . . .

Up the main street everywhere was horrible evidence that *they* had been at work. Mingled with dead and wounded combatants were bodies of women and children, many terribly mutilated . . .

But there was one thing which, for the men who saw it, dwarfed all else. Hanging up in the open window of a shop, strung from a hook in the cross-beam, like a joint in a butcher's shop, was the body of a little girl, five years old, perhaps. Its poor little hands had been hacked off, and through the slender body were vicious bayonet stabs . . .

Small wonder, if tales like that were circulating, that another soldier (Lance-Corporal Stanley Thomas, 1/South Wales Borderers), quoted in *The Times* on 16 September, could speak of a bayonet charge and say: 'The Germans don't like the cold steel. They were falling on their knees and praying, but our blood boiled at the way they were treating the civilians, and we had no mercy.'

'We had no mercy'; in those words the mission of the evil myths finds fulfilment. The 'smoke' was doing its work; truth was being asphyxiated. However, in fairness to the soldiers, it has to be said that such a frame of mind as Corporal Thomas's became rare at the front after 1914 (by contrast with 'Home'). Indeed, one soldier-writer said of 1918: 'Only in the trenches (on both sides of No Man's Land) were chivalry and sweet reasonableness to be found.'[21] And it is to another, very famous soldier-writer, Robert Graves, that I owe this fascinating demonstration of how a myth is born, how the evil is injected into it:

Kölnische Zeitung:
'When the fall of Antwerp became known, the church bells were rung' (i.e. at Cologne and throughout Germany).
Le Matin:
'According to the *Kölnische Zeitung,* the clergy of Antwerp were forced to ring the church bells when the fortress was taken.'
Corriere della Sera:
'According to what *The Times* has heard from Cologne, via Paris, the unfortunate Belgian priests who refused to ring the church bells when Antwerp was taken have been sentenced to hard labour.'
Le Matin:
'According to information which has reached the *Corriere della Sera* from Cologne, via London, it is confirmed that the barbaric conquerors of Antwerp punished the unfortunate Belgian priests for their heroic refusal to ring the church bells by hanging them as living clappers to the bells with their heads down.'[22]

Enough has perhaps been said about such myths, the 'fire' and the 'smoke'. They are, evidently, to some extent self-defeating. Admittedly, during the war itself a large number of people on both sides remained in the grip of myth until the very end – thus, on 3 July 1918 *The Times* printed a letter from a Mr T. B. Napier on the notepaper of the Reform Club, in which he said:

'[The British People] are beginning to think that with a nation so polluted and polluting [as Germany], whose ideals are so false and whose human feeling is so dead, no people acknowledging the morals of Christianity, or even of civilization, ought, as it values its own soul, to have truck or dealing or even speech . . . To the people the war is becoming a holy war – a war of right against wrong, of Heaven against Hell . . .'

Yet a degree of saturation had been reached, despite the Mr Napiers, and despite continuing hysteria on the subject of enemy aliens in Britain. When the War produced its one clear act of genocide, the great massacre of Armenians by the Turks between 1915 and 1917 (reliable authorities estimate the Armenian dead at between 1 and 1½ million), though the event was noticed it produced no uproar even faintly comparable to that aroused by *Schrecklichkeit* in Belgium in 1914.

After the war, of course, there was a very violent reaction against atrocity stories, whether true or false. Lord Ponsonby of Shoulbrede wrote, referring to people who had been sincere in their patriotic zeal and unconscious at the time of being duped by myth:

'Finding now that elaborately and carefully staged deceptions were practised on them, they feel a resentment which has not only served to open their eyes but may induce them to make their children keep their eyes open when the next bugle sounds.'[23]

This was an understandable reaction; but when the next bugle did sound, it would be across landscapes containing such place-names as Guernica, Lidice and Oradour and the whole dire country of the Holocaust. The fires of 1914–18 were hidden to some extent by their own smoke; the fires of 1939–45 are not so easily lost to view.

---

1   Barbara W. Tuchman, *The Guns of August,* Macmillan (New York), 1962, p. 317.
2   Michael Howard (*The Franco-Prussian War,* Rupert Hart-Davis, 1961, p. 252) informs us: 'one company was dressed in the romantic if impractical style of Alexandre Dumas's Musketeers, with plumed hats, huge cloaks, boots, sabres and daggers. The *francs-tireurs* of Nice wore grey Tyrolean jackets and hats, the *francs-tireurs* of the Pyrenees berets; the *Partisans du Gers* carried black banners ornamented with crossbones; a mounted company from South America appeared with lassos; and a company from North Africa wore the burnous.'
3   Ibid., p. 251; when Jules Favre pointed out to Bismarck that the *francs-tireurs* were only doing what the Germans themselves had done during the War of Liberation, the Prussian statesman replied: 'That is quite true; but our trees still bear the marks where your generals hanged our people on them.' Mr A. J. P. Taylor, on the other hand, in *The Course of German History* (Hamish Hamilton, 1945; Methuen University Paperback, 1961, pp. 39–40) speaks scathingly of 'the myth of the national uprising against Napoleon'. He says: 'Of any movement of the masses against the French there was no trace at all. The French were never troubled in Germany, as they had been in Spain and Russia, by guerillas. French couriers travelled across Germany without escort, and Napoleon received his regular post from Paris even on the day of the battle of Leipzig.'
4   Fred Majdalany (*Cassino: Portrait of a Battle,* Longmans, Green and Co., 1957, p. 249) says that they carried rifles, but preferred their knives: 'They had a habit of bringing back evidence of the number of victims they had killed, which made them an unpleasant enemy to face.'
5   Walter Laqueur, *Guerilla: A Historical and Critical Study,* Weidenfeld and Nicolson, 1977; pp. 84–5.
6   Howard, op. cit., p. 381.
7   General Erich Ludendorff, *My War Memories 1914–1918,* Hutchinson, 1919, pp. 31–2.
8   H. W. Wilson and J. A. Hammerton, *The Great War: The Standard History of the All-Europe Conflict,* Amalgamated Press, 1914, 1, p. 200.
9   Ibid., p. 197.
10   Gordon A. Craig, *Germany 1866–1945,* O.U.P., p. 317.

11 *The Private War of Seaman Stumpf,* ed. Daniel Horn, Leslie Frewin, 1969, p. 29.
12 Walter Bloem, *The Advance from Mons, 1914,* Peter Davies, 1930, pp. 20–1.
13 Tuchman, op. cit., p. 318.
14 Peter J. Parish, *The American Civil War,* Eyre Methuen, 1975, pp. 479–80.
15 Sir J. E. Edmonds, *A Short History of World War I,* O.U.P., 1951, p. 26.
16 Tuchman, op. cit., p. 319.
17 Wilson and Hammerton, op. cit., i, p. 442.
18 Tuchman, op. cit., p. 320.
19 Sven Hedin, *With the German Armies in the West,* John Lane, The Bodley Head, 1915,
    p. 55.
20 Ibid., p. 240. One of Sven Hedin's embellishments consists in obscuring the date of the
    Louvain episode; he says that German troops were fired on by civilians 'on entering the
    town' – i.e. on 19 August. In fact, the burning took place between 25 and 30 August.
    Another embellishment is that the damage round the Hôtel de Ville was caused by
    artillery fire: 'The German artillery had given a magnificent proof of its unerring
    accuracy of aim. It had hit everything round this building but without injuring as much
    as a cornice of any of the six turrets.' He had already accepted from von Moltke the
    story that German soldiers tried to extinguish fires in buildings near the Hôtel de Ville
    in order to save it and 'were shot down during their work by *francs-tireurs*'.
21 Charles Edmonds, *A Subaltern's War,* Peter Davies, 1929, p. 188.
22 Robert Graves, *Goodbye to all That,* Penguin Edition, 1960, p. 61.
23 Lord Ponsonby of Shoulbrede, *Falsehood in War-time,* Allen and Unwin, 1928, p. 26.

III

THE GREAT CASUALTY MYTH:
The 'Lost Generation'

'For 50 years the Great War has been the British wooden leg . . . .
The wooden-leg legend runs thus: British casualties were so
colossal that the national life was enfeebled by the absence of a
"Lost Generation"; the war itself was so hideous an experience
that the national faith and confidence were justifiably
undermined; economically, the war shattered our predominance
by forcing us to sell our overseas investments.
  This wooden-leg legend is historically absolute rubbish.'
  (Correlli Barnett: *The Sunday Telegraph Magazine*, 7.11.68)

We turn now to post-war myth. Few wars escape the infection of
mythology – we have seen (p. 33, Note 3) that Mr A. J. P. Taylor
scorns the myth of a German national uprising against Napoleon in
1813; Professor Michael Howard equally pricked the bubbles of
misguided verbiage about French national resistance in 1870–71;
we shall shortly examine a powerful myth about the American Civil
War which had grave distant consequences; the myths of the
Second World War are still in process of exhumation (and much
remains to be done in that field). The mythology of the First World
War endures with all the strength of religious doctrine, particularly
in Britain and America. At its very centre, its emanations
spreading to infect all parts, is the great Casualty Myth.

  This myth is, briefly, the fixed belief that the First World War
was the deadliest experience in human history. It has flourished in
Britain since the 1920s; Americans, for a long time, since their own
325,876 casualties (115,660 dead, including those who died of
disease in the U.S.A.)[1] did not exactly confirm it, were
unimpressed. They were unimpressed by the First World War
itself, to tell the truth. But in recent years they too have caught the
infection, largely from British writing concerned, usually, only
with British experience. Thus a book (widely acclaimed) by

Professor Paul Fussell of Rutgers University, written in 1975, entitled *The Great War and Modern Memory,* proved to be an examination of British war literature in terms, really, of a private contest between the literate British middle class and the German Empire. Another eminent American author, recipient of numerous literary awards, Mr William Manchester, writing about General Douglas MacArthur in 1978,[2] is forced to pay some attention to the First World War, because MacArthur became, at thirty-eight, its youngest divisional commander. The depth of Mr Manchester's understanding of the War may be judged by the statement: 'In World War I Douglas Haig butchered the flower of British youth in the Somme and Flanders without winning a single victory.' This sentence completely encapsulates that particular mythology, with a significant ramification well displayed. I have myself recently (August 1979) been accused of 'fantastic philistinism' by *The New Statesman* for 'trying to suggest that the generals who presided over the demolition of a whole British generation were something more respectable than idiots'. I shall return to the question of generalship in due course; for the time being it is more rewarding to consider the phrases 'the flower of British youth' and 'a whole British generation', containing as they do the very heart of the myth.

Britain is a collection of islands; and though, intellectually, the British know that air power and missiles have long ago abolished island status, and in spite of all economic or political associations with the mainland of Europe, the island mentality persists. It is sheer myopic insularity which inspires the great Casualty Myth. Its believers and perpetrators speak and write as though virtually every dead soldier on the Western Front between 1914 and 1918 wore khaki. Table A (p. 44), which shows the percentage of casualties to total numbers mobilized by the various belligerents, reveals how vastly wide of the mark this belief is. It dates from the year 1916 (which I shall examine more closely later), and in particular from awareness of the calamitous 1 July of that year, the worst day in the British Army's history.[3] The year as a whole cost the British Army some 660,000 casualties, a figure which produced an enduring national trauma, already firmly lodged among some who possessed knowledge and influence, before the year was ended. Chief among them was the Secretary of State for War, Mr Lloyd George, who denounced the 'military Moloch' to Colonel Repington of *The Times* on 25 October 1916. To Lloyd George, loss on this scale (it implies about 200,000 dead) was something uniquely horrible. Horrible it certainly was but, regrettably, it was also commonplace – and that was something he was never able to reckon with. For example, as the year began, French losses (from a smaller population) already stood at about two million, compared with Britain's half million. According to one authority, even by March 1915, the Austro-Hungarian Army had lost over two million;[4] the Russians lost that number in 1915 alone. The truth is that the only really exceptional thing about Britain's experience in 1916 was that she had been spared so long.

There is, to my mind, something very morbid and unhealthy about this blinkered concentration down the decades on British loss, irrespective of anyone else's – and equally irrespective of British achievement. Comparison with the very much smaller losses of 1939–45 only helps to compound the mythology. The fact that the British dead of the Second World War amounted to less than half the total for the First shows only that never at any time during that war was the British Army engaged with the main body of the main enemy, and that the only sure way to avoid casualties is to avoid fighting. Certainly, as regards real comparison between the two wars, it serves only to conceal a terrible reality.

Nothing is more frustrating for the historian than trying to reach some firm ground on the subject of casualties.[5] All that can be said with assurance of the war dead of 1914–18 is that no exact total can ever be given; the records to support it do not exist – in some cases never did exist. Nevertheless, historians tend to circle round a maximum of about thirteen million for all belligerents (though some would include in this Russian losses in the Civil War, which continued until 1920). It is a figure high enough and awful enough to justify the revulsion of the Twenties and Thirties, but since 1945 we have had another yardstick, which makes the persistence of so palpable a myth less forgivable. We need now to take into consideration, when contemplating the thirteen million dead of the First World War, the Soviet Union's 13,600,000 military dead of 1941–45, with about seven million casualties in addition.

Exact figures for the total mortality of the Second World War are no more available than for the First World War.

An article by M. Jacques Mordal, entitled 'Les Pertes Humaines dans les deux Guerres Mondiales' ('Human Losses in the two World Wars'), in the journal *Miroir de l'Histoire* in September 1961, states that German deaths amounted to 6,500,000 (four million military) and that the total for the Soviet Union was 20,600,000 (quoting Colonel Kalinov of the Soviet Headquarters in Berlin). M. Mordal also quotes a table for the rest of Europe prepared by Dr Helmut Arntz:

Country	Military Dead	Civilian Dead
	in thousands	
Austria	230	104
Belgium	12	76
Bulgaria	10	10
Denmark	00·4	1
Finland	82	2
France	250	350
Greece	20	140
Great Britain	326	62
Hungary	140	280
Italy	330	80
Luxemburg	4	1
Norway	6	4
Holland	12	198
Poland	100	4,200
Romania	200	260
Czecho-Slovakia	150	215
Yugoslavia	300	1,400
Total	2,172,400	7,383,000

This gives a European total of 36,655,000 (clearly a very 'round' figure); M. Mordal points out that for the countries of the Far East – Japan, China, the Philippines, Burma, Malaya, etc., we have no figures at all. He suggests that the full world total may well be 55 million – admitting that such a figure cannot pretend to be precise, though it is broadly accepted by most statisticians. It can, he says, only be an approximation, but it is a reasonable approximation. It is more than four times the total for the First World War. Even if the reality behind the great Casualty Myth is not quite so bad as that, it is terrible enough.

———

1 C. R. M. F. Cruttwell, *A History of the Great War 1914–1918*, O.U.P., 1934, p. 631.
2 William Manchester, *American Caesar: Douglas MacArthur 1880–1964*, Hutchinson, 1979, p. 345.
3 See Table B, p. 45.
4 Norman Stone, *The Eastern Front 1914–1917*, Hodder and Stoughton, 1975, pp. 122–3.

5 My files record the attempt to arrive at a casualty total for France in the First World War:

Source	Total	
Paul-Marie de la Gorce, *The French Army,* Weidenfeld and Nicolson, 1963, p. 103. This repeats General de Gaulle, *France and Her Army,* Hutchinson, 1944, p. 99.	4,926,000	(addition of yearly totals)
Statistics of the Military Effort of the British Empire (henceforth *Statistics*) p. 352.	2,521,600	('incomplete', including 1,385,300 dead)
Cruttwell, op. cit.	2,831,600	('incomplete', including 1,385,300 dead; this total includes 447,000 'discharged owing to wounds', but Cruttwell says the total of seriously wounded 'is commonly given as about 2,000,000', which gives a revised total of
	4,384,600	
D. C. Watt, *A History of the World in the Twentieth Century,* Hodder and Stoughton, 1967, p. 264.	'6 million casualties'	
Jacques Mordal, in *Miroir de l'Histoire,* Sept. 1961.	No total, but 1,393,515 dead	

[Similar problems are presented by every nation engaged except America.]

IV

AN ASIDE ON CASUALTIES

The great Casualty Myth does not merely lend itself to the propagation of serious and dangerous untruths; it also obscures important areas of truth itself. Professor Paul Fussell, in *The Great War and Modern Memory,* provides a useful illustration of this. Like so many other writers on the First World War, he is obsessed by the British casualties – and obsession is rarely an aid to understanding. In the opening sentence of his book, Professor Fussell tells us: 'By mid-December, 1914, British troops had been fighting on the Continent for over five months. Casualties had been shocking . . .' Like the playwright Webster in T. S. Eliot's poem, he is 'much possessed by death'; the pages that follow are full of graves and corpses. Clearly profoundly affected, soon he tells us: 'At the beginning of the war, a volunteer had to stand five feet eight to get into the army. By October 11 the need for men was such that the standard was lowered to five feet five. And on November 5, after thirty thousand casualties in October, one had to be only five feet three to get in.'[1]

Two pages further on we reach the Battle of Loos in September 1915: '. . . 60,000 more British casualties had been added to the total. Now volunteers were no longer sufficient to fill the ranks.'

The truth is somewhat different.

British casualties in 1914 were 92,915; British recruiting in that year was 1,186,357, of which no less than 898,635 *before* the end of October, with its 'thirty thousand casualties'.

By the end of 1915 British casualties had mounted to 532,700; British recruiting totalled 2,466,719.[2]

Those are the stark statistics of army manpower, which make sad havoc of Professor Fussell's idea that recruiting at that period (or any other) was linked to specific casualty returns. But it is the misinterpretation of the lowering of the height requirement that is most unfortunate; Professor Fussell completely misses a significant piece of social revelation.

The great mass of nearly 2½ million voluntary recruits in the first seventeen months of the War were, of course, the men who responded to Lord Kitchener's famous call. They came from all walks of life, from fields, factories, docks and mines, as well as from shops, professions, universities and overseas. One may say that for the first time the British Army met the British people, and in so doing introduced Britain herself to her people. The shock was considerable; the image of a sturdy, strapping population (by comparison with weedy foreigners) was rudely dispelled when the results of callous nineteenth-century industrial expansion flocked into view. Robust enough in spirit, the men of the narrow streets of the industrial towns, offspring of long working hours, low wages, persistent poverty and persistent malnutrition, simply did not meet the physical standards laid down by a small professional army which could normally pick and choose its recruits. If the Army had not lowered its physical requirements, hundreds of thousands of these eager volunteers would have had to be turned away – which was unthinkable. When conscription came, the same applied, and in the later stages of the war many noted the contrast between the small British soldiers from the cities, the tall, powerful frames of the Dominion troops and even the hefty appearance of the French, digging deep into their reserves of tough peasantry.

Particular modes of suffering and sorrow are concealed behind the bald statistics of recruiting height. In December 1914 a battalion (17th) of the Royal Scots was formed of men who could not even reach the five feet three inches minimum; the best they could manage was five feet to five feet two. They were called 'Bantams', and for some reason the name and the ardour which lay behind it caught the imagination of the public. Other battalions of the same characteristics were raised and formed into a division, the 35th; it contained two Scottish battalions, a whole brigade from Lancashire and battalions from Cheshire, Gloucestershire, Nottingham, Yorkshire, Durham and Northumberland. They had this in common: they were, in the words of Sir Philip Gibbs, then war correspondent of the *Daily Chronicle,* 'the dwarfed children of Industrial England and its mid-Victorian cruelties'. In trench warfare, says Gibbs, 'they did well . . . . In actual battle they were hardly strong enough, and could not carry all that burden of fighting kit – steel helmet, rifle, hand-grenades, shovels, empty sandbags – with which other troops went into action.'[3] Long route marches in full kit especially tried them. It was difficult to keep their ranks filled with men of the right type, with the consequence that 'they deteriorated in physique and morale and, although they passed through the ordeal of the Somme with considerable credit, it was found necessary to reconstitute the infantry of the 35th Division at the end of 1916 with men of normal physique, most of whom came from the Yeomanry.'[4] The truth is that they should never have been recruited as infantry at all; some who had been miners found a proper form of service in the Tunnelling Companies of the Royal Engineers – of which, of course, nobody even dreamed in 1914.

The last word on this sad subject may be given to an officer who, after a long stint on the Western Front, had the task of training eighteen-year old conscripts in 1918:

'The skinny, sallow, shambling, frightened victims of our industrial system, suffering from the effect of wartime shortages, who were given into our hands, were unrecognizable after six months of good food, fresh air, and physical training. They looked twice the size and, as we weighed and measured them, I am able to say that they put on an average of one inch in height and one stone in weight during their time with us . . . Beyond statistical measurement was their change in character, to ruddy, handsome, clear-eyed young men with square shoulders who stood up straight and were afraid of no one, not even the sergeant-major. "The effect on me," I wrote in a letter, "is to make me a violent socialist when I see how underdeveloped industrialism has kept them, and a Prussian militarist when I see what soldiering makes of them." Then I added, rather inconsequently, in a phrase that dates: "I shall never think of the lower classes again in the same way after the war." An odd forecast but true; I never have.'[5]

Compassion does not need to wander far to discover its right objects.

---

1   Paul Fussell, *The Great War and Modern Memory*, O.U.P., 1975, p. 9.
2   British casualty figures are from the Official History (henceforward O.H.), *Military Operations, France and Belgium*, compiled by Sir J. E. Edmonds, Macmillan, H.M.S.O., *1914*, ii, p. 467, and *Statistics*, for other theatres of war. Recruiting figures are from the table of monthly enlistments on p. 364 of the same work.
3   Philip Gibbs, *Realities of War*, Heinemann, 1920, pp. 329–30.
4   O.H., *1916*, ii, pp. 92–3, f.n.2.
5   Charles Carrington, *Soldier from the Wars Returning*, Hutchinson, 1965, p. 230.

V

ANTI-MYTH:

Some Casualty Statistics

A casualty is a man blown to pieces, disintegrated, nothing left of him but a name on a war memorial . . . or a man killed with horrible mutilations . . . or killed with nothing to show on his body at all, or just a tiny hole – but dead; or sightless, or limbless, or scarred for life . . . or happy in possession of a 'Blighty one', a wound bad enough to take him out of the war, but ultimately curable; or neither dead nor wounded, but irretrievably mentally and spiritually damaged; or taken prisoner to face humiliation, hardship, starvation, cruelty. These are the circumstances of the individual casualty. But casual*ties,* on the national and international scale, in their terrible plural, can only be presented intelligibly as statistics. I make no apology for the following tables.

Table A

First World War Casualties expressed as percentages of forces mobilized:

Country	Killed (million)	Wounded (million)	Prisoners (million)	%
Austria-Hungary	1·2	3·6	2·2	90
Russia	1·7	4·9	2·5	76·3
France	1·3	4·3	·5	73·3
Romania	·33	(·12)	(·08)	71·4*
Germany	1·8**	4·2	1·2	64·9
Serbia	·04	·13	·15	46
Italy	·65	·94	·60	39·1
British Empire	·90†	2·0	·19	35·8
Belgium	·01	·04	·03	34·9
Turkey	·32	·40	·25	34·2††

Source: D. C. Watt, *A History of the World in the Twentieth Century*, Hodder and Stoughton, 1967, p. 264. Unfortunately Professor Watt does not tell us what *his* source is; his total mortality figure ('over eight million killed') is definitely too low.

* This statistic is highly suppositional. The compilation, *Statistics*, in a table of 'Allied and Enemy Casualties' (p. 353), can only offer a total of 335,706 officers and other ranks killed and missing, supplied by the Romanian Embassy on 6 January 1919. It adds that '265,000 of the civilian population are stated to have been killed or are missing'.

** Official German sources now say that 2,037,000 German soldiers were killed.

† The Commonwealth War Graves Commission, whose burials go up to 31 August 1921, gives a total of 1,114,786. The British Official Historian says 996,230. The percentage for the United Kingdom is, as usual, variable. Calculation based on Mr C. R. M. F. Cruttwell's figures (*History of the Great War*, 1914–1918, O.U.P., 1934) makes it 42·1 per cent; based on *Statistics*, 34·8 per cent.

†† Again, highly suppositional; *Statistics*, (p. 357) gives a total of 725,000 'accounted for' (including 240,000 died of disease) and a further 1,565,000 'unaccounted for' (prisoners, deserters, invalids and missing).

Table B

Some Occasions of Heavy Loss, 1914–18

1 July, 1916, the opening day of the Battle of the Somme, was the worst day in the history of the British Army, whose losses on that day (almost all of them killed or wounded) were probably greater than those of any army in any war on one single day. They were, in detail:

	Killed (or died of wounds)	Wounded	Missing	Prisoners	Total
Officers	993	1,337	96	12	**2,438**
Other ranks	18,247	34,156	2,056	573	**55,032**
					57,470

It is an appalling figure; but as a measurement of time a day is no more significant than a week, a fortnight, a month or a year. Every army involved in a major campaign had its occasions of disastrous loss; the British had no monopoly of catastrophe; indeed, never again did they experience anything remotely like that First of July. It is worth looking at some other periods and other armies for perspective:

Period	Dates	Army	Losses
1 week	4–10 June 1916	Austro-Hungarian	**280,000 approx.**
Fortnight (16 days)	16–31 Aug. 1914	French	**210,993**
Month (26 days)	18 Aug.–12 Sept. 1917	Italian	**165,000***
6 weeks	21 Mar.–30 April 1918	German	**348,300**
Year	1915	Russian	**2 million approx.†**

* Compared with a British total of 164,709 for the whole month of July 1916 (thirty-one days).

† Some of these figures represent losses in attack, others in defence; as General Mangin remarked, comparing the casualties of various divisions at Verdun, *'quoi qu'on fasse, on perd beaucoup de monde'* ('whatever you do, you lose a lot of men').

Table C

Casualties in Five Major British Battles, 1916–18

Battle	Duration	Days	Casualties	Daily Rate
1916, Somme	1 July–18 Nov.	141	415,000	2,950
1917, Arras	9 April–17 May	39	159,000	4,070
3rd Ypres (Passchendaele)	31 July–12 Nov.	105	244,000	2,121
1918, Picardy, Lys (German Offensive)	21 March–30 April	41	239,793	5,848
Final Offensive	8 Aug.–11 Nov.	96	350,000	3,645

This table offers a grim commentary on the myth that the defensive was cheaper than the offensive.

Table D
Some Losses in Mass Warfare, 1861–1945

Battle	Date	Confederate Forces Total Engaged	Casualties and %	Union Total	Casualties and %
Antietam*	17 Sept. 1862	50,000	**13,700** **27·8%**	70,000	**12,400** **17·7%**
Fredericksburg	12–13 Dec. 1862	72,000	**5,309** **7·3%**	113,000	**12,653** **11·1%****
Gettysburg	1–3 July 1863	70,200	**20,000** **28·4%**	90,000	**23,000** **25·5%**
Wilderness/ Cold Harbour/ Spotsylvania	4 May–3 June 1864	61,000 (original)	**39,000†** **59·0%**	105,000 (original)	**54,929†** **52·0%**

* Antietam has been called 'the bloodiest one-day battle of the entire war' (R. E. Dupuy and T. N. Dupuy, *The Compact History of the Civil War*, Hawthorn Books [N.Y.], 1960; this is the source of almost all the above statistics).

** The Union army only brought about 80,000 men into action, which makes their proportionate loss 15·8 per cent.

† '[Grant] could afford the loss; Lee could not' (Dupuy and Dupuy, op. cit., p. 300); rightly, they call these figures 'the grim arithmetic of attrition', which was *not*, contrary to myth, an invention of the First World War. In the course of the American Civil War, 115 regiments (sixty-three Union, fifty-two Confederate) sustained losses of more than 50 per cent in a single engagement. The 1st Texas (C.S.A.) lost 82·3 per cent at Antietam; the 1st Minnesota (U.S.A.) lost 82 per cent at Gettysburg. In that battle the 26th North Carolina (C.S.A.) had the highest losses of any regiment on either side in any battle: 549 out of 800. Three Confederate divisions had over 50 per cent loss: Pickett's, 67 per cent; Pettigrew's, 60 per cent; Trimble's, 52 per cent.

Campaign	Date	German Casualties and %	Russian Casualties and %
Operation BARBAROSSA	22 June–10 Dec. 1941	**775,078*** **24·2%**	**4,500,000*** **37·5%**
Stalingrad	23 Nov. 1942– 2 Feb. 1943	**280,000**** **330,000†** **100%**	
Siege of Leningrad	Sept. 1941–Jan. 1944		**632,000 dead** **900,000 dead††**
Battle of Berlin	16 April–8 May 1945		**305,000 (total)*†** **?%**

* Alexander Werth, *Russia at War 1941–1945*, Barrie and Rockliff, 1964, pp. 259–60, quoting German sources; p. 401, quoting a contemporary Soviet comparative table *intended to encourage the Soviet population*.

**Peter Young, *World War 1939–1945*, Arthur Barker, 1966, p. 245.

†Werth, op. cit., p. 542.

††Ibid., p. 324; 632,000 is the Soviet official figure; 900,000 is the figure that the composer Shostakovich, who was in Leningrad throughout the siege, gave to Werth.

*†*Marshal Zhukov's Greatest Battles*, ed. Harrison E. Salisbury, Macdonald, 1969, p. 288 f.n.

VI

MYTH-MAKING:
'The Indirect Approach'

'When in the course of studying a long series of military campaigns, I first came to perceive the superiority of the indirect over the direct approach, I was looking merely for light upon strategy. With deepening reflection, however, I began to realize that the indirect approach had a much wider application – that it was a law of life in all spheres: a truth of philosophy.'
(Sir Basil Liddell Hart, *The Way to Win Wars*, p. 5)

'During this survey one impression grew ever stronger – that throughout the ages decisive results in war have only been reached when the approach has been indirect. In strategy the longest way round is apt to be the shortest way home!' (Ibid., p. 15)

As I have said, the great Casualty Myth of the First World War lies at the root of all misinterpretations of that event; it lies also at the root of the false theories arising out of the experience of that war. The foregoing tables are intended to help towards a clearer perspective of the war's casualties by comparing like with like. But the comparison has to be made coolly; history must not be forced 'to yield the appropriate lessons'.[1] Myth-making flourished between 1918 and 1939, and was enabled to do so precisely by the process of making history conform to preconceived ideas or lend support to a fixed frame of mind. Two famous men who, in their day, contributed copiously to the mythology of war were Major-General J. F. C. Fuller and Captain B. H. Liddell Hart.

Fuller and Liddell Hart both had direct experience of the First World War, Fuller always as a Staff Officer, Liddell Hart as a regimental officer (King's Own Yorkshire Light Infantry). Both, like so many others, were emotionally deeply marked by the War; indeed, Liddell Hart's brief[2] experience of the Western Front left him in a permanent state of shock or trauma. Under the guise of cool, scientific reasoning, he evolved theories which stem not from science but from shock. The most famous of these was his theory of 'The Indirect Approach' which, as he said, 'owed much to a study I made in reflection on the entrenched deadlock of 1914–1918, of ways and means by which an earlier case of deadlock had been overcome in the American Civil War, particularly by Sherman in the Western theatre'.[3]

Major-General J. F. C. ('Boney') Fuller was Liddell Hart's 'early mentor and later friend, rival and colleague'; the turning point of his life had come in 1916, when he became G.S.O.2 at the headquarters of what later became the Tank Corps. The new instrument of war which he now encountered proved to be a catalyst in his mind, bringing thoughts about the past to a vision of the future. His ideas about armoured warfare put a stamp on him for evermore, giving him fame or notoriety according to the prevailing point of view. In considering the lessons of the First World War, Fuller and Liddell Hart were 'working along the same lines. These lines were obviously a violent reaction against the destruction, slaughter and linear entrenchment of that war.'[4] From this springboard of understandable revulsion both men proceeded – Liddell Hart to the inspection of 280 campaigns which demonstrated to him the unwisdom of 'direct strategic approach to the main *army* of the enemy', and from this to the evolution of the theory which was to become a cornerstone of myth; Fuller to a great body of controversial writing, but ultimately to *The Decisive Battles of the Western World* (1954–56), which though it does contain some theory, is a true work of history, and *The Conduct of War, 1789–1961* (1961), which is a distillation of collected knowledge.

It is significant that, seeking light in the darkness, both turned to the American Civil War – though they extracted very different lessons from it. Fuller, in particular, came to see the strong link between that war and the two World Wars of the Twentieth Century. Other campaigns during the period 1861–1945 (e.g. the Franco-Prussian War, the South African War and the Russo-Japanese War), while containing valuable special lessons,[5] are in fact deceivers; each for its own reasons failed to reveal the fundamentals of the warfare of its time, though each revealed some of its particular attributes. The Franco-Prussian War was a palpable freak: to weakness in numbers the French added staggering inefficiency and unrealistic strategy. Small wonder that France was defeated in ten months – the misfortune is that this quick victory bolstered a hope and belief amounting to a myth in its own right that brilliant generalship could always make wars short. The South African War, despite interesting technical features (stemming from the modern weapons used), remained nevertheless a colonial campaign. So, in effect, did the Russo-Japanese War; this again displayed much of technical interest, but its central fact is that it was fought at the extremity of the Russian Empire.[6] It was never a war *à outrance* between Russia and Japan.

With the American Civil War and the two World Wars, it is quite a different story. It is in some ways ironical that the clearest exponent of the links between the three is 'the Unconventional Soldier', Fuller. It is Fuller who says:

The first of the unlimited industrial wars was the Civil War in America. It was the first great conflict of the steam age, and the aim of the Northern, or Federal, States was unconditional surrender – that is, total victory. Its character was, therefore, that of a crusade, and because of this, as well as because it put to the test the military developments of the Industrial Revolution, it opened a radically new chapter in the history of war.[7]

Tracing the links between 1861–65 and his own war, 1914–18, Fuller goes even further:

The war fought by Grant and Lee, Sherman and Johnston, and others closely resembled the first of the World Wars. No other war, not even the Russo-Japanese War of 1904–1905, offers so exact a parallel. It was a war of rifle bullets and trenches, of slashings,[8] abattis, and even wire entanglements . . . It was a war astonishing in its modernity, with wooden wire-bound mortars, hand and winged grenades, rockets, and many forms of booby traps. Magazine rifles and Requa's machine gun were introduced and balloons were used by both sides . . . Explosive bullets are mentioned and also a flame projector, and in June, 1864, General Pendleton asked the chief ordnance officer at Richmond whether he could supply him with 'stink-shells' which would give off 'offensive gases' and cause 'suffocating effect'. The answer he got was: 'stink-shells, none on hand; don't keep them; will make if ordered.' Nor did modernity end there; armoured ships, armoured trains, land mines and torpedoes were used, together with lamp and flag signalling and the field telegraph. A submarine was built by Horace L. Huntley at Mobile . . . On February 17, 1864, she sank the U.S.S. *Housatonic* off Charleston and went down with her. Had the nations of Europe studied the lessons of the Civil War and taken them to heart they could not in 1914–1918 have perpetrated the enormous tactical blunders of which that war bears record.[9]

The technological base of the Civil War was the First Industrial Revolution, expressing itself in the apparatus of steam and iron, which remained the dominating technical factors of the First World War. The sociological base of both wars was the mass population created by the Industrial Revolution. Mass populations breed mass armies. It has been estimated that the Northern States, from first to last, mobilized over 1½ million men, out of a male population of 4,010,000 between the ages of fifteen and forty. For the South the same source gives an estimate of 1,082,119 mobilized out of 1,140,000 white males of similar age; but this may be a rather high figure, and 850,000-900,000 may be nearer the mark. Either way, we see that something approaching 2½ million men took up arms.[10]

During the First World War the technological base expanded. This was the result of advances in chemicals and electronics, the introduction of a new power of motion through oil, and the development of the internal combustion engine, leading in turn to the research of light metals. A Second Industrial Revolution in fact took place. In the next World War these new factors, while not displacing the older needs for coal and iron, increased very largely in importance.

By 1914 populations, also, had expanded considerably (in 1860 the total population of the United States was 31,443,321; in 1900 it was 75.9 million). The result was, as may be supposed, even greater mass armies than before. France, for example, between 1914 and 1918 called up 7,800,000 men – one fifth of her total population. Britain mobilized, either by voluntary recruitment or by conscription, 5,704,416.[11] This represented about 10 per cent of the total population, as compared with just over 8 per cent of the American population mobilized in 1861–65. The British Empire as a whole mobilized 8,654,467 men between 1914 and 1918.[12] Of course, by 1939 populations had expanded again, and the result – inevitably, and in spite of all the theories – was an even greater mobilization of the masses than in 1914: for the United Kingdom (*excluding* Women's Services, Civil Defence, the Merchant Navy and the Royal Observer Corps – all vital to the war effort) the total was 5,896,000; for the Empire, over 10 million.[13] By May 1945 the United States had more soldiers in Europe alone (2,618,023) than the whole Civil War recruitment for both sides. As the British Official History tersely remarks: 'War in 1944–1945 was still basically a matter of flesh and blood.'[14]

For the historian, then, the inescapable feature of the great wars of the First and Second Industrial Revolutions has been the participation of the human masses. All three were manpower wars, and all ways of writing about them, or theories evolved from them, which blur this fact are mischievous. The fundamental problems of manpower wars are: mobilization, movement (to and on the battlefield), armament, and control – all of them vastly complicated because of the great numbers involved. A useful exercise of theory, at any time after 1865, would have been the examination of these problems – and for Britain in particular the first of them, bedevilled as it was by the British devotion to the Voluntary System, with all its inequalities and wastefulness. Continental nations at least had a start here, and the United States, whose condition of unreadiness in 1941 was lamentable, drew upon past experience to produce at the twelfth hour a method whose results were sensational – at their peak in 1945 the American Armed Forces reached a total of 12,294,000 men (compared with 12,500,000 for the Soviet Union)[15] or 12.5 per cent of the population. But it was precisely the manpower war that the theorists of the Twenties and Thirties abhorred and preached constantly *against*.

The exigencies of such wars were strict. In all cases they made nonsense of the notion of a short war: the American Civil War lasted exactly forty-eight months, the First World War fifty-one months, the Second World War (in Europe) sixty-eight months. Expanding populations and developing technology were thus extending the duration of wars while laymen and politicians were recoiling from this fact and its distressing implications, and theorists offered tempting promises of a 'shorter way', either through alternative manoeuvres or through weaponry, or both. But the historical truth is that there *was* no shorter way – until the possession and use of the atomic bomb by one side created it. (We still don't know, of course, what happens in a war in which both sides possess nuclear weapons and have to take the decision whether to use them or not.) What the past has shown is that armies of millions, equipped by modern technology, cannot be defeated quickly, and that war economies show an almost incredible capacity for survival even under the most intense duress – as Germany proved under air attack in 1944 and 1945.[16] It requires the fullest, sustained pressure on both the military and the economic fronts (to say nothing of the psychological) to achieve 'victory' – a word in inverted commas because, by the time it comes, such is the destruction of life and *matériel* involved that its meaning can only be measured by what has been averted, rather than by what has been gained.

Under the eye of history, the strategy of mass manpower wars becomes a very limited exercise within a narrow margin of possibility. Whatever delightful prospects might be conjured up by the use of stimulating rhetoric – 'the strategy of the indirect approach', 'knocking away the props', 'the soft under-belly of the Axis', etc. – they proved to be delusions. The inexorable compulsions of Industrial Revolution war allowed no cheap rates. This Fuller came to perceive, and it is interesting to see how he treats, for example, those operations of General Sherman in 1864 which so much inspired Liddell Hart.

Eighteen sixty-four was the year in which Lieutenant-General Ulysses S. Grant became General-in-Chief of the United States armies. Sherman's operations then, for the historian – certainly for Fuller – form only a part of an overall strategy decided by Grant (though Grant and Sherman were friends who were able to discuss the conduct of the war with great frankness, and who were always receptive to each other's ideas). The strategy arrived at by Grant in 1864 involved four major armies, two in the east, two in the west, operating simultaneously against the two main Confederate forces, the Army of Northern Virginia, commanded by General Robert E. Lee, and the Army of Tennessee, commanded by General Joseph E. Johnston. On the Union side the pivotal army was General George G. Meade's Army of the Potomac, facing the main body of the Confederacy under Lee on the line of most direct approach to the Confederate capital, Richmond, Virginia. Others might manoeuvre; Meade must attack. Grant's orders were explicit:

'Lee's army will be your objective point. Wherever Lee's army goes, you will also go . . .'

Fuller writes: 'Meade's attack . . . was to be an attack in such overwhelming force that Lee would suffer so heavily that the Confederate Government would be unable to reinforce any other army . . . It was also to be a continuous attack, in order to prevent Lee's army recuperating, and to impede his sending men on furlough or to work in the fields or the workshops . . . Further than this, no exchange of prisoners was to take place.'[17] He says further:

'Grant's grand tactics were based, therefore, on the attrition of Lee, an attrition which was to lead to such an attenuation of his strength that he would be compelled to use his entire force on the defensive; this would deny him freedom of movement, and would consequently fix him.'[18]

The fixing of Lee enabled Sherman to march. Grant's orders to
his lieutenant in the West (4 April) were: 'You I propose to move
against Johnston's army, to break it up, and to get into the interior
of the enemy's country as far as you can, inflicting all the damage
you can against their war resources . . .' We have noted (p. 26) how
thoroughly Sherman carried out these instructions. But before he
could begin, Meade had to move against Lee; his advance into
Virginia began on 4 May, and four days later Sherman set out from
Chattanooga on the long march which ultimately took him through
Georgia to the sea and up into the Carolinas – the very stuff of
which myths can be made.

While Sherman advanced the price of his mobility was paid by
Meade's army. To fix a general of Lee's quality, leading an army
hardened in many battles whose morale was still high with the
memory of many victories, was never likely to be an easy task. By
12 June, following hard, slogging battles in the Wilderness and at
Spotsylvania and Cold Harbour, Meade's Army of the Potomac,
under Grant's personal direction, had sustained some 55,000
casualties, which represented no less than 52 per cent of its original
strength (see Table D, p. 47). What it represented in terms of
human suffering became all too clear as the boatloads of wounded
men returned to Washington with tales of Bloody Angle and other
savage fights under drenching rain with mud halfway to the knees.
Grant's reputation also became a casualty; Fuller writes: 'The
newspapers, ever eager to feed the masses on the carrion of events,
turned on Grant – he had failed, he was no more than a butcher,
and "had provided either a cripple or a corpse for half the homes of
the North." . . . Even today . . . in the opinion of many, Grant still
represents the butcher type of general.'[19]

Liddell Hart is only one of many who have been impressed by the
heavy casualties sustained by the Union forces in the East under
Grant's direction, and the much lighter casualties produced by
Sherman's war of manoeuvre in the West. Indeed, this comparison
is the very core of the myth of the 'indirect approach'. But Grant
had not failed. He had done what he set out to do; he had imposed
his will on Lee, who was consequently so weakened and so firmly
fixed in Virginia that he could do nothing to stop Sherman from
going on marching. He certainly could not send any help to
Johnston. Yet Liddell Hart, seeing the Virginia campaign as an
early 1914–18-style 'Western Front', argued that the Civil War was
won not by the great battles between Washington and Richmond,
but by blows against the Confederate economy down the
Mississippi and in the western theatre: 'The indirect approach to

the enemy's economic and moral rear had proved as decisive in the ultimate phase as it had been in the successive steps by which that decision was prepared in the west.'[20]

It is Fuller, however, who makes the point that, contrary to Liddell Hart's beliefs, there was no antithesis between the operations of Grant and Sherman – they were interdependent. So far from Sherman's movements being a means to 'overcome' the deadlock in the east, it was precisely that deadlock that made them possible. In other words, the 'indirect approach' was completely dependent on the hard grind of heavy battle against the enemy's main army on the direct line.

The two World Wars hammered home this lesson. In the First, Field-Marshal Lord Haig, whose reputation suffered even more severely than Grant's had done, enunciated as early as March 1915 a truth which held good for both:

'We cannot hope to win until we have defeated the German Army.'

Again it is Fuller who has most devastatingly displayed the foundations of this thought: 'Should Clausewitz's statement be accepted, that in a war against an alliance the aim should be the defeat of the principal partner, because "in that one we hit the common centre of gravity of the whole war", then, in 1914, the allied aim was to defeat Germany, since her defeat would carry with it the collapse of her allies.'[21]

Many people, including Mr Lloyd George, who became Prime Minister at the end of 1916, and Lord Hankey, the industrious and influential secretary to the War Cabinet, were ardent advocates of an 'indirect approach' to Germany via her allies; this strategy was called 'knocking away the props'. As expounded after the War, it nicely illustrates how one myth can beget another. Fuller deals with it summarily:

In what locality could Germany be most profitably struck? The answer depended on the most practical allied line of operations, which, in its turn, was governed by the location of the allied main bases. They were France and Great Britain, and in no other area than France could the ponderous mass armies of this period be fully deployed and supplied in the field. The main bases and the main theatre of war were fixed by geography and logistics, and no juggling with fronts could alter this.[22]

Historically, this is the crushing rejoinder to the myths and the theories – happily, Fuller the historian had supplanted Fuller the theorist by the time this was written. War has a habit of being

governed by great simplicities (to the dismay of complex minds).
The great simplicities of the First World War were these:
the presence of the main body of the German Army in France
supplied the objective;
the French road and railway networks supplied the essential
communications;
British and French industry supplied the technological base,
and all combined to lodge the Allied effort inexorably in France.
The difficulty was that from October 1914 the line of battle had
become continuous from the sea to the Swiss mountains; there
were no flanks to turn; there was only a front to be assaulted – a
front rendered practically impenetrable (as long as it was held by
determined troops) by the conjunction of quick-firing weapons,
wire and concrete. The costly attempts of the Allies to penetrate
this front between 1915 and 1917, often with poorly trained troops,
often by inept tactical methods and with inadequate technical
resources, created the dreadful picture of the Western Front which
haunted so many minds and contributed so powerfully to
mythology in the decades after the War. Fuller writes:

Exasperated by these unprofitable assaults, and ignorant of tactical
considerations, the allied statesmen accused the soldiers of lack of
imagination, and set out to recapture mobility by a change of front, as if
the locality itself was to blame for the stalemate. What they were unable
to appreciate was, that should another locality be found in which the
enemy's resistance was less formidable than on the Western Front, it
would only be a matter of time before the same tactical conditions
prevailed. It was the bullet, spade and wire which were the enemy on
every front, and their geographical locations were purely incidental.[23]

Ironies abound in such studies as these; it is one such that
President Abraham Lincoln had reached the same conclusion as
Fuller, starting from a somewhat different position, exactly ninety-
nine years earlier. Allied statesmen, between 1914 and 1918, tried
to discourage their generals from attacking on the Western Front;
in 1862, Lincoln bent his efforts to trying to make General George
B. McClellan attack *somewhere,* while McClellan contrived
endless delays by searching for an 'indirect approach'. Finally (9
April) Lincoln addressed him in set terms: 'You will do me the
justice to remember I always insisted that going down the bay[24] in
search of a field, instead of fighting at or near Manassas, was only
shifting and not surmounting a difficulty; that we would find the
same enemy and the same or equal entrenchments at either place
. . . But you must act.'[25]

The quest for an alternative front continued through the First World War until March 1918, when the German General Staff taught the amateur strategists of the Allies a final lesson by nearly winning the war outright on the Western Front. And in the event, of course, the war *was* won on that front – not surprisingly; it is hard to see where else the 2,562,000 Frenchmen, 1,794,000 British, 1,876,000 Americans, 145,000 Belgians and 55,000 Italians required to defeat the 3,527,000 Germans and Austrians[26] could have been assembled and maintained. Meanwhile, however, the quest had extorted an exorbitant price in terms of dispersion of British Empire effort and manpower. I have discussed this in detail elsewhere,[27] but this reminder seems appropriate:

The official statistical record lists ten major theatres of operations, besides France and Flanders, during the First World War. Unquestionably, the Western Front predominated: it swallowed up 5,399,563 men, compared with 3,576,391 for all the rest together. Yet three and a half million is no small number, and further inspection reveals more of interest. Five of those ten fronts accounted for just under 250,000 men between them, so that the remaining subsidiary campaigns used over three and a quarter million. This means, in effect, that although 'subsidiary', 'secondary', or whatever adjective one may care to use, they were, in fact, pretty big affairs. Egypt and Palestine, for example, from first to last, gave employment to 1,192,511 men; Mesopotamia to 889,702; the Dardanelles to 468,987; Salonika to 404,207; and, surprisingly, East Africa to 372,950 (against German forces which never totalled more than 15,500). And these were only the British Empire's contribution; there was a considerable French contingent at the Dardanelles, while at Salonika the French played the larger part. But for an Empire which, at the outbreak of war, had only been able to muster an Expeditionary Force of 100,000 men, these 'side-shows' alone represented an astonishing military expansion and effort.

Fuller's final comment on all this is scathing: 'All these peripheral endeavours to discover a penetrable front were a waste of effort, and in expenditure of man-power – the vital factor in mass warfare – costly in the extreme. The stalemate laughed each to scorn.'[28] It is Fuller who has pronounced the deadly epitaph of the 'strategy of the indirect approach' in that war; he called it 'the strategy of evasion'.[29]

'Evasion' meant evasion of obligations to allies, evasion of the unpleasant necessity to fight. The alternative was, of course, attrition, as in 1864 but on an immeasurably vaster scale – and it was this that aroused so much revulsion in Liddell Hart, in Fuller himself, and in many others. Yet, looking across the three wars whose characteristics are so akin, the mass casualties of attrition would appear to be an inevitable concomitant of wars of masses. The truth about this has never been better expressed than by the British soldier most concerned with applying it: by Haig in his Final Despatch – but largely due to the efforts of Liddell Hart and Fuller it became unfashionable to regard the victorious Commander-in-Chief as an important contributor to military thought. Yet from his first days in the Army Haig had been a serious student of war. As Chief of Staff in India (1909–11) he preached on Staff Tours the four necessary phases of battle:

the manoeuvre for position,

the first clash of battle,

the wearing-out fight of varying duration,

the eventual decisive blow.

'Attrition' was the 'wearing-out fight'. His war experience suggested no reason for departing from this analysis, and so he wrote in 1919:

In the stage of the wearing-out struggle losses will necessarily be heavy on both sides, for in it the price of victory is paid. If the opposing forces are approximately equal in numbers, in courage, in moral[e] and in equipment, there is no way of avoiding payment of the price or of eliminating this phase of the struggle. In former battles this stage of the conflict has rarely lasted more than a few days, and has often been completed in a few hours. When armies of millions are engaged, with the resources of great empires behind them, it will inevitably be long. It will include violent crises of fighting which, when viewed separately and apart from the general perspective, will appear individually as great indecisive battles. To this stage belong the great engagements of 1916 and 1917 which wore down the strength of the German Armies . . . If the whole operations of the present war are regarded in correct perspective, the victories of the summer and autumn of 1918 will be seen to be directly dependent upon the two years of stubborn fighting that preceded them.[30]

It took a second world war to prove the point (to those who had eyes to see) that evasion would not work, and that attrition would always be grim. In the 1914–18 war, the Western Front in North-West Europe came into being as soon as the German armies began to march, and it remained in being uninterruptedly, exercising continuous compulsions on all belligerents, from first to last. The Western Front of 1939 collapsed in 1940 – and had to be recreated in 1944 by a hazardous assault landing from the most elaborate amphibious operation in history. Once again, there were compelling reasons for making the supreme effort of the Western Allies in northern France, and they closely resembled those which had reigned in the previous war: 'Between D-Day and VE-Day, a cumulative total of almost 5,500,000 Allied troops had entered western Europe, along with 970,000 vehicles and over 18,000,000 tons of supplies.'[31] No such deployment could have taken place at a greater distance from the base – the United Kingdom; one has only to reflect on the vital importance of such devices as the Mulberry harbours or PLUTO[32] to perceive this truth. There is also food for reflection in the fact that General Eisenhower employed greater human masses in eleven months in this theatre than the British Empire had sent there in the fifty-one months of the First World War – and this despite the immensely increased armour and mechanization of 1944–45. War, as the British Official Historian says, was still 'basically a matter of flesh and blood'.[33]

The ultimate irony, however, is that, even so, this was not the main front. The main front was where the enemy's main army stood, and would have to be beaten; in 1864 that was Virginia, between 1914 and 1918 it was the Western Front, from 1941 to 1945 it was the Eastern Front.[34] It was on that front, as Table D (p. 47) shows, in battles more fierce, more dreadful, more destructive of human life than any of those fought in the First World War, that the German Army was ground down in the classic manner of the 'wearing-out struggle'. And the further irony is that it was also on the Eastern Front that the style of warfare advocated by Fuller and Liddell Hart – the fast-moving warfare of the armoured thrust under air supremacy – came nearest to its fulfilment. German generals have freely confessed their intellectual debt to these two British writers; but history shows that the lessons they learned enticed them only to their doom. The great clashes of armour supported by air power, the *Blitzkrieg* in its most powerful form,[35] produced casualty bills which put the 'blood-baths' of the First World War quite in the shade. In 1916, for example, in ten months of agonizing attrition at Verdun, the French and Germans between them suffered about 750,000 casualties; Germany alone sustained that number in the first six months of Operation BARBAROSSA in 1941 – and this was the period of her sensational victorious advances. Progressing technology, and the battle practice based upon it, had only hugely increased the cost of war.

This is the grim truth which military history, as opposed to military theory and mythology, has to teach us. (A further grim truth is that the only way so far devised of shortening a war of mass armies based on mass populations has been the invention of a weapon of mass extermination). It is difficult to resist the conclusion that much military theory between the wars, no matter how seemingly thoughtful, was really only mythology, an emotional reaction to the (then) unprecedented losses and destruction of the First World War. Because, for special reasons, both Britain and America were able to avoid similar losses in the Second – chiefly because neither was at any time engaged with the main body of the main enemy – there remains a difficulty in evaluating the theories in the light of history. 'Passchendaele' still seems much more real than Stalingrad – there are people still alive and whom one can talk to in English who were there. Yet history does tell us that, valuable though the theorists were in keeping minds awake which might otherwise have slumbered gently through the lullaby of peacetime military routines, they were missing the main point about war in their time, and thus failing to awaken their nation to its real coming needs. Fuller, of course, did see the point – when it was too late, when it had become history, and history had claimed him entire. The lesson of all this, I would suggest, is that it is unwise, at the end of a war, to set aside for purely emotional reasons the distilled experience of educated soldiers:

In this, my final Despatch, I think it desirable to comment briefly upon certain general features which concern the whole series of operations carried out under my command. I am urged thereto by the conviction that neither the course of the war itself nor the military lessons to be drawn therefrom can be properly comprehended, unless the long succession of battles commenced on the Somme in 1916 and ended in November of last year on the Sambre are viewed as forming part of one great and continuous engagement.

To direct attention to any single phase of that stupendous and incessant struggle and seek in it the explanation of our success, to the exclusion or neglect of other phases possibly less striking in their immediate or obvious consequences, is in my opinion to risk the formation of unsound doctrines regarding the character and requirements of modern war. If the operations of the past 4½ years are regarded as a single continuous campaign, there can be recognised in them the same general features and the same necessary stages which between forces of approximately equal strength have marked all the conclusive battles of history.[36]

Unfortunately, 'the character and requirements of modern war' were not appreciated; the lesson was not learned; and the consequences were accordingly painful. With regret the historian must attribute this result to seeking comfort in theory and mythology at the expense of fact.

1   Brian Bond, *Liddell Hart, A Study of his Military Thought*, Cassell, 1977, p. 44:
    'Liddell Hart was already (1925) forcing history to yield the appropriate lessons.'
2   He served in France from late September 1915 until mid-July 1916, when he was
    invalided home.
3   Sir Basil Liddell Hart, *Memoirs*, Cassell, 1965, i, p. 165.
4   Brigadier (then Lieut.-Col.) A. J. Trythall, letter in the *Journal* of the Royal United
    Services Institution, June 1970, pp. 71–2. Brigadier Trythall's *'Boney' Fuller: The
    Intellectual General* (Cassell) appeared in 1977.
5   The Chassepot breech-loading rifle, sighted up to 1,600 yards, with which the French
    infantry was equipped in 1870–71, was responsible for 'a small landmark in military
    history' (Michael Howard, *The Franco-Prussian War*, Rupert Hart-Davis, 1961,
    p. 335) when it forced the Prussian Guard to adopt a widely spaced attack formation full
    of significance for the future, but forgotten by both French and Germans in 1914. The
    steel Krupp guns with which the German artillery went to war also provided a preview
    of what 'artillery wars' might be like.
        In South Africa the British were the first to encounter the disconcerting phenomenon
    of the 'empty battlefield', the product of the combination of long-range, low trajectory,
    rapid small-arms fire and smokeless powder. This caused a revolution in tactics which
    the Regular B.E.F. of 1914 well understood but the new armies had to relearn at great
    cost.
        In the Russo-Japanese War modern heavy artillery displayed its crushing power
    against fortifications, while quick-firing field artillery exerted a dominant influence in
    the field. The fearful conjunction of machine-guns and barbed wire was also
    encountered.
6   The distance from Moscow to Port Arthur is 5,500 miles; only the single track of the
    Trans-Siberian Railway existed to supply the Russian armies.
7   Major-General J. F. C. Fuller, *The Decisive Battles of the Western World*, Eyre and
    Spottiswoode, 1956, iii, p. 6.
8   'Slashings' is an odd word; the conjunction with 'abattis' and 'wire entanglements'
    suggests that the meaning here is associated with the *Shorter Oxford English
    Dictionary's* 'the debris of felled trees'. Both sides in the Civil War felled trees freely to
    construct field defences.
9   Fuller, op. cit., p. 89.
10 Clement Eaton, *A History of the Southern Confederacy*, The Free Press (N.Y.), 1954,
    p. 93.
11 *Statistics*, p. 740; C. R. M. F. Cruttwell (*A History of the Great War, 1914–1918*,
    O.U.P., 1934) says 6,211,427.
12 *Statistics*, p. 740.
13 'Strength and Casualties of the Armed Forces and Auxiliary Services of the United
    Kingdom 1939 to 1945', H.M.S.O., Cmd. 6832, 1946.
14 L. F. Ellis and A. E. Warhurst, *Victory in the West*, H.M.S.O., 1968, ii, p. 405.
15 Charles B. MacDonald, *The Mighty Endeavour*, O.U.P., 1969, p. 514.
16 Despite the Allied Strategic Air Offensive, 'the German armaments production index
    rose from 100 in January 1942 to 153 in July, 229 in July 1943, 322 in July 1944' (Max
    Hastings, *Bomber Command*, Michael Joseph, 1979, pp. 226–7). In June 1941 German
    tank production was 310 of all types; for December 1943 the total was 1,229, reaching
    an all-time record of 1,669 in July 1944 (Richard Humble, *Tanks*, Weidenfeld and
    Nicolson, 1977, p. 104). German aircraft production rose from 25,094 in 1943 to 39,275
    in 1944.
17 Fuller, *The Generalship of Ulysses S. Grant*, John Murray, 1929, p. 225.
18 Ibid., p. 224.
19 Ibid., p. 274.
20 Liddell Hart, *The Way to Win Wars*, Faber, 1952, p. 146.
21 Fuller, *The Conduct of War, 1789–1961*, Eyre and Spottiswoode, 1961, p. 161.
22 Ibid., pp. 161–2.
23 Ibid., p. 161.

24 Chesapeke Bay; McClellan attempted to take Richmond by a flank attack from the Yorktown Peninsula, only to find Lee awaiting him behind strong entrenchments.
25 T. H. Williams, *Lincoln and His Generals,* Hamish Hamilton, 1952, pp. 69–70.
26 *Statistics . . .,* p. 628.
27 John Terraine, *The Western Front,* Hutchinson, 1964, pp. 53–4.
28 Fuller, *The Conduct of War,* p. 165.
29 This is the sub-title which Fuller gives to the section of *The Conduct of War* on pp. 160–5.
30 Sir Douglas Haig's *Despatches,* ed. Lieutenant-Colonel J. H. Boraston, Dent, 1919, pp. 320–1; see also the 1979 edition, with foreword by the author.
31 MacDonald, op. cit., p. 513.
32 Petrol Pipe-Lines Under The Ocean to supply the invading forces. A line from the Isle of Wight to Cherbourg was not very successful. Three were laid from Dungeness to Boulogne, later increased to six and ultimately eleven; average daily output in March-April 1945 was 3,100 tons.
33 L. F. Ellis, *Victory in the West* (H.M.S.O. 1968), ii, p. 405.
34 The resemblance between 1864 and 1944 is close. Just as Grant's fixing of Lee made possible Sherman's attack on the Confederate rear, so the Russian fixing of Hitler's main force made the Allied landings possible. Had Hitler been permitted to divert any significant part of his strength, particularly the attenuated Luftwaffe, against the Allies, their task would have been vastly more dangerous than it already was, and might have ended in a terrible disaster.
35 For Operation BARBAROSSA, in June 1941, the Germans deployed nineteen armoured and twelve motorized divisions, with some 2,000 aircraft. In the Battle of Kursk, July 1943, the Germans used seventeen Panzer divisions (1,800 tanks) and the Russians threw in 3,600 tanks. This was 'the greatest tank battle in history', but what decided it was probably the 6,000 Russian anti-tank guns.
36 Boraston, op. cit., pp. 319–20.

VII

ANTI-MYTH:
Soldiers and Politicians

*'La guerre est un malheur, mais il est encore plus malheureux qu'il
faut la confier aux militaires.'*
('War is a misfortune, but what makes it even more so is that it
has to be entrusted to the military.')
        (Aristide Briand, quoted by Lord Esher, August 1916)

'It is so important that soldiers and politicians should work
together in this war. It is only by the most complete
understanding and co-operation between the military and
civilian elements that we can hope to win.'
        (Lloyd George to Haig, November 1916)

Autocracies – absolute monarchies or dictatorships – have no
immunity from mythology; indeed, some of them are firmly
founded on it. It was unquestionably the vast body of myth
surrounding Napoleon I, rather than any inherited personal
quality, that gave Napoleon III his throne. Myth-laden Wagnerian
thunders have supplied background music for Imperial Germany
and the Third Reich, but one of the strongest inspirations of the
latter was the myth of 'the stab in the back' – the 'betrayal' of the
'undefeated' German Army by Communists, Jews and other
sinister elements in 1918. To uphold the Soviet autocracy, myth has
been elevated to the level of religion, and heresies have been
stamped upon with much ferocity; if the worst brutalities are now
unfashionable, a stream of exiles nevertheless reminds us that
disbelief in the prevailing mythology still earns heavy punishment.
But it is the *prevailing* mythology; in democracies every citizen can
be his own myth-maker. Once more it will be instructive to look at

the American Civil War and the two World Wars together, to see
how democracy has faced the problems of waging war.

In a democracy, the contrast between civilian and military is
sharp; most authoritarian régimes have a strong military content,
in peace as well as in war. But there is no mistaking the civil and
military sides of democracies – indeed, the normal posture of the
two elements is to eye each other askance. There is always, at the
back of the mind of the civilian of a democratic country the lurking
fear that the man in uniform may one day put a stop to democracy
altogether, while the military man reflects that but for the likes of
him and their willingness to spill their blood on its behalf,
democracy might well have been stopped long ago. A certain
degree of distrust, a hesitancy between civilian leaders and military
commanders, is virtually inevitable, and well illustrated by Aristide
Briand's well-known remark (itself embodying what has now
become enduring myth) which I have quoted above. In April 1864,
however, we find something very different.

On 30 April President Lincoln was composing a letter to General
Grant. The next day Grant was going to commit the Army of the
Potomac to the crossing of the Rapidan River, thus opening the
campaign in Virginia on which, as we have seen, his whole
ultimately victorious strategy pivoted. With sensitive awareness of
history in the making, Lincoln felt it appropriate to mark the
moment, and he wrote:

Not expecting to see you again before the spring campaign opens, I wish
to express to you in this way my entire satisfaction with what you have
done, so far as I understand it. The particulars of your plans I neither
know nor seek to know. You are vigilant and self-reliant, and pleased
with this, I wish not to obtrude any constraints or restraints upon you.
While I am very anxious that any great disaster or capture of our men in
great numbers shall be avoided, I know these points are less likely to
escape your attention than they would be mine. If there is anything
wanting which is within my power to give, do not fail to let me know it.
And now, with a brave army and a just cause, may God sustain you.

It was a model letter; as an American historian has written, 'a
perfect statement of the command relationship he expected to exist
between himself and Grant'.[1] It is also, in the light of later
experiences in democracies, full of ironies.

Lincoln's words to Grant have clear echoes. In May 1917, for
example, the civil and military leaders of France and Britain met in
Paris to mend the wreckage of Allied strategy after the disastrous
opening of General Robert Nivelle's offensive on the Aisne. It was,

ANGEL OF MONS

valse

by PAUL PAREE

THE LAWRENCE WRIGHT MUSIC Cº
8 DENMARK Sᵀ (Charing Cross Road)
LONDON W.C.
AUSTRALIA & NEW ZEALAND, E W COLE BOOK ARCADE, MELBOURNE

COPYRIGHT

'. . . the angel of the Lord faced the advancing Germans at Mons and forbade their further progress'.

SCHRECKLICHKEIT, 1864: '. . . systematic destruction of railroads, bridges, mills, workshops and many public buildings . . .'. Sherman's army in Atlanta.

SCHRECKLICHKEIT, 1942: all the male inhabitants of Lidice, in Bohemia, were killed and the village completely wiped out as a reprisal for the assassination of Reinhard Heydrich, Nazi 'Protector' of Czechoslovakia.

SCHRECKLICHKEIT, 1914: '. . . the feeling of the people was everywhere the same. They hated the Germans . . .'. Belgian civilian under arrest; was he a *franc-tireur*?

'. . . of all military costumes in 1914, the least inspiring . . .'. A group of Belgian Civil Guards in 1914.

LOSSES IN MASS WARFARE: some of the 43,500 men of both sides killed, wounded or missing at Gettysburg, 1863.

as I shall emphasize again later, one of democracy's darkest hours. Nivelle's replacement was in the air, and for the time being Field-Marshal Sir Douglas Haig was enjoying the unexpected and unusual favour of the British Prime Minister, Mr Lloyd George. As Lord Esher said, '[Lloyd George] has shelled off his Gallic proclivities in a remarkable degree. He has got to distinguish matter from form, and his notions of French superiority in everything are obliterated. He sees, with his serene Celtic forgetfulness, the British Commander-in-Chief and the British soldier through a more gracious stratum of air.'[2] Haig had already discovered this, recording in his diary (no doubt with some astonishment, in view of previous experiences) that Lloyd George had

'made two excellent speeches in which he stated that he had no pretensions to be a strategist, that he left that to his military advisers, that I, as C.-in-C. of the British Forces in France had full power to attack where and when I thought best. He [Mr. L.G.] did not wish to know the plan, or where or when any attack would take place. Briefly, he wished the French Government to treat their Commanders on the same lines. His speeches were quite excellent.'[3]

No doubt they were – as speeches. Equally excellent were parts of the first telegram from Winston Churchill to General Sir Claude Auchinleck on 1 July 1941, on the latter's becoming Commander-in-Chief, Middle East, in replacement of General Sir Archibald Wavell. Churchill said: 'You take up your great command at a period of crisis. After all the facts have been laid before you it will be for you to decide whether to renew the offensive in the Western Desert and if so when . . .' Churchill then offered a brief 'shopping list' of strategic preoccupations, and continued:

'You will decide whether and how these operations can be fitted together. The urgency of these issues will naturally impress itself upon you. We shall be glad to hear from you at your earliest convenience.'[4]

'Full power to attack where and when I thought best . . .', 'for you to decide . . .' In both these communications we seem to hear distinct echoes of Lincoln's letter to Grant. But there was an important difference: the American President meant what he said; the two British Prime Ministers did not. Grant, though neither he nor Lincoln could know this on 1 May 1864, was about to embark on the bloodiest campaign of the Civil War, that sequence of bitter battles in northern Virginia whose effect on his reputation we have already seen (p. 54). And though this was, indeed, to be the final campaign, ending with Lee's surrender at Appomattox Courthouse, that event was still a whole year away. Yet Lincoln never withdrew his confidence and support from Grant. Lloyd George's friendliness towards Haig, on the other hand, evaporated as swiftly as it had appeared, and turned, later that summer, when the Third Battle of Ypres ('Passchendaele' – the 'squalid catastrophe', as he called it) reached its height, to relentless dislike. And Churchill, for all his fair words, lost no time in thrusting his own strategic ideas upon Auchinleck, and pushing his general towards courses of action which the latter could not favour, until at last they had to part company. Yet Auchinleck had just become the first British general to beat a German general in battle in that war, when he defeated Rommel at the First Battle of El Alamein in July 1942, an event which Churchill scarcely seemed to notice.

All this would seem to suggest that the Democracies had actually regressed in their understanding of how to wage war. In some respects that was true, but in at least one important respect it was the opposite of the truth – in fact, a great and significant advance had been made in the seventy years which separated Lincoln from Churchill. As I shall shortly show, a remarkable *system* had been evolved, despite the fact that some of the personalities associated with it did not always use it properly.

---

1   T. H. Williams, *Lincoln and His Generals,* Hamish Hamilton, 1952.
2   John Terraine, *The Road to Passchendaele,* Leo Cooper, 1977, p. 88.
3   *The Private Papers of Douglas Haig 1914–1919,* ed. Robert Blake, Eyre and Spottiswoode, 1952, p. 228.
4   John Connell, *Auchinleck,* Cassell, 1959, p. 249.

VIII

ANTI-MYTH:
'The Proper Application of Overwhelming Force'

'Lincoln . . . was a better natural strategist than were most of the trained soldiers. He saw the big picture of the war from the start . . . He grasped immediately the advantage that numbers gave the North and urged his generals to keep up a constant pressure on the whole strategic line of the Confederacy until a weak spot was found – and a break-through could be made.'

(T. H. Williams, *Lincoln and His Generals*)

'Hitler's fate was sealed. Mussolini's fate was sealed. As for the Japanese, they would be ground to powder. All the rest was merely the proper application of overwhelming force.'
(Winston Churchill, *The Second World War;* comment on Pearl Harbour)

Three great modern democracies have conducted war on the grand scale – that is to say (for reasons intimately connected with Democracy itself) total war, war for the highest stakes. Of the three, two are republics, France and the United States, and one a constitutional monarchy, Great Britain. For all three the experience has been, in different ways, traumatic – again, for reasons intimately connected with Democracy itself. Before we compare the dilemmas posed by each war, and their solutions or otherwise, it may be as well to consider the structure upon which democracies must build all their war-making apparatus.

It need hardly be said that in a democracy, whether in peace or war, the conduct of affairs is decided by the political machinery (as opposed to, say, an autocrat's whim). At the very centre of the democratic political machinery, and linked by special relationships to the military machinery, stands the head of state. Nowhere is his relationship to the Armed Forces more special than in the United States, because there the President is also, *ipso facto,* the Commander-in-Chief. Lincoln's story is of particular note because, as we shall see, he not only held the title, but actually had at certain critical times to perform some of its practical functions, owing to the shortcomings of the military. In Britain, the monarch is, of course, the titular Commander-in-Chief of the Armed Forces, but there has been no practical significance attaching to that since the Battle of Dettingen in 1743, when George II became the last British monarch to command his army in the field. Indeed, with their entertaining aptitude for confusion, the British managed to retain the post of Commander-in-Chief of the Army in the hands of a serving officer, irrespective of the monarch's title, until 1904 (the last incumbent was Field-Marshal Lord Roberts). In the French Republic once, but only once, did a head of state perform to some extent the practical functions of a Commander-in-Chief in war. By coincidence, the same man also united the posts of head of state and head of government: he was M. Adolphe Thiers,[1] who played a large part in directing the military operations which ended the Paris Commune in 1871. But thereafter, in army matters, the Minister of War emerges as the man of power, responsible to the Prime Minister and advised by the General Staff.

Though no two of these three great democracies had similar systems, yet the same major problem sooner or later faced them all. That problem, fundamentally, was how to make military action conform fruitfully to the requirements of national policy – in other words, how to evolve and apply a successful grand strategy. In democracies, this is always complicated by the need to carry public opinion along. What does this opinion consist of? Clearly, a very considerable number of human beings possessing varying degrees of influence, holding different beliefs and all subject in varying degrees to the pressures of mythology.

First of all, the chief executive – in America the President, in France and Britain the Prime Minister – has to be in working accord with his Government, his Cabinet or War Cabinet colleagues who have been carried to their eminent positions by the varying processes of the democratic system, and whose duty is to make the separate parts of the state machine act efficiently. Next, there is the assembly of elected representatives of the nation: Congress, the House of Commons, the *Assemblée Nationale.* However apparently united behind a war effort, it remains the duty of this body to keep a vigilant and critical eye on the national interest, whether in its civil or its military aspect. Behind this powerful assembly stand the organs of the various vested interests – political parties, industry, trade unions, churches, and so on. And behind all of these stands that somewhat mysterious but ineluctable force, public opinion itself, with all the prejudices and passions which impel it to choose its representatives, and then to support them or throw them out.

Throughout the period of the great wars of the industrial democracies, the chief influence upon public opinion, the source of most of its information and most of its myths, has been the Press, which has thus been a power factor in its own right. This was never more frankly recognized than by Lloyd George, who included no fewer than three Press barons in his administration in 1917: Lord Rothermere (Air Minister), his brother Lord Northcliffe (Director of Propaganda in Foreign Parts) and Lord Beaverbrook (Minister for Propaganda). In all three of the wars with which we are concerned, the Press could not fail to exercise a powerful guidance of public opinion in the area of grand strategy.[2] It could, and did, lodge strategic objectives in the public mind, often with baleful results: 'On to Richmond!' – what disasters *that* inspired! '*A Berlin!*' – how many Frenchmen, I wonder, really thought that the French Army could march to Berlin in 1914? Yet the contrast between this bombast and the dismal reality of the Battles of the Frontiers could not fail to be discouraging. In the Second World War 'Save Finland!' could have produced disaster if acted upon, and 'Second Front NOW!' at certain stages could have produced total catastrophe. Such slogans, endlessly repeated and difficult to silence, can exert a hypnotic effect well able to undermine a weak government.

Democracy or otherwise, grand strategy – relating the waging of war to national policy – is central. In 1861, policy was not difficult to decide: for the newly formed Southern Confederacy it was simply to survive, to continue to be; for the North, the representative of Union, it was to suppress by force the 'combination' of the Southern States, and bring them back into the fold. When it came to working out a grand strategy for the fulfilment of these policies, neither side found the matter quite so simple.

In the wars of the industrial democracies, grand strategy involves a good deal more than the adoption of particular strategies or stratagems; it has resolved itself, in the end, around two elements – mass and command. They are closely interlinked. All three of the great wars fought by the modern democracies have involved the very large, if not total, mobilization of national resources in order to avoid defeat. This constitutes the mass: mass armies, drawn from mass populations, supported by mass production. It has immensely complicated the functions of command; in 1861 the difficulties revealed themselves very quickly.

In order to overthrow the Confederacy, the Union Government had to find a means of effectively re-occupying the Southern States with sufficient force to compel their allegiance to the Federal Government in Washington. This problem was difficult enough in the light of fanatical Southern determination to resist, but made the more so by the vast size of the Confederacy and the primitive condition of its communications. There was another problem, too: in 1861 the United States Army numbered 16,367 officers and men, the Navy 7,000. The bulk of the Army was scattered in 'penny packets' on the Indian frontiers. To officers and enlisted men alike, the Civil War posed an immediate problem of loyalty. For the latter, of course, this problem was simplified by the fact that a transfer of allegiance could only be made by desertion, and less than fifty all told were prepared to do that. The officers, on the other hand, could resign their commissions, with the result that 286 out of 1,036 Army officers and 322 out of 1,300 in the Navy did so and joined the forces of the states supporting the Confederacy. But the real point is that, at their fullest strength in 1861, neither the regular Army nor the Navy of the Union was adequate to carry out the grand strategy that the nation required. How little the difficulties of that strategy were at first appreciated may be seen from President Lincoln's call, on 15 April, three days after the outbreak of war, for 75,000 militia enlisting for three months' service.

Fortunately for the survival of democracies, there is usually some leading figure who at least glimpses military realities in moments of crisis. In the United States in 1861 this person was seventy-five-year-old Winfield Scott, General-in-Chief of the Army. He stated his view that 300,000 men would be needed to defeat the Confederacy.[3] He was wrong, of course: in the event the Union would raise one and a half million soldiers, and its armies would rise to a peak of 622,000 present for duty in April 1865.[4] Lord Kitchener was equally wrong in 1914, when he pronounced that Britain would need three million men for the war against Germany; in fact, the British Empire raised eight and a half million. But both men performed a valuable service in setting the sights high when others were still thinking in terms of limited liabilities and quick results.

It was not long before Lincoln, who had a natural aptitude for strategy never again quite matched by a democratic statesman, grasped the point that Scott was making. As soon as he did so, the war assumed its modern character. To apply the superior manpower of the North to the struggle involved, necessarily, also the application of its superior economic resources; in due course both military and economic warfare would require to be backed by political warfare, and thus the picture would be complete. A percipient recent historian of the Civil War says this of the way it had developed by 1865:

What happened on the field of battle had become more than ever the tip of the military iceberg. The great submerged mass was a matter of equipment, supply, transport and communications, of industrial power, and technical skill, and also of public opinion, civilian morale, and sheer will to resist. War had become a matter of management and organisation more than individual heroism or feats of derring-do. A policy of attrition by the stronger side ultimately wore out the weaker. This was now the way of reaching a military decision, less spectacular and dramatic than the old, but ultimately more relentless and inescapable. It was all summed up in a few words written in 1863 by one of the organisation men of the new warfare, Quartermaster-General Meigs: 'It is exhaustion of men and money that finally terminates all modern wars.'[5]

In 1861 these grim and prophetic truths were not yet apparent; Lincoln himself had yet to arrive at them, and in order to conduct war in this new style he would need to find modern generals, and to work out a system of using them. Because the whole thing was so new and unfamiliar, this naturally took a little time. What is important is that it was done; what is sad is that, this having been done, the lessons were so generally ignored elsewhere.

The correct grand strategy for the Union, which Lincoln was perhaps the first to grasp, was to bring all its strength, military, naval, economic and political, to bear simultaneously. Within that broad picture there were various particular strategies which needed to be conducted: a military strategy concerned with at least neutralizing Lee's Army of Northern Virginia and its permanent threat to Washington; a naval-economic strategy of blockade and capture of the Southern ports to cut off essential supplies from Europe and prevent the export of cotton; a military-naval-economic strategy of control of the Mississippi basin to divide the Confederacy; a political strategy of slave emancipation to isolate it and rule out European support. The command structure at the centre would need to have all these objectives continuously in mind.

In 1864 such a structure was achieved. Lincoln's own self-confidence had grown with each of his encounters with military ineptitude: timid McClellan, indecisive Halleck, egregious Pope, pathetic Burnside, hesitating Hooker, equally hesitating Meade. Certainly after Gettysburg (July 1863) but probably earlier, Lincoln had formed a clear idea of where the key to the war lay. The U.S. Navy, greatly expanded,[6] was playing its part well; the economic attrition of the Confederacy was mounting; General Grant's capture of Vicksburg on the day after Gettysburg had effectively cut the Confederacy in half down the Mississippi line. But there was a flaw. General George G. Meade and the Army of the Potomac had actually beaten the famous Robert E. Lee in battle, and caused the Army of Northern Virginia to retire from Union soil. But that was all; there had been no harrying pursuit, no clinching of the victory at Gettysburg; the Army of Northern Virginia remained in being, Lee remained in command, and still possessed the confidence of his men. And as long as this continued to be the case the North's advantages would continue to risk being nullified, either by bold strokes in the sensitive vicinity of Washington, or by swift reinforcement of threatened Confederate armies in other theatres.

Lincoln was quite sure by now what the answer was; he expressed it with perfect clarity in a letter to General Henry W. Halleck (General-in-Chief at that time) on 19 September: '. . . I have constantly desired the Army of the Potomac to make Lee's army, and not Richmond, its objective point.' Halleck might agree, but, as Lincoln knew only too well, Halleck was not the man to go after Lee. Neither was Meade; the very idea appalled him. 'His defensive victory at Gettysburg ruined him as an offensive general.'[7] So who could Lincoln find who shared his strategic views and had the ability to put them into practice?

The answer, of course, was Grant. Grant's advent as General-in-Chief, with the revived rank of Lieutenant-General,[8] on 9 March 1864, was the decisive element in the new command structure which would at last carry out the grand strategy of the Union. There was no dispute about what that should be between Grant and Lincoln; 'Grant's strategy was Lincolnian.'[9] Quickly recognizing the vital sector, he realized that he would have to remain with the Army of the Potomac in the East; but as General-in-Chief he now had responsibility for seventeen commands containing over half a million men. To ease the burden of co-ordinating all these into the overall design and release Grant for the field, Halleck was appointed Chief of Staff of the Army in

Washington. Mr Williams writes: 'The arrangement of commander-in-chief, general-in-chief, and chief of staff gave the United States a modern system of command for a modern war. It was superior to anything achieved in Europe until von Moltke forged the Prussian staff machine in 1866 and 1870.'[10]

It was not merely the system that was modern; so was the man himself. Mr Henry T. Williams contrasts Grant with his famous opponent, Robert E. Lee, who is (not without reason) generally regarded as one of the 'great captains' of history:

Fundamentally Grant was superior to Lee because in a modern total war he had a modern mind, and Lee did not. Lee looked to the past in war as the Confederacy did in spirit. The staffs of the two men illustrate their outlook. It would not be accurate to say that Lee's staff were glorified clerks, but the statement would not be too wide of the mark. Certainly his staff were not, in the modern sense, a planning staff, which was why Lee was often a tired general . . . Most of Lee's staff officers were lieutenant-colonels . . . Grant's staff was an organization of experts in the various phases of strategic planning. The modernity of Grant's mind was most apparent in his grasp of the concept that war was becoming total and that the destruction of the enemy's resources was as effective and legitimate a form of warfare as the destruction of his armies. What was realism to Grant was barbarism to Lee. Lee thought of war in the old way as a conflict between armies and refused to view it for what it had become – a struggle between societies. To him, economic war was a needless cruelty to civilians. Lee was the last of the great old-fashioned generals, Grant the first of the great moderns.[11]

It has been the fate of the modern generals to encounter very new dimensions of once familiar problems; the great armies of modern times with all their equipment are difficult to handle, and with their mass and their fire-power they are hard to beat. Even with the right idea, a sound system and a numerically superior and better equipped army, it took Grant a punishing year to accomplish his purpose. Distance, climate, the very mass that he wielded, to say nothing of Lee's great tactical skill and the fighting qualities of the Confederate soldiers, all told against him. But he never faltered, and in the end his cumulative, crushing pressure on the Confederacy produced its result. So it came about that with Grant in overall command, Sherman ably handling the Western theatre, General George H. Thomas savaging the Confederates in Tennessee and General Philip H. Sheridan 'taking out' that important strategic and economic asset to the Confederacy, the Shenandoah Valley, Lincoln at last found the men who could interpret his approach to war and turn it into battlefield reality.

And what Lincoln struggled to achieve between 1861 and 1864 was what the Anglo-French Alliance unsuccessfully fumbled for between 1914 and 1918, and the Anglo-American Alliance somewhat surprisingly arrived at between 1941 and 1945.

In 1914 Britain and France, and in 1917 the United States, were involved in war against the Central Empires of Europe. In 1939 Britain and France, and in 1941 the United States, were at war with the Third German Reich. Only France, on each of these occasions, was able to avoid the initial disadvantage suffered by the United States in 1861 – the lack of mass force for what was clearly going to be a mass war. This fact alone is a striking illustration of the special hazards that democracy undergoes in total war. Admittedly, in 1914, Britain did possess the largest navy in the world, but a navy is not the most obvious instrument for defeating countries whose capitals are Berlin and Vienna. Britain had had a warning, after all: the South African War, fought against an enemy never numbering more than about 60,000 mounted farmers, had required Britain to place 448,435 soldiers in the field. Against great European industrial nations, the probability of requiring a great army was not remote; but when such a thing was advocated – even by such admired figures as Lord Roberts – the democratic outcry was exceedingly violent. To pursue the matter would have spelt political suicide.

A complicating factor in the search for grand strategy in both the First and Second World Wars was that they were wars of coalitions, and unless one member of a coalition occupies the dominating position that Germany enjoyed *vis-à-vis* her allies, it is bound to be more difficult for a coalition to come to a conclusion than for a single government. For Britain in 1914, and for America later, the initial grave weakness of their armies increased the difficulty. Britain entered the war with a 'paper army' of 733,514 officers and men (including Reservists); yet the Expeditionary Force in August only numbered about 100,000. With the help of contingents from the Empire's only other regular land force, the Indian Army, and the Territorial Army, this figure rose to 163,897 in mid-September, 245,197 at the end of December, 601,000 by May 1915, and topped the million mark in February 1916 – nineteen months after the outbreak of war.[12] By contrast, the French mobilization order in August 1914 affected some four million men; between 2 and 18 August 3,781,000 men were carried to their appointed postings by the French railway system. Such disparity could only mean one thing: that the British voice in deciding grand strategy would necessarily be a quiet one – he who pays the piper calls the tune.

The misfortune was that the French themselves, through a faulty plan, immediately lost the strategic initiative, with the result that until almost the end of the War the Allies were reduced to the simple strategy of trying to seize this initiative back. Or, to put it another way, the French were forced to dance to the German tune, and, being the junior partner, so were their British allies.

This was still the situation when America entered the War in April 1917. Her own military position was worse than Britain's three years earlier: her regular Army, fortified by Federal National Guards (called up for the war with Mexico in 1916) numbered 208,034, and there were just over 100,000 National Guards in State service. In one respect, learning from its own Civil War experience as well as from that of its allies, the United States Government showed greater wisdom than Britain, in bringing in conscription immediately, whereas the British had waited two years before doing so, with inevitably wasteful results. Thanks to conscription, America was able to raise nearly five million men for the Forces in the nineteen months of war which remained. By November 1918 there were nearly two million American troops in France[13] –which seems to compare well with the British effort in the same span of time, but in fact does not.

The ineffectiveness of the vast amount of American manpower available and tapped is one of the continuing mysteries of the First World War.[14] The outstanding difference, clearly, between 1861 and 1914 was that mere manpower was no longer sufficient for a modern army. Equipment and organization were of vital importance, and in April 1917 the United States did not have a single formed division equipped for the field; ten months later, she only had one in the line of battle in France. By comparison, the British put four high-quality divisions in the line straight away; five months later they had eleven divisions in line, and after twelve months they had twenty-eight. Twelve months after entry into the War, the United States had two divisions in line. Nineteen months later, at the very end, the United States had eighteen divisions in the line; at the comparable stage Britain had had forty. Nor was this only a matter of delay in deploying men. In the first great 'American' battle of the War, St Mihiel on 12–13 September 1918, the United States Army used 3,000 guns, not one of which was of American manufacture. The first American-designed and American-built tank (a 2-man 2½-tonner) arrived in France in October 1918; only fifteen were ever constructed. The American Air Force was only effective during the last weeks of the War, and in order to be so acquired 2,676 aircraft from the French. No doubt, given another year of war, American manpower and productivity would have played a far greater part; but in the time given there was no comparison with the finely appointed army which General McClellan was able to take almost to Richmond within a year of the outbreak of the Civil War, or the lavishly equipped hosts which began to appear in 1942.

It is not surprising then, in view of these weaknesses, that the United States, like Britain at the beginning, spoke with a weak voice in the debates about grand strategy. But there was a yet more powerful reason: the fact is that there was very little grand strategy to debate. By the time the American forces became at all effective, the Germans had hammered home the military strategic lesson of the War. (From the beginning, economic and political strategies had been invoked; the Germans had scored the chief successes with these: the U-boat blockade, bringing in Turkey and Bulgaria on their side, stimulating the collapse of Russia – a great coup.) As regards Western military strategy, its central truth was as stated by Haig in March 1915 (see p. 55): 'We cannot hope to win until we have defeated the German Army.' Lincoln and Grant would have understood him perfectly, and as far as the French were concerned he was only stating something which was obvious enough, since the bulk of the German Army was on their soil. Nor were the Americans in 1917 disposed to argue; defeating the Germans was what they had come to France to do and they had practically no interest in any other activity. The crises produced by the great German offensives of March-July 1918 finally demonstrated that there was no other way.

The sheer brutal simplicity of the necessary strategy repelled many Allied statesmen, particularly some of the British, who were unused to the exigencies of continental war, and preferred not to know too much about them, even while the War was on. As a tart political observer remarked in July 1915: 'The Government were content to remain in a kind of dusk with regard to military operations.'[15] Needless to say this frame of mind, evolved across decades of Victorian Liberalism, did not make the integration of policy and command – the fundamental of grand strategy – any easier. So for sound reasons, chief of which was the French Army's heavily preponderant rôle, General Joseph Jacques Césaire Joffre exercised most of the functions of an Allied Commander-in-Chief. Because he never held the title, many people in Britain who should have known better quite failed to grasp the point; even some twenty years later, Lloyd George was posing in all seriousness the question whether Mr Asquith's government should have 'vetoed'

Joffre's double offensive in Artois and Champagne in September 1915. There was no possibility of 'veto'; the only decision the British could have taken was whether to give support to their Allies, or risk a breakdown of the Alliance by standing aloof. Soldiers, closer to the realities of war, could see the matter more clearly. Thus Haig, less than a fortnight after becoming C.-in-C. in December 1915, interviewed the Head of the French Mission at British G.H.Q.: 'I pointed out that I am *not under* General Joffre's orders, but that would make no difference, as my intention was to do my utmost to carry out General Joffre's wishes, as if they were orders.'[16]

It was the only way. And in 1916, for the first time, Joffre made the attempt to bring all the forces of the Entente simultaneously to bear, as Lincoln and Grant had done for the Union in 1864. It was not easy: the Russians participated, but in their own time and in their own way; Italy also picked her moments; Romania practically committed suicide by failing to co-ordinate with others; the British played their part with honour. Yet the attempt failed, and no similar attempt was made until two years later, in September 1918, by which time, of course, the Eastern Front had ceased to exist.

Two significant experiments in grand strategy-making were carried out in the First World War. The first was the setting up of the Supreme War Council, with political and military representatives of France, Britain, Italy and the U.S.A., in November 1917. This was an organ which appealed to politicians because it gave scope to their favourite activity, talk. It was swept into paralysed oblivion in the crises of the great German offensives of 1918, because a debating society cannot be an instrument of command.[17] The same crises themselves produced the next experiment – an Allied Generalissimo, General (later Marshal) Ferdinand Foch. Under this institution the Allies conducted the remainder of the War, and because the War ended in victory the institution received much credit; its apparent revival in the next war, in the persons of the Supreme Allied Commanders of the various theatres, also put it in a rosy light. The truth is somewhat less friendly. Foch's mode of command was very much akin to Lee's: it was inspirational, operating through a small staff (about twenty all told) of relatively junior officers, quite unlike the great planning organizations over which the Supremos of the Second World War presided. Indeed, one must correct Mr T. Henry Williams's verdict (p. 73); Lee was not 'the last of the great old-fashioned generals' – the very *last* was probably General Douglas MacArthur, but Foch was certainly one of the breed.

Foch himself was well aware of the limitations of the command function reposed in him; as he said:

What later on was known by the term 'unified command' gives a false idea of the powers exercised by the individual in question – that is, if it is meant that he commanded in the military sense of the word, as he would do, for example, in the French Army. His orders to Allied troops could not have the same characteristic of absolutism, for these troops were not his, especially in the sense that he could inflict punishment in case this became necessary. But by persuasion he could stimulate or restrain their Commanders-in-Chief, decide upon the policy to follow, and thus bring about those concerted actions which result in victory, even when the armies concerned are utterly dissimilar.[18]

With Haig, Foch had occasional disputes, but by and large their relationship was cordial and fruitful; it was Haig, after all, who had asked for Foch to be given the command-in-chief, and it was Haig's armies, during the last three victorious months of the War, which were setting the pace, so there was not a great deal for them to dispute about. With the American Commander-in-Chief, General John J. Pershing, the story was different. Pershing was determined that America's large forces should preserve their national identity, that they should fight and win great American battles, as behoved the representatives of the great American Democracy in arms. This policy necessarily clashed with the urgency, for the weary Europeans, of ending the War – but there was very little that Foch could do about it. The breakdown of the American administrative services in the Argonne at the end of September was a chastening experience; fortunately the Allied advance fared better further north, the British broke through the Hindenburg Line, the collapse of the German Army accelerated, and Franco-American discords faded out in the reek of Germany's sunset.[19]

When war came again, against a revived Germany in 1939, once more it was only France that could immediately field a mass army; 2,776,000 men in front-line units, 2,224,000 more in the interior. As in 1914, Britain could only offer five divisions, rising to nine on the eve of the German attack in May 1940, though this time the British had so far overcome rooted prejudice as to bring in conscription in peacetime (April 1939) as well as doubling the Territorial Army.[20] The result of this discrepancy between the efforts of the two countries was precisely what it had been before: the British voice in determining strategy was feeble, the direction of the Allied armies passed without question to France – and

France proved to be far more the broken entity which she became for a time in 1917 than the determined (if misguided) one of 1914. Six weeks of violent combat in 1940[21] revealed the extent of the psychological and political rot that had set in between the wars, and the military backwardness beneath the appearance of French strength.

With France gone, and the remains of the Expeditionary Force back on home ground, British grand strategy in 1940 became a very simple matter: like that of the Confederacy in 1861, it really had only one object – survival. The inspiring leadership of Churchill encouraged in the British an optimism not justified by realities; the unpalatable truth was, as Sir Basil Liddell Hart has said, that

'By refusing to consider any peace offer the British Government had committed the country to a course that . . . was bound, logically, to lead through growing exhaustion to eventual collapse – even if Hitler abstained from attempting its quick conquest by invasion. The course of no compromise was equivalent to slow suicide.'[22]

However, as Liddell Hart adds, 'the British people took little account of the hard facts of their situation. They were instinctively stubborn and strategically ignorant.' They decided to hang on like grim death, and mobilize as they had never done before; the entire national economy of Great Britain was geared to the war effort, and at the same time imperial resources were greatly expanded. Yet the fact remains that in 1940 and 1941 Britain possessed only sufficient strength for peripheral operations. She could, and did, trounce the Italians in Africa, but as regards defeating her main enemy, Germany, there could be no possibility of such a thing without the intervention of a powerful ally. There were only two possible candidates: the Soviet Union (ruled out by several considerations, not least the Nazi-Soviet Pact) and the United States, still in the fetters of the Neutrality Acts. In the event, it required the combination of both of these, added to the full weight of the British Empire, to do the job.

The entry, first of the U.S.S.R., then of the U.S.A., into the conflict in 1941 provided at last the manpower masses that this war, like the First, was going to demand. The Soviet Union, of course, had always been the land of masses (the 'Russian steam-roller' was no novelty); the Red Army in 1941 was estimated at twelve million men. At its peak strength in 1945 it was estimated at twelve and a half million, which, taking into account the enormous casualties already suffered, represents a prodigious mass deployment.

America's situation in 1941 has been well described by one of her Official Historians: 'At the time of Pearl Harbour the United States still was unprepared for war, but it stood much nearer the threshold of preparedness than it had at the start of any previous war.'[23]

The reason for this is worth a brief inspection. It is apparent that President Roosevelt, formally bound though he was by the Neutrality Acts, had nevertheless been edging the United States towards belligerency from the beginning. In May 1940, as the German blows fell upon France, he was telling his *confidant* Harry Hopkins that there must be a 'complete reorientation' of United States policy.[24] By December 1941 this had already gone a long way; under the cloak of 'defence of the Western Hemisphere', Roosevelt had assumed some decidedly un-neutral positions, favourable to Britain, hostile to Germany. A notable example was the decision to designate some three-quarters of the North Atlantic as 'defensive waters' of the United States, within which merchant shipping (including British convoys) would enjoy the protection of the U.S. Navy. Of course, this measure proved to be to America's own advantage when war came, but the methods by which Roosevelt achieved it and others can hardly be described as a triumph of democratic procedure.[25]

It was the results that counted. In 1941 the United States Army already numbered 1,750,000 men, and although only one entirely ready division existed, thirty-seven others were in training – a very great contrast with 1917, let alone 1861. The navy, especially after the Pearl Harbour losses, was weak for its rôle, and the army air force was down to a mere 807 combat planes (though here again the contrast with 1917–18 is striking). But this was not the point:

The real accomplishment of the preparedness program . . . would have to be sought not in what had been completed but in what had been started. Keels had been laid and substantial work accomplished on eight new battleships, while construction was so far along on new aircraft carriers that within two years the Navy would have ten, plus thirty-five of a new class, a small escort carrier. Eleven government shipyards and over a hundred private yards were working three eight-hour shifts a day, including Sundays . . . Some of the planes that would prove to be the workhorses of the air war were already in production . . .[26] More than 425,000 people were working in aircraft plants, and already the industry had expanded to the point that almost 3,000 planes would come off the assembly lines during the first month of 1942.[27]

In January 1942 President Roosevelt laid down production targets for the year: 60,000 planes, 45,000 tanks, 8 million tons of merchant shipping. Mr MacDonald comments: 'The figures sounded incredible, even to those intimately involved in achieving them; but most would be met.'[28] The manpower story was of similar dimensions: at their peak the United States Armed Forces very nearly equalled those of the Soviet Union. In north-west Europe alone, General Eisenhower's command reached a maximum of four and a half million – ninety-one divisions, of which sixty-one were American. This was certainly democratic war-making with a new look.

The system of command devised to direct these unprecedented masses was also new. Britain, between the wars, had evolved the admirable Chiefs of Staff Committee (an innovation so obviously useful that one can only wonder at its being so slow in coming). The function of this committee was to present the Government with the balanced joint advice of all three services in the framing of its military (and sometimes foreign) policy. In war, this body (headed by the Prime Minister in his capacity as Minister of Defence) became the strategic arbiter. America lost no time in setting up similar machinery, which in both countries was now called the Joint Chiefs of Staff. At the *Arcadia* Conference in Washington in December 1941, during the happy, beaming honeymoon of Anglo-American relations, the two groups of Joint Chiefs were fused into a Combined Chiefs of Staff Committee, with a permanent apparatus. This body became the ultimate strategy-making institution for the two Western Allies; Supreme Commanders in their theatres of war received their orders through it, and reported back formally to it. Churchill wrote: 'It may well be thought by future historians that the most valuable and lasting result of our first Washington conference . . . was the setting up of the now famous "Combined Chiefs of Staff Committee" . . . There never was a more serviceable war machinery established among allies . . .'[29] Field-Marshal Lord Alanbrooke, who was to become one of its most distinguished members, was sceptical at first, but later fully endorsed Churchill's opinion:

'My views altered completely as time went on and I grew to have the greatest faith in the Combined Chiefs of Staff organization as the most efficient that had ever been evolved for co-ordinating and correlating the war strategy of two allies.'[30]

Naturally, like all other human institutions, the Combined Chiefs of Staff Committee was subject to the qualities or failings of the high officers who sat upon it. National differences (what often looks like the contest between American dogmatism and British pragmatism, or, from the other side of the table, American determination and British timidity) inevitably contributed discords. There were seemingly incorrigible conflicts between the American Navy, chiefly interested in the war against Japan, and the American Army, with its commitment to the European theatre. Above all, there were the personalities of the two great leaders, Roosevelt and Churchill, both of them always liable, in the eyes of their military advisers, to take up far-fetched schemes and fly off at tangents. The professionals had to evolve their method of dealing with this problem, well summed up in a piece of advice given to Brooke by Field-Marshal Sir John Dill at the Casablanca Conference in 1943: 'You know that you must come to some agreement with the Americans and that you cannot bring the unsolved problem up to the Prime Minister and the President. You know as well as I do what a mess they would make of it.'[31]

Of course, there were bound to be *some* messes; but the organization was sound. It was perhaps never sounder than at the very beginning, when it took the bold decision to continue to treat Germany as the main enemy, although it was Japan that had attacked America. This immediate formulation by the Democracies of a correct grand strategy is the measure of the advance from Lincoln's long drawn-out perplexities between 1861 and 1864, and the stumbling of the Entente throughout the First World War.

---

1 Thiers was also, of course, a famous historian of the French Revolutionary and Napoleonic Wars.
2 In the Second World War a new medium, radio, deeply affected public opinion. Hitler and Mussolini used it to excite their people; Roosevelt and Churchill used it as a steadying force. In Britain, certainly, the contrast between the public moods in the two World Wars was very marked. Despite much greater danger and hardship, the British public was far steadier in the second war than in the first. It is hard to believe that this is not largely due to the B.B.C.'s News Service, in particular the 'Nine O'Clock News', which became a national institution. The calm, even voices of Alvar Liddell, John Snagge, Stuart Hibbert and their colleagues, in bad times as well as good, were the very antithesis of the screaming headline and the strident tone of a cinema newsreel.
3 R. E. Dupuy and T. N. Dupuy, *The Compact History of The Civil War,* Hawthorn Books (N.Y.), 1960, p. 25.
4 Clement Eaton, *A History of The Southern Confederacy,* The Free Press (N.Y.), 1954, p. 94.
5 Peter J. Parish, *The American Civil War,* Eyre Methuen, 1975, p. 159.
6 1861: forty-two vessels in commission (no armour-clads); 1865: 670 vessels in commission, including armour-clads.
7 T. H. Williams, *Lincoln and His Generals,* Hamish Hamilton, 1952, p. 219.

8 Only two officers in the history of the United States Army had previously held the rank of lieutenant-general: George Washington and Winfield Scott.

9 Williams, op. cit., p. 251.

10 Ibid., p. 248.

11 Ibid., pp. 256–7.

12 There were, of course, British expeditionary forces in other theatres of war besides France during this time.

13 'Ration strength': 1,876,000; 'Combatant strength': 1,175,000 (*Statistics*, p.628.)

14 See John Terraine, *To Win a War,* Sidgwick and Jackson, 1978, pp. 15–20.

15 F. S. Oliver, *The Anvil of War,* Macmillan, 1936, p. 109.

16 Robert Blake (ed.), *The Private Papers of Douglas Haig 1914–1919,* Eyre and Spottiswoode, 1952, p. 122.

17 For fuller discussion of the Supreme War Council see Terraine, *The Western Front,* Hutchinson, 1964, pp. 101–8.

18 Marshal Foch, *Memoirs,* (trans. Colonel T. Bentley Mott), Heinemann, 1931, pp. 210–1.

19 See Terraine, *To Win a War,* Sidgwick and Jackson, 1978, esp. pp. 132–4 for a serious disagreement between Foch and Pershing.

20 Unfortunately the immediate effect of the paper doubling of the Territorial Army seriously damaged the efficiency of its units.

21 Because of the completeness of the débâcle in 1940, exact figures for the French casualties in the Battle of France cannot be given. Alistair Horne, in *To Lose a Battle* (Macmillan, 1969), puts them at around 300,000 killed and wounded, which yields a daily rate of loss (forty-six days) of 6,521 – very considerably higher than that of any of the big British battles of the First World War referred to in Table D (p. 47).

22 Sir Basil Liddell Hart, *History of the Second World War,* Cassell, 1970, p. 141.

23 Charles B. MacDonald, *The Mighty Endeavour,* O.U.P., 1969, p. 44.

24 Joseph P. Lash, *Roosevelt and Churchill 1939–1941,* André Deutsch, 1977, p. 126.

25 Ibid., pp. 415–9.

26 P–38 Lightning, P–47 Thunderbolt, P–51 Mustang, A–20 Havoc, B–17 Flying Fortress, B–24 Liberator.

27 MacDonald, op. cit., p. 43.

28 Ibid., p. 44.

29 Sir Winston Churchill, *The Second World War,* Cassell, 1950, iii, pp. 608–9.

30 Arthur Bryant, *The Turn of the Tide,* Collins, 1957, p. 316.

31 Ibid., p. 350.

IX

ASIDE:
Making Things Difficult

The tribulations of the United States during the American Civil War repay study from all angles. Being a civil war, the event was naturally steeped in politics, as the Cold War is and always has been, as the Korean War was, as all phases of war in Vietnam were, as terrorism and guerilla (urban or otherwise) clearly remain. And if democracy seems ever to relish new political aberrations to hamper its military conduct of a fight for survival, that was certainly no less the case between 1861 and 1865. Indeed, as Mr Peter Parish has said, 'The only really surprising thing about the intermingling of political and military matters during such a war is that so many people have found it remarkable. It was not merely inevitable, it was right and proper – which is not to say that such matters were always conducted in a right and proper way.'[1]

Politics were present from beginning to end, and permeated the war through and through. We have seen that, at the outbreak in 1861, the total strength of the United States Forces on land and sea was less than 25,000 men – nothing like enough to inflict quick defeat on the South. So, despite the blissful ignorance which encouraged many intelligent men to think otherwise, it was going to be a long war. Mass armies would have to be raised – and organized into glittering commands far beyond the imaginings of peacetime soldiers. This meant that 'civil leadership, civilian participation, and citizen-soldiers shaped the conduct of the war at every turn'.[2]

This, of course, also meant an intensification of the political character of the war: 'if ever there was a war that met the textbook definition and was simply an extension of politics – ward and county and state-house politics, politics at the most lived-in levels – it was this one, and nobody but professional soldiers was especially shocked thereby.'[3] What followed from this, something that certainly did shock professional soldiers (even if only for the human reason that they felt cheated when passed over), was that every one of the glittering new commands became a political prize.

Whatever British officers may have had to contend with in their transactions with politicians in modern times – and often it has been bad enough – at least they have been spared that degree of jobbery. It is a long time now, in this country (part, indeed, of long abandoned traditions of aristocratic privilege handed down from the feudal system, purchase of commissions, etc.), since the raising of a military unit has been a matter of political patronage; yet in the volunteer army of the Union, raised by the States themselves, such patronage was the perquisite of each State Governor and the political machine which he conducted. And as though this was not bad enough,

Partly out of faith in grass-roots democracy, partly for lack of any available alternative, captains and lieutenants were elected by the rank and file of their own company. Election of officers was pernicious nonsense from an orthodox military standpoint, but probably a necessary evil in a situation, a society and a conflict of this kind. It also meant that the permeation of army life by political influence and political considerations extended from top to bottom; even an election for corporal in one Confederate company turned into a lively debate between the two candidates over Unionism and states rights, although the winner was the candidate who had taken the precaution of providing two jugs of whisky 'to treat the boys' – another time-honoured electoral practice.[4]

It was fortunate for the Union that the Confederacy decided to saddle itself with parallel absurdities.

As at the bottom, so, but even more so and with more serious results, at the top: brigade and divisional commands were generally distributed on political grounds, even when the most elementary professional qualifications were lacking in the men appointed. It frequently required a minor disaster in the field (sometimes a major one) to get rid of such incompetents. And at the army corps level, the very organization itself was a political matter – in the Army of the Potomac a subject of dispute between senior Republican officers who resented the ascendancy of their Democratic army commander, George B. McClellan, and the younger officers of the same political persuasion as himself whom he had brought forward. The army corps system was imposed on McClellan not, primarily, for reasons of military efficiency –the Union never did have enough really competent officers at that level of command[5] – but for reasons of political balance.

If corps commands within armies were political appointments, how much more was that true of independent army commands. Grant himself, in the Western theatre, had to cut the egregious McClernand down to size, and, if he had not pulled off some spectacular successes in battle, might well have found himself ousted by the other's political influence. Politically powerful but professionally lustreless generals like Nathaniel P. Banks or Benjamin F. Butler proved to be utterly irremovable. For the professional officer, the West Pointer, generally scorned and envied simultaneously by his political colleagues, this deadweight became a hazard of war as normal as facing the enemy, and no one was immune: 'Grant was supposed to see that in many cases the political general had to be used because it would cost too much to discard him. The lieutenant-general commanding was not expected to come running to the White House every time he found such a person in his path.'[6]

One event, in two of its aspects, of those distant times may make the British serviceman or student of military affairs boggle even now, in these days of constant political wonders. This was the Presidential Election of 1864. Not even the crisis of a war for the survival of the Union itself could disturb this sacred democratic ritual, but what is really astounding is that the man who opposed Lincoln's re-election was a general – none other than McClellan himself, no longer holding a command, but still adopting an inappropriate air of martial glory. With Grant and Lee firmly locked in their decisive combat, and Sherman shortly to begin his march to the sea, McClellan stood on a platform of negotiated peace, based on the assumption (though he carefully refrained from saying so himself) that the conduct of the war was a failure. Even with Sherman's timely victory at Atlanta, and Sheridan's final conquest of the Shenandoah Valley, Lincoln was only able to defeat McClellan by the narrow margin of 2,216,067 popular votes to 1,808,725 – though this result, in the electoral college, gave Lincoln the massive majority of 212 to 21. It was an impressive view of democracy at war – the British, after all, did wait until Hitler had been defeated before conducting that majestic exercise of democratic prerogative by which they dismissed Churchill in 1945. But there was an even more remarkable element within the vote for Lincoln.

In this election, the soldiers themselves had voted. Election day was 8 November, and in those closing months of 1864 war-weariness had become a powerful motive in the nation and also in the army – the Army of the Potomac above all. Conscription was

universally unpopular: 'successive drafts looked as likely to lose
votes as raise men.'[7] The battles in Virginia in the early summer had
been desperate, bloodthirsty affairs and there was every indication
that future battles would be as hard. And there was no visible end
in sight. At this critical juncture, for the first time in history, the
soldiers of a large modern democracy were given the vote – 'even
though it was clear that a soldier who wanted to fight no more,
disliked his generals or had lost track of what he was fighting for
would assuredly vote for the opposition, which if it won would be
under a strong compulsion to call off the war altogether. To give
soldiers that much control over their own destiny was
unprecedented, and it might be very risky, but it was
unavoidable.'[8]

In the decision to let the soldiers vote Grant, as General-in-
Chief, naturally played an important part; he explained his views at
length in a letter to the Secretary of War, Mr Edwin M. Stanton,
which may be considered a fundamental document for the
understanding of citizen armies and democracy at war:

The exercise of the right of suffrage by the officers and soldiers of armies
in the field is a novel thing. It has, I believe, generally been considered
dangerous to constitutional liberty and subversive of military discipline.
But our circumstances are novel and exceptional. A very large proportion
of legal voters of the United States are now either under arms in the field,
or in hospitals, or otherwise engaged in the military service of the United
States.

Most of these men are not regular soldiers in the strict sense of that
term; still less are they mercenaries, who give their service to the
Government simply for its pay, having little understanding of the political
questions or feeling little interest in them. On the contrary they are
American citizens, having still their homes and social and political ties
binding them to the States and districts from which they come and to
which they expect to return.

They have left their homes temporarily to sustain the cause of their
country in its hour of trial. In performing this sacred duty they should not
be deprived of a most precious privilege. They have as much right to
demand that their vote shall be counted in the choice of their rulers as
those citizens who remain at home. Nay, more, for they have sacrificed
more for their country.

As a West Point soldier, one of the most outstanding of the breed,
Grant then added this:

I state these reasons in full, for the unusual thing of allowing armies in the
field to vote, that I may urge on the other hand that nothing more than the

fullest exercise of this right should be allowed, for anything not absolutely necessary to this exercise cannot but be dangerous to the liberties of the country. The officers and soldiers have every means of understanding the questions before the country. The newspapers are freely circulated, and so, I believe, are the documents prepared by both parties to set forth the merits and claims of their candidates.

Beyond this nothing whatever should be allowed. No political meetings, no harangues from soldiers or citizens, and no canvassing of camps or regiments for votes . . .[9]

Within these limits (bearing in mind that in such an army every camp fire was potentially a political meeting) the experiment was carried out, and Grant's trust was seen to be justified. The soldiers did not, in any significant numbers, try to vote themselves out of the war. Their vote went to Lincoln by four to one – far more than can be accounted for by manipulation or fraud, though both were in some degree undoubtedly present. And the Union prevailed in the war, after all. So democracy, in taking this most alarming risk, found in it its strongest vindication. It must be admitted, of course, that United States democracy, in 1864, was still youthful, moving towards the crest of an unrivalled economic, technological and numerical expansion, and basically bursting with self-confidence. Conditions today are not the same, either in America or in Britain. Yet we may draw some encouragement from this story. There are signs – not as many as one might wish, not often as dramatic as one might hope, but signs nevertheless – that appeals made to a broadly enough based democracy can still win assent, even when it hurts. When that happens, we see democracy rise again above its self-inflicted impediments, as it did in 1864. But how it does make things difficult!

----

1   Peter J. Parish, *The American Civil War,* Eyre Methuen, 1975, p. 154.
2   Ibid., p. 129.
3   Bruce Catton, *Grant Takes Command,* Dent, 1968, p. 145.
4   Parish, op. cit., p. 152.
5   Neither did the Confederacy – but it took care to have fewer army corps. The British Expeditionary Force between 1914 and 1918 experienced the same difficulty in finding officers able to perform the important duties of this command level. That is one of the drawbacks of a small peacetime army.
6   Catton, op. cit., p. 145.
7   Parish, op. cit., p. 531.
8   Catton, op. cit., p. 375.
9   Grant to Stanton, 27 September 1864; quoted by Catton, op. cit., pp. 375–6.

X

ANTI-MYTH:
Democracy's Dark Hour

'The point is that all our best soldiers agree, and yet the politicians will not accept their opinion.'
(Colonel Repington, 30 December 1916)

'The old coat of democracy, never intended for wear at Armageddon, was showing white at the seams.'
(Major-General Sir Edward Spears, *Prelude to Victory*)

There were bad moments for democracy in the course of the American Civil War, but nothing that approached the nadir of democratic war direction which was arrived at by the Entente Powers in 1917. In fact they had been working towards this crisis for most of the previous year, a period of deep historical significance whose meanings I shall hope to expound later. Let us merely remark now that it had been a year of continental suicide; the five great nations of Europe (France, Britain, Italy, Germany and Austria-Hungary) had sustained among them about four million casualties, of whom probably about a quarter, perhaps more, were dead. And the worst of it was that outwardly there seemed to be nothing to show for this immolation.

Like candles before they expire, the two great Western battles of 1916 had thrown up their last brief brilliancies. On the Somme, the 51st (Highland) Division captured Beaumont Hamel, of evil fame, on 13 November – an operation in very sharp contrast to the disaster that had taken place there on 1 July (see p. 124). At Verdun, a month later, the French, inspired by General Robert Nivelle, carried out a four-day attack which won them 11,000 prisoners and 115 guns as well as a further slice of that sacred, ravaged field. Then both these terrible conflicts quietened down. Already one of the bleakest winters in European history had arrived; the whole Western Front soon petrified under sleet and snow and ice which froze the rivers and canals and the Channel beaches to the low-tide mark.

It was in this atmosphere of gloom that the stock-taking of the war's worst year so far was conducted – in happy ignorance that the next year was going to be far worse. A dreadful stalemate appeared to have gripped all the battle-fronts as firmly as the winter frosts: the Russians, in General Brusilov's great offensive, had inflicted tremendous losses on Austria-Hungary – yet Austria-Hungary was still in the field, still able to check all the furious assaults of the Italians in their tracks; at Verdun, ten months of battle of legendary fierceness had left the front lines almost where they had been at the beginning; the British on the Somme were still, after four and a half months, short of objectives which they had set themselves for the first day. The war had reached an intolerable equilibrium.

In fact, of course, as with a tidal river at the turning moment, this equilibrium was an illusion. For Russia, for Austria-Hungary, for Germany, the ebb had begun. It would proceed at varying speeds; as yet it was not something you could see, but it was something you might sense, by training, by instinct, by disposition. You *might;* alternatively, you might not. The training and usual background of politicians in liberal democracies are not generally helpful at such times.

Fundamentally what is involved is the ability, at a certain stage of a hard, bloody, daunting fight, to project your mind 'over the hill', to take into account what you are doing to the enemy as well as what he is doing to you. Soldiers, it need hardly be said, are not infallible in this matter; military history is littered with the unhappy names of the generals who couldn't manage it – names like McClellan, or Sir Redvers Buller, or the younger von Moltke. But in democracies generals do have two important advantages over politicians: they are taught that in a fight it is normal for *both* sides to be hurt, and this helps to fortify their resolve; and they are free of the necessity to win votes. The way to win votes is to show yourself much concerned with the lot of your own constituents – not somebody else's. If things are bad, you tell the voters you will try to make them better. It is no good telling them that other people are worse off – that will be poorly received; nor are blood, toil, tears and sweat recommended as a *steady* diet for democratic consumption.

Politicians in Britain and France at the end of 1916 were in an understandably nervous condition. They were horrified at what had been happening to their voters – genuinely horrified, not just politically horrified, because the experiences of that year seemed to be a negation of everything that a democratic, progress-seeking, liberal-minded society stood for, and nothing in their backgrounds had prepared them for such a state of affairs. There was no mistaking, by the end of 1916, what the landscapes of Verdun and the Somme were like: they were like Hell. There was no mistaking the meaning of some of the things that happened to people in those landscapes – being practically blown apart, or gassed, or incinerated by flame-throwers: these were veritable tortures of Hell. Small wonder if politicians – or anyone, for that matter – recoiled from such spectacles. And, as it happened, in both Britain and France there were new governments, headed by men whose recoil was very profound indeed. On 7 December Mr Lloyd George became Prime Minister of Great Britain, and on the same day M. Aristide Briand, the French Prime Minister, won a vote of confidence which enabled him to form a new administration.

Already Lloyd George was making his view of the War known; on 1 November he had been lunching with Sir Maurice (later Lord) Hankey, who was soon to become Secretary of his War Cabinet, a post entirely new in the British constitution. Lloyd George, Hankey recorded,

'considered that the Somme offensive had been a bloody and disastrous failure; he was not willing to remain in office, if it was to be repeated next year; he said that Thomas [French Minister of Munitions], Bissolati [Italian Socialist leader] and others thought the same; they would all resign simultaneously and tell their fellow-countrymen that the war was being run on the wrong lines, and that they had better make peace rather than repeat the experience of 1916 . . .'[1]

Both in Britain and in France the political leaders were deeply dissatisfied with their military advisers, General Joffre, French Comander-in-Chief (who was virtually generalissimo of the Western Front), Field-Marshal Sir Douglas Haig, British C.-in-C., and General Sir William Robertson, Chief of the Imperial General Staff. It is, indeed, not too much to say that a head-on collision was now taking place between the soldiers and the politicians. A conference of the military representatives of the Allies at Joffre's headquarters at Chantilly on 16 November agreed that, as far as the deadly winter permitted, offensive operations should be continued, and the grand offensive on the Western Front should be resumed, if possible, by the first week of February. In other words, the Germans were to be given no respite. 'The essential idea which governed me,' wrote Joffre, 'was that the battle of 1916 had so thoroughly disorganized the enemy's defences and the German reserves had been used up to such an extent that, if we now made a supreme effort, we could hardly fail to obtain decisive results.'[2]

'Decisive results' – it is too easy, contemplating the blood-baths that the generals ordered, to forget that the reason for them, the aim behind them, was to end the killing, end the war. The politicians, like Lincoln in 1864, also wanted to end the war; but, unlike Lincoln, many of them could not believe that hard fighting was the only way to do it. The German High Command, Field-Marshal von Hindenburg and First Quartermaster-General Erich Ludendorff, had no such doubts about the portents. The High Command, wrote Ludendorff,

'had to bear in mind that the enemy's great superiority in men and material would be even more painfully felt in 1917 than in 1916. They had to face the danger that "Somme fighting" would soon break out at various points on our fronts, and that even our troops would not be able to withstand such attacks indefinitely, *especially if the enemy gave us no time for rest* and for the accumulation of material . . . Our position was uncommonly difficult . . . If the war lasted our defeat seemed inevitable.'[3]

This was no rationalization after the event; it was a conclusion forced upon the German leaders by grim necessity. As far back as September, when they took up their appointments at the head of the German Army, Hindenburg and Ludendorff had departed from Germany's hallowed strategic principles and ordered the construction of that strong system of rear defences which Germans called the Siegfried Position and the Allies somewhat misleadingly called the Hindenburg Line. The whole purpose of this formidable fortification (still far from complete) was to avoid having the German Army knocked to pieces in another Somme. How delighted the High Command would have been had they known that their staunchest allies in this intention would be their enemies' political leaders.

In the event it was not Lloyd George, much as he distrusted his top soldiers and detested their strategic advice, who gave the Germans the breathing space they desired. Partly, it was the winter of 1916–17; but chiefly it was Aristide Briand. On 12 December he removed Joffre from his post as Commander-in-Chief, and with Joffre's departure the whole strategy agreed at Chantilly fell apart. Briand replaced Joffre with General Nivelle, whose Verdun honours were fresh upon him; Briand saw in Nivelle the prophet of a new style of war whose advent would bring an end to old Joffre's long-drawn out 'nibbling' battles with their terrible casualty lists. Nivelle said he knew how to break through the German lines in forty-eight hours; then he would roll them up and drive the enemy out of France. The method, he claimed, was infallible; but if, by some incredible lapse of natural law, anything did go wrong, he would break it all off at once. No more attrition, that was absolutely certain. What more could a politician ask? Victory –and no one doubts Briand's patriotism – without a bloodbath – and Briand was nothing if not humane. It was perfect.

Then came a miracle. The British, who were already preparing to play their part in Joffre's orchestra, and who also had plans of their own (prompted by the U-boat campaign) for a further offensive in Flanders if needed, had to be won over. Not only would Briand and Nivelle have to persuade British G.H.Q. in France and the War Office General Staff, but Lloyd George himself – and Lloyd George (this was his fundamental quarrel with the General Staff) hated the Western Front and never ceased his restless search for other theatres where, he felt sure, the war could be won at lower cost. He was, in other words, the arch-apostle in that war of General Fuller's 'strategy of evasion' (see p. 57). Sometimes Lloyd George favoured Salonika and the Balkans as a decisive theatre, sometimes landings in Asia Minor or Syria, sometimes the long haul up from Egypt to the Bosporus; but in 1917 his steady favourite was to supply massive material backing which would enable the Italians to knock out Austria. Whatever the chosen ground, one thought runs through these proposals like a golden thread: someone else would be doing the hard fighting, someone else would be paying the price. Whether this strategy would appeal to the people concerned was, of course, another matter, but it was in order to advocate it that he travelled to a conference in Rome in early January – only to find that his trusted colleague Briand had succumbed to the blandishments of a Western Front general after all.

Briand told Lloyd George of the clockwork precision of Nivelle's Verdun advances: 'General Nivelle had described exactly how he could conduct the operation, and had stated that he would send telegrams to him at such and such an hour from such and such points which he had captured. Eventually, M. Briand sanctioned the attack, and General Nivelle carried it out exactly as he had forecast. This naturally had created a most favourable impression . . .'[4] Lloyd George was also impressed, and when he met

Nivelle even more so. The general had an English mother; he spoke English perfectly, and with great eloquence; he possessed considerable charm, and put it to good use. And that was not all:

'Another point in General Nivelle's favour was that Mr Lloyd George liked the shape of his head. He was a great believer in his own powers as a phrenologist. He often judged men in this way; he either liked the shape of a man's head or he did not, and General Nivelle's cranium found favour in his eyes.'[5]

So the Nivelle Plan was 'on', whether the British generals liked it or not.

They did not like it very much. It was not that they disliked Nivelle personally (Haig at first thought him 'a most straightforward, soldierly man'). Nor had they any objection to him winning the war in forty-eight hours. It was just that experience had taught them to be less sanguine; they doubted if it could be done. They were also worried in case the enemy were allowed respite while Nivelle's redispositions were completed, and in any case, for sundry weighty reasons, they were unwilling to lose sight of the offensive in Flanders. However, G.H.Q. and the General Staff were overruled; cogent objections put forward by Robertson (who questioned in particular whether it was really possible to break off a great modern battle at will, as Nivelle had promised) were brushed aside; Haig was ordered to release French troops by taking over more front and to prepare to support Nivelle with an attack in the Arras sector in early April. Robertson was instructed to inform Haig that the Government expected him to carry out this order 'in the letter and the spirit . . . On no account must the French have to wait for us owing to our arrangements not being complete.'[6]

This was indeed a *volte-face* on the part of Lloyd George. Furthermore, it was setting a dangerous precedent (as Lincoln could have told him) to make military minutiae – e.g. dates and the extent of relief of one army by another – matters for political intervention. But the whole of the 'Nivelle episode' was charged with such misconceived dealings, which would shortly produce the rock-bottom of civil-military relations in British history. At the root of it – as so often in history – lay personalities; every hackle in Lloyd George rose against the stubborn, tongue-tied (but on paper unanswerable) objections of Robertson and Haig to his various essays in 'the strategy of evasion'. Principles, military or political, held out little appeal to a temperament which has been described at different times as 'quicksilver', 'disingenuous' or just 'shifty'. The fact is that Lloyd George would greatly have liked to part with both his senior generals, and, irrespective of the rights and wrongs of the strategic theories involved, it can be strongly argued that, since he so distrusted his advisers, he should have dismissed them. Why did he not do so? He tells us:

'In considering whether we should have gone further and taken more drastic action by replacing Haig and Robertson, I had always to bear in mind the possibility that such a step would inevitably have given rise to political complications. Both had a considerable backing in the Press and the House of Commons and inside the Government. The Asquithian Opposition were solid behind them. Northcliffe strongly supported both . . .'[7]

So Lloyd George, being too skilful a politician not to recognize weak ground when he saw it, decided to try some trickery.

The remorseless winter supplied the opportunity. Alternate biting frosts and destructive thaws produced very nearly a breakdown of the Nord Railway system on which the B.E.F. depended. All military traffic in the Nord area was jeopardized; only strenuous efforts by both French and British could put this right, and yet another inter-Allied conference was accordingly arranged at Calais for 26 February. As far as the War Office or G.H.Q. were concerned, this was a conference about transportation – a vital enough subject indeed. For Lloyd George, however, it was a heaven-sent chance to strike at both those hostile bodies and cut down their authority. In secret collusion with Nivelle (through a French liaison officer in London) but without informing the War Cabinet of his intentions, and in particular deliberately concealing the matter from the Secretary of State for War (Lord Derby), the Army Council and the C.I.G.S., Lloyd George set off for Calais with the firm intention of reducing the British Commander-in-Chief to a subordinate of his French colleague. In the words of Sir Edward Spears, in the manner of later American gang warfare, the British generals 'were to be "taken for a ride" to Calais, and there "put on the spot".'[8]

This is not the place to relate again the full proceedings of the notorious Calais Conference. General Spears has left a brilliant account of it in his *Prelude to Victory;* Robertson subjected it to caustic review in *Soldiers and Statesmen;* Lloyd George's *War Memoirs* have revealingly little to say about it; Lord Hankey's diary, and Haig's, make valuable contributions; I have discussed it at length in *Douglas Haig: The Educated Soldier* and *The Western Front.* It is an extraordinary tale: the great cautionary example of how a democracy should not conduct a war. In brief what happened was this: a short discussion of transportation took place, quickly transferred from the principals to their accompanying experts; Lloyd George then raised the question of 'plans' and asked Nivelle to speak. Again the discussion became somewhat technical (Haig wanted the Vimy Ridge to be included in the British front of attack, Nivelle dissented); Lloyd George became restive and asked the French to draw up proposals for a *system of command* before dinner. As Nivelle had been amply forewarned, this proved to be well within their powers; he produced a formula which would have reduced the forces of the British Empire to a mere contingent in the French Army and the Commander-in-Chief of the greatest army in British history to a glorified Adjutant-General.

Naturally, Robertson and Haig were outraged; Lloyd George himself was somewhat taken aback by the scope of these proposals. The French, too, were startled when they saw that this memorable *démarche* had been made without any prior agreement on the British side. In the end Hankey found a compromise solution (his speciality): Haig's subordination to Nivelle would be solely for the duration of the coming great offensive, and he would have the right of appeal to the British Government at any time if he thought the safety of his army was being endangered. Nivelle was content with this, since he believed that he was going to win the War, and this formula made him supreme for the duration; Robertson and Haig contented themselves because they believed no such thing and saw they could play a waiting game. But they were very far from pleased.

So that was the Calais Conference. What prompted Lloyd George to this appalling step? What did he think he was doing? What did he hope to gain by setting aside all constitutional, strategic and political considerations in this blundering manner –to say nothing of considerations of relations with men whom he would have to continue to work with? These questions are unanswerable in terms of logic or reason, just answerable in terms of instinct and emotion. If his military advisers were so intolerable to him, for his own sake and the nation's it was his plain duty to dismiss them; if too many important people retained enough confidence in them to make that politically impossible, then it was equally his plain duty to accept that fact, and treat the generals with respect despite private misgiving. But he could not bring himself to do either of these things, and so, impelled to do *something,* he tried to diminish the British generals by subterfuge, not seeing that this must also diminish the Army, the nation, and the Government itself.

And so, of course, it fell out, with gruesome precision. Ironically, on the day before the Calais Conference the Germans

'1,393,515 DEAD':

Village war memorials, such as these, all over France commemorate the cost of her immense effort in the First World War.

GUERRE 1914-1918

632,000 DEAD: the memorial to the fallen of Leningrad, 1941—44; but the composer Shostakovich estimated the true figure at 900,000.

**'THE LAST OF THE GREAT
OLD-FASHIONED GENERALS':**
General Robert E. Lee (1807–1870)
Marshal Ferdinand Foch (1851–1929)
General Douglas MacArthur (1880–1964)

'GREAT MODERNS':
Lieutenant-General Ulysses S. Grant (1822–1885)

Field-Marshal Sir Douglas Haig (1861–1928)

General Dwight D. Eisenhower (1890–1969)

Marshal Georgi Konstantinovich Zhukov
(1897–1974)

(in war the enemy in the field often displays a tiresome habit of butting in at awkward moments) had begun to spoil the whole Nivelle Plan. Observing his well-advertised preparations, they began to retire upon the Hindenburg Line, thus wrecking his attack along a wide front (and, incidentally, justifying Joffre's strategy, which the politicians had scorned). For a long time Nivelle closed his eyes to what was happening, but Haig knew, and so did the senior French generals and other officers; confidence in the Commander-in-Chief declined rapidly. As long as he had Briand's backing Nivelle could (just) afford to ignore this; but Briand's position, too, was vulnerable, and on 17 March (less than a month after the Calais Conference) his government fell. In the new ministry of M. Alexandre Ribot, Paul Painlevé became Minister of War. Painlevé was in touch with many officers who now felt deeply apprehensive about Nivelle and his plan – not least among them General Philippe Pétain, commanding the *Groupe d'Armées du Centre* (G.A.C.), who enjoyed all the prestige of having been 'the saviour of Verdun' in 1916.

Retribution for the follies of Calais now descended. Obedient to Nivelle's somewhat discourteous instructions (and the British Government's ruling), Haig pressed on with his preparations for the attack at Arras in early April; there was no question now of 'the French having to wait for us' – the boot was on the other foot. The German withdrawal to the Hindenburg Line was completed, practically without hindrance, leaving behind a zone of 'scorched earth' and wrecked communications across which movement was exceedingly difficult. This left the whole of Nivelle's left wing, the *Groupe d'Armées du Nord* (G.A.N.), 'in the air'; yet he flatly refused to adapt or reconsider his plan. In Olympian terms, detached from all reality, he stubbornly announced his decision 'to make no fundamental modification in the general plan of operations which has been drawn up'.[9]

As the date of the great attack approached, Painlevé was becoming desperate, filled with the sense of a horrible disaster impending, but not knowing what to do. On 6 April, with only ten days to go (only three to the opening of the British subsidiary attack at Arras) Painlevé took a remarkable step. Prompted by a frantic appeal from one of his predecessors in office (Adolphe Messimy, now a colonel at the front), to intervene for the safety of the Army and the nation, the War Minister persuaded the President of the Republic to convene a special meeting at Nivelle's headquarters at Compiègne. This occasion provided another rock-bottom of democratic war-making. The purpose of the meeting was for the political chiefs, President Poincaré, M. Ribot and Painlevé, to test the true feelings of the senior generals about the attack and reach a decision. But armies do not function by public debate; the conference proved totally inconclusive; Nivelle, affronted by the entire proceeding, offered to resign, but this was refused. No decision was taken either way – which meant that the attack would go on, though no one now, except Nivelle, professed any real faith in it. The whole dismal business, as General Spears said, 'stands as a monument to the inefficiency of democracy at war, to the helplessness of Ministers facing technicians, and their total inability to decide between different professional opinions'.[10]

For the British, thanks to Lloyd George, there were further considerations concerning the Compiègne Conference. Supposing the French *had* decided to call off their attack, what would have happened to the B.E.F., whose whole effort had been subordinated to it, whose bombardment at Arras had begun on 25 March (a matter of a mere 2,687,653 rounds of ammunition, fired off in fifteen days) and whose own strategy had been abandoned for this purpose? Once more it is Spears who points the ugly moral:

The seed planted at Calais bore fruit at Compiègne. The British forces were under the orders of the French Commander-in-Chief, but the French C.-in-C. was under the control of the French Cabinet, who, in an emergency such as occurred, did not hesitate to use their powers without reference to the British Government. It was now quite evident that our Cabinet had abdicated its powers in favour not of a French general but of the French Government.[11]

And this was still not the full reckoning for Lloyd George's duplicity – and democracy's fallibility. The Battle of Arras opened on 9 April with considerable success, nowhere more spectacular than at Vimy Ridge, stormed by the Canadian Corps in a brilliant feat of arms. Ludendorff wryly remarked: 'The consequences of a break through of 12 to 15 kilometres wide and 6 or more kilometres deep are not easy to meet . . . A day like April 9th threw all calculations to the winds.'[12] The battle then developed into the familiar hard grind of the Western Front, drawing in German reserves as intended. That was, indeed, its chief purpose – to assist the main stroke by Nivelle, delivered on 16 April. It immediately became obvious that this had failed. The actual results of Nivelle's attack were, by the standards of that period of the War, quite good, but in relation to his grandiose promises they were a disaster. This brought swiftly in its train Nivelle's own downfall, the mutinies which racked the French Army for months ahead (and, indeed, put a stamp on it for the rest of the War), and a nearly fatal crisis of confidence in France herself – only righted with the advent of Georges Clemenceau as Prime Minister in November, when 'democracy temporarily died in France. And died unmourned.'[13]

For Britain, the fruits of the Calais Conference, in a year which saw the British Army necessarily carrying the burden of the War (since Russia collapsed, America was unready and France gravely weakened), were not merely the 150,000 casualties sustained at Arras to no purpose[14] but, far more important, a permanent rupture of relations between soldiers and politicians. Calais, wrote Sir William Robertson, 'created an atmosphere of distrust between Ministers and military chiefs which never afterwards disappeared'.[15] In 1918 this would nearly cause the War itself to be lost – democracy's dark hour indeed.

---

1 Lord Hankey, *The Supreme Command 1914–1918*, Allen and Unwin, 1961, ii, p. 556.
2 Marshal Joffre, *Memoirs* (trans. Colonel T. Bentley Mott), Geoffrey Bles, 1932, ii, p. 515.
3 General Erich Ludendorff, *My War Memoirs, 1914–1918*, Hutchinson, 1919, i, p. 507; my italics.
4 Lloyd George, *War Memoirs*, Odhams, 1936, i, p. 852.
5 Sir Edward Spears, *Prelude to Victory*, Jonathan Cape, 1939, p. 40.
6 Minutes of War Cabinet No. 36, 17 Jan. 1917 (CAB 23/1).
7 Lloyd George, op. cit., ii, pp. 1370–1.
8 Spears, op. cit., p. 134.
9 John Terraine, *The Road to Passchendaele*, Leo Cooper, 1977, p. 47.
10 Spears, op. cit., p. 376.
11 Ibid., p. 437.
12 Ludendorff, op. cit., ii, p. 421.
13 Richard M. Watt, *Dare Call It Treason*, Chatto and Windus, 1964, p. 237. For France's internal crisis, see Terraine, *To Win a War*, Sidgwick and Jackson, 1978, pp. 20–27.
14 See Table C, p. 46; it will be noted that the daily rate of loss at Arras was only exceeded during the German offensives of 1918.
15 Field-Marshal Sir William Robertson, *Soldiers and Statesmen 1914–1918*, Cassell, 1926, ii, p. 214.

XI

A FOUNT OF MYTH:
The Year of Attrition

'Our great commanders, having refused or neglected to organise a break-through where and when it was feasible . . . being unable to think out anything more original, had fallen back on attrition – always the game of the poor player.'
(Lloyd George, *War Memoirs*)

'. . . better make peace than repeat the experience of 1916 . . .'
(Lloyd George to Sir Maurice Hankey, 1 November 1916)

'1916 spoke a language which made itself heard.'
(Field-Marshal von Hindenburg)

Delusion about history is a serious matter; it can gravely affect the history that is waiting to be made. That state of nervous delusion which, as we have just seen, possessed the Allied statesmen in 1917, has been perpetuated in the whole damaging mythology surrounding the First World War ever since. As I have said earlier in this book (see p. 36) the central British myth, the great Casualty Myth, dates from the year 1916; indeed, most of the delusion, most of the frame of mind that gave birth to the mythology, dates from that year. This is not surprising, because it was *par excellence* the year of attrition, or, as the late Captain Cyril Falls named it, 'the year of killing'. For the British, it was, of course, pre-eminently the 'Year of the Somme', a battle about which myth and delusion remain virtually unlimited.

It helps to establish useful perspectives of 1916 if we begin by examining Captain Falls's phrase, 'the year of killing'. What did he mean by it? Let us start with Germany, since it was a German initiative (at Verdun) that set the year's sombre train of events in motion. The German Official History (Vol. xi, p. 41), quoted in the British Official History (*France and Belgium 1916,* vol. ii, pp. xiv–xv), says: 'the great losses . . . of 1916 since the beginning of the year, without the wounded whose recovery was to be expected within a reasonable time, amounted to a round figure of 1,400,000, of whom 800,000 were between July and October.' Great controversy has surrounded the phrase 'the wounded whose recovery was to be expected within a reasonable time'; the British Official Historian, Sir James Edmonds, asserted that German sources showed that this category amounted to some 30 per cent, which figure he then proceeded to add to all German casualty returns. I have discussed this question elsewhere;[1] all we need to note here is that the fearful figure of 1,400,000 is a 'round' one, which the Germans themselves do not pretend to be complete.

France also presents problems: I have two French totals for 1916, and they are widely different. The historian Paul-Marie de la Gorce (*The French Army*, p. 103) says that France lost 900,000 men, killed, wounded or captured, during the year. Sir James Edmonds, however, says that 'French losses for the year appear almost to balance those of the British' (op. cit., p. 528, f.n. 1) which would make them just over 600,000. France's overseas commitments during the year cannot possibly account for a discrepancy of nearly 300,000. Edmonds may have underrated French losses on so-called 'quiet' sectors of the Western Front. Whatever the reason, we are left with one figure which seems substantially too high, and another which seems substantially too low; but in either case, it is another large number to be added to the toll of European manhood.

Mystery also veils the losses of Austria-Hungary and Italy during the year. According to Dr Norman Stone (*The Eastern Front 1914–1917,* Hodder and Stoughton, 1975, p. 266) the Austro-Hungarian Army had sustained 614,000 casualties in the East alone by the end of August. In addition there were five battles on the Isonzo front against Italy and one with heavy fighting on the Trentino; for all these I can find only incomplete totals, and there is also, of course, another figure to be added for the Eastern Front, for September to December. The sum of all the actual figures that I have for Austria-Hungary is 797,000, which means that the full total for the year might easily be about 1 million. For Italy I have an incomplete 'low' total (there is a big divergence between C. R. M. F. Cruttwell and Captain Cyril Falls concerning the Trentino losses) of 272,000 and an incomplete 'high' total of 411,000. The latter seems to me far more likely to be near the truth. For Russia there is only an estimate: about 1 million. British losses are recorded with far greater exactitude: 607,784 on the Western Front, 58,305 in other theatres.

As I have said earlier (see p. 102), for the five powers of Western and Central Europe these totals, whether we take the 'high' of not less than 4,174,000 or the 'low' of not less than 3,742,000, constitute an act of continental suicide. They signal the beginning of the departure of European power. In terms of the war itself, they represent a high-water mark of manpower expenditure. In the following year the Eastern Front virtually ceased to exist, following the collapse of Russia, which greatly reduced the losses of Germany and Austria-Hungary; Italy's losses increased, but France did less fighting and accordingly suffered less; Britain did more, and suffered more. By then all the major belligerents were in the grip of manpower crises of varying intensity, thanks to the ravages of 1916. And these have, indeed, left a mark on the minds of those who lived through them that has never been expunged and has been handed on 'with advantages' to succeeding generations.

For the British, far more than for their friends and enemies, the mass casualties of mass warfare came as a dreadful novelty in 1916, because that was the first time they had ever fielded a mass army. The Battle of the Somme was the initiation of that army into the true practice of mass warfare, and the shock reverberates still. Let it be said at once, however, that this shock was chiefly in the minds of people at home, of civilians and politicians when the truth sank in, not in the minds of the soldiers, who displayed exemplary fortitude under unimaginable stress. Yet even this quality was turned against the real understanding of what they had actually achieved. In a famous passage, Winston Churchill supplied the central mythology of the Somme:

If two lives or ten lives were required by their commanders to kill one German, no word of complaint ever rose from the fighting troops. No attack, however forlorn, however fatal, found them without ardour. No slaughter however desolating prevented them from returning to the charge. No physical conditions however severe deprived their commanders of their obedience and loyalty. Martyrs not less than soldiers, they fulfilled the high purpose of duty with which they were imbued. The battlefields of the Somme were the graveyards of Kitchener's Army.[2]

The Somme is irrevocably associated with 'Kitchener's Army', otherwise known as the New Army, that surge of eager volunteers which accounts for the amazing recruiting figures in 1914 and 1915 to which I have referred on p. 40. Twenty-five out of the fifty-three

British and Dominion divisions which fought on the Somme in 1916 were New Army. The nine Dominion divisions present were volunteers of similar spirit, and more of the same kind were by now present in all the rest (Regular, Territorial, Naval) as reinforcements. Lloyd George (then Secretary of State for War) was quite correct in saying: 'The battle of the Somme was fought by the volunteer armies raised in 1914 and 1915. These contained the choicest and best of our young manhood.'[3] What horrified him at the time and ever after, and many others with him, was the thought that 'over 400,000 of our men fell in this bull-headed fight and the slaughter amongst our young officers was appalling'.[4] Viewed beside the trifling gain of ground at the end of four and a half months of struggle, it was this that later caused him, with all the authority of an ex-premier, to brand the Somme as 'horrible and futile carnage',[5] one of 'the most gigantic, tenacious, grim, futile and bloody fights ever waged in the history of war.'[6]

The 'ghastly notoriety' conferred upon the Battle of the Somme by Lloyd George and Churchill, and by a whole school of historians and mythologists who followed them, had more serious repercussions upon later generations than the battle itself on those who fought it. It was surely the steady repetition of the word 'futile' that did the damage, the clear implication that such losses had never been necessary, that they were the fruit of incompetence and brutal lack of imagination. The fact that the experience of the American Civil War and of every other warring nation between 1914 and 1916 showed mass casualties to be of the very essence of mass warfare was something to be firmly rejected. So this thinking (or lack of it) became a powerful ingredient in the 'disenchantment' of the Twenties and Thirties.

The harvest came in the humiliation of increasing powerlessness in the face of the aggressive dictators in the 1930s − ironically Churchill, who had made a substantial contribution to the Appeasement mentality by his writing about the First World War, then turned into a leading opponent of Appeasement. The sick joke of Munich underlined Britain's powerlessness; it was underlined again in the military feebleness of 1939 − a distinct regression from 1914. In June 1940, when the birds finally came home to roost bringing with them outright defeat in the field, General Ironside, Chief of the Imperial General Staff, wrote in his diary: 'The saying that we were never again to have "the bloody massacres of the Somme" has deluded the people. Nobody has been educated to the horrors of modern war. I don't believe the people understand it yet.'[7]

He was right; they never did understand it. Neither did their new Prime Minister. Flung out of Europe in 1940, the British were yet able to do severe damage to the Italians in Africa, but for the Germans that theatre was never more than a sideshow. Not until America entered the war in December 1941 could Britain engage more than detachments of the forces of the main enemy. The Americans were not interested in making war against detachments, or in peripheral operations. From the first, they braced themselves for an assault on Hitler's 'Fortress Europe' and the re-creation of a Western Front. There was for a time a strong element of unreality in the American approach: American planners were slow to grasp the need for special weapons and equipment which did not exist (especially landing craft); they underestimated the difficulties of producing these things quickly in the large numbers that were required. But American productivity tended to make light of material deficiencies – they could be, and usually were, made good. Overcoming the British Prime Minister's detestation of the Western Front of the previous war was another matter. The strategic argument was fierce, at times threatening the solidarity of the alliance itself. Churchill is quite frank about it:

'I was not convinced that [invasion of Europe] was the only way of winning the war, and I knew that it would be a very heavy and hazardous adventure. Memories of the Somme and Passchendaele and many lesser frontal attacks upon the Germans were not to be blotted out by time and reflection.'[8]

For Churchill, like Lloyd George before him, any 'indirect approach' was better than a head-on assault: a massed air offensive, despite heavy losses of bomber crews for sometimes equivocal results; expeditions against 'the soft under-belly of the Axis', even though this turned out to be a hard spine. Like his predecessor, he was privately dedicated to 'the strategy of evasion'. As Churchill's doctor told the American Chief of Staff, General George C. Marshall, in arguing with the Prime Minister 'he was fighting the ghosts of the Somme'.[9]

It is time these ghosts were laid – long past time for a true perspective of the 'year of the Somme'. The statistics quoted above tell us plainly that the British experience in 1916 was by no means exceptional; there was nothing in it (except perhaps the surrender of a British Indian force of some 12,000 men at Kut-al-Amara) attributable purely to British incompetence or stupidity or bad luck. Britain's losses during the year indicate only that she had begun at last to play a serious rôle in the land war. The much smaller losses of 1914–15 were simply due to the fact that the Army, though expanding fast, was still too small to fight large battles, just as the even smaller losses of the Second World War show only (as I have said) that the British Army was never at any time during that war pitted against the main force of the main enemy.[10]

It was on the Somme, in 1916, that the British Army first took on that task (a rôle confined uniquely to that war); that is the clue, the *only* clue, to the battle. By the time it ended, in November, according to Professor Sir Charles Oman,[11] whose wartime duty it was to examine the German Order of Battle and casualty lists, eighty-three German divisions out of 125 on the Western Front had fought on the Somme, many of them twice, some even three times. On the Eastern Front at that time the Germans had forty-eight divisions. These figures speak for themselves; there is no doubt about where their 'main body' was, and though the French (despite their Verdun losses) made a considerable contribution, there is no doubt either that the Somme was primarily a British battle.

There is a further consideration. At the centre of the War, its 'motor', the thing that made it 'go', was the German Army, the most powerful military machine in the world. This was not just a matter of numbers, though the German Army was, indeed, very big. It was a matter also of sound organization and administration, directed by the Great General Staff; of hard peacetime training, chiefly conducted by a corpus of about 100,000 regular N.C.O.s, who were the very backbone of the whole organism; of severe though not cruel discipline; of good and plentiful equipment thanks to long preparation for the need; of fortitude, courage, self-confidence and initiative born of a good general standard of education, in all ranks. A British officer, in mid-1915, reported with wonder that

when the war began we were all prepared for the Germans to be successful *at first* owing to their study of war and scientific preparation, but we argued that very soon we should become better than they, not being hidebound by a system. The exact contrary had been the case. The Germans with their foundation of solid study and experience have been far quicker to adapt themselves to the changed conditions of war and the emergencies of the situation than either we or the Russians have been – possibly even more so than the French.[12]

Captain Cyril Falls (who met them in battle) sums up the quality of the German soldiers: 'The commanders who had such troops to rely on in days of adversity were fortunate. It was almost impossible to ask or expect of them more than they were ready to give and capable of giving.'[13]

By 1916 this war machine had already performed wonders. It had rescued its Austrian ally from disaster; it had inflicted terrible defeats on the Russians; it had lent support to its Turkish allies; it had played a large part in overthrowing Serbia; it had conquered all of Belgium except a small triangle round Ypres; and it had occupied a huge area of north-eastern France. Every day M. Georges Clemenceau's newspaper, *L'Homme Enchaîné*, reminded the French people (and the French General Staff) that *'les Boches sont à Noyon'* — that is to say, as close to Paris as Canterbury is to London. The German Army, in 1914, had seized an initiative which it still possessed; Allied strategy, in 1915 and 1916, danced to Germany's tune. That is what a strategic initiative is about. To understand 1916 it is essential to remember that Germany had it, the Allies did not.

It would, indeed, be fair to say that until 1916 there was no such thing as an *Allied* strategy. There were the strategies – or stratagems – of the Allies, which sometimes coincided and sometimes did not coincide at all. In an attempt to remedy this unprofitable state of affairs, Joffre had convened a conference of Allied military leaders at his headquarters at Chantilly in December 1915 (not to be confused with the similar conference in November 1916 which we have noted on p. 91). By now the vast Russian Army – the 'Russian steam-roller', which had seemed to promise the Allies inexhaustible manpower – appeared to be on its knees; if the Allies had a 'motor', it was unquestionably the French Army, with its ninety-five divisions on the Western Front. As its Commander-in-Chief, Joffre was, as we have seen, to all intents and purposes the Allied C.-in-C. on that front, and his view of the War was very clear, very simple:

'The best and largest portion of the German army was on our soil, with its line of battle jutting out a mere five days' march from the heart of France. This situation made it clear to every Frenchman that our task consisted in defeating this enemy, and driving him out of our country.'[14]

If it *had* been Canterbury, and not Noyon, few Englishmen would have challenged this proposition.

The Chantilly Conference prescribed the means of ridding French soil of the German presence; Joffre says:

It was agreed upon that a decisive result should be sought through co-ordinated offensives on three fronts, Russian, Franco-British and Italian. These offensives were to be launched simultaneously, or at least on dates sufficiently near each other to prevent the enemy from moving his reserves from one front to another.

The general action would be begun as soon as possible.[15]

Joffre calls the Chantilly Conference 'a vital date in the history of the conduct of the war'. So it should have been, but as we have seen (p. 77) the great co-ordinated assault on the Central Powers did not succeed – and the chief reason for that was exactly what we might suppose: the German Army had more to say. In 1914 the German initiative had been directed westward, with dramatic results; in 1915 it was directed eastward, with results scarcely less dramatic (the great Gorlice-Tarnow offensive); in 1916 the Germans came west again. On 21 February General Erich von Falkenhayn (Chief of Staff) launched the Battle of Verdun, whose explicit object was not to capture forts, or ground, or the historic town, but to 'bleed to death' the French Army in defence of those features. Falkenhayn, in fact, made the French Army his objective in 1916 in exactly the same way as Grant had made Lee's army his objective in 1864. This was the real beginning of attrition in the First World War; it was something quite different from Joffre's attempts to win back ground. It was not ground that was the objective now, but the taking of human lives.

This is the background against which the British effort on the Somme has to be viewed; it was not developed in isolation, nor, indeed, at first as a specially British enterprise, but as part of an agreed strategy, with the French in the main rôle. But the unremitting thunder of the guns of Verdun while the British assembled turned it instead into a rescue operation. With what seemed painful slowness to the French, but sometimes uncomfortable speed to themselves, Kitchener's divisions, the Canadians and the Anzacs came to France, set up their camps and bases, marched and trained, tried to pick up a quick military education, took part in trench fighting which cost them over 120,000 casualties in six months, but did nothing which could in any way ease the German pressure on Verdun, or give reality to Joffre's strategy of co-ordinated Allied attacks. As crisis succeeded crisis at Verdun, Sir Douglas Haig endured repeated urging, often couched in the most passionate terms, from Joffre, from the French President and other notables, and no doubt from his own conscience, aware as he was of the critical position of his allies. But Haig stuck it out, because he knew the truth: 'I have not got an Army in France, really, but a collection of divisions untrained for the field. The actual fighting Army will be evolved from them.'[16]

By June there was no holding back any longer; on 31 May

President Poincaré told Haig 'that he had just returned from Verdun where he had seen the senior generals – Pétain, Nivelle and another general. They told him *'Verdun sera prise'* ['Verdun will be taken'] and that operations must be undertaken without delay to withdraw pressure from that part.'[17] On 13 June the head of the French Mission at G.H.Q. 'reported that the situation at Verdun is serious. Not only men, but generals and staffs are getting tired out and jumpy. General Joffre is anxious that our infantry attack should be launched on 25th June . . .'[18] Ominously he added that a political crisis was brewing up in Paris and that 'a scapegoat for Verdun is wanted'.

It had already become quite clear that the French would not be playing the major rôle on the Somme as originally intended; indeed, it was a question whether they might not collapse altogether. The British would *have* to take on the main body of the main enemy, prepared or not. And this they began to do on 1 July, known in Britain for evermore as the first day of the Battle of the Somme, but not to be properly comprehended except as also the *132nd day* of the Battle of Verdun. Furthermore, it was the twenty-eighth day of the offensive launched by a miraculously revived Russian Army under General Brusilov. In August the Italians would also join in with yet another attack on the blood-stained Isonzo, as agreed at Chantilly back in December 1915. It requires a dense and impenetrable insular mythology, unforgivable after so many years, to allow the British experience on 1 July to obscure this context.

The British experience on 1 July was undoubtedly disastrous. Only on the extreme right of the 25,000-yard front of attack was any gain made; the day's casualties amounted to 57,000, about 20,000 of them dead. It was a dreadful blow. The Army recovered from it almost immediately; the nation never recovered. It is possible to say, with assurance, that the Army recovered because, as we shall now see, the Army continued the battle implacably for 141 more days. It is also possible to say that the nation never did because, to this day, books and articles are written, television and radio programmes made, that see practically nothing of the battle but its first day. By implication they seem to ask, in effect, why, on the 133rd day of the Battle of Verdun, the British Command did not tell the French (and Russians) that one day of this sort of thing was quite enough; the retort may be imagined.

Fortunately, 1 July was a freak; the contrast between that first day's loss and the daily rate for the whole battle (Table C, p. 46) shows that quite clearly. When at last the fighting died down, after the capture of Beaumont Hamel on 13 November, the British had lost some 415,000 men, and the French, even in a secondary rôle, over 200,000.[19] But battles – even such battles as this – are not only about casualties. The Germans concealed their figures, but not their meaning – which was, in fact – the meaning of the battle itself. General Ludendorff summed it up:

'The Army had been fought to a standstill and was utterly worn out.'[20]

Hindenburg wrote of the prospects for the next year: 'We could be in no doubt that the military machine with which we were now working was not to be compared with those of 1914 and 1915, or indeed with that of the opening months of 1916.'[21]

That is the reality of 1916, what makes that year the watershed of the First World War: this fatal damage to what I call the 'motor' of the War itself, thanks to 299 days of Verdun, 142 days of the Somme, and the four months of Brusilov's offensive. In the Second World War the German Army was once again the 'motor', and once again it was fatally damaged by battles of attrition – outside Moscow, at Stalingrad, at Kursk, at Orel, and at many other Russian places whose significance is precisely that of Douaumont, Mort-Homme, Delville Wood, Thiepval, and all the other grisly signposts of 1916. It was the 'texture' of the Eastern Front between 1941 and 1945 that gave the Russians their victory; the British began to earn their victory in 1918 by the 'texture' of the Somme.

---

1 See John Terraine, *The Road to Passchendaele,* Leo Cooper, 1977, p. 343, 'A Note On Casualties'.
2 Sir Winston Churchill, *The World Crisis,* Odham's Ed., 1938, ii, pp. 1091–2.
3 Lloyd George, *War Memoirs,* Odham's, 1936, i, p. 321.
4 Ibid.
5 Ibid., p. 514.
6 Ibid., ii, p. 1247.
7 *The Ironside Diaries,* ed. Colonel Roderick Macleod, Constable, 1962, p. 352.
8 Churchill, *The Second World War,* Cassell, 1950, v, p. 514.
9 Forrest C. Pogue, *George C. Marshall: Ordeal and Hope,* Macgibbon and Kee, 1966, pp. 316–7.
10 See Table F (p. 128).
11 Sir Charles Oman, 'German Losses on the Somme' *(The Nineteenth Century and After,* May, 1927).
12 See F. S. Oliver, *The Anvil of War,* Macmillan, 1936, p. 113.
13 Cyril Falls, *The First World War,* Longmans, 1960, p. 200. The phrase 'a year of killing' is also from this book, p. 155.
14 Marshal Joffre, *Memoirs* (trans. Colonel T. Bentley Mott), Geoffrey Bles, 1932, ii, p. 327.
15 Ibid., p. 414.
16 Author's papers: Haig Diary, 29 March, 1916.

17 Robert Blake (ed.), *The Private Papers of Douglas Haig 1916–1919*, Eyre and Spottiswoode, 1952, p. 146.
18 Author's papers: Haig Diary, 13 June, 1916.
19 O.H. *1916*, ii, p. xvi.
20 General Erich Ludendorff, *My War Memories 1914–1918*, Hutchinson, 1919, i, p. 304.
21 Field-Marshal von Hindenburg, *Out of My Life*, Cassell, 1920, pp. 262–3.

XII

ANTI-MYTH:
The True Texture of the Somme

'The German artillery, with targets no gunner could resist . . .
concentrated on the British. For long minutes this line or that of
the many waves succeeding each other was completely invisible
in the smoke of explosions a mile long, and when seen again,
though showing gaps of hundreds of yards where there had been
men before, was perceived to be slowly advancing at the same
even pace. As a display of bravery it was magnificent, as an
example of tactics its very memory made one shudder . . .'

(Major-General Sir Edward Spears, *Prelude to Victory*)

'The extended lines started in excellent order, but gradually
melted away. There was no wavering or attempting to come
back, the men fell in their ranks, mostly before the first hundred
yards of No Man's Land had been crossed.'

(Official History)

'And to Private Ball it came as if a rigid beam of great weight
flailed about his calves, caught from behind by ballista-baulk
let fly or aft-beam slewed to clout gunnel-walker
below below below.
　　　When golden vanities make about,
　　　　　　you've got no legs to stand on.
　　　He thought it disproportionate in its violence considering
the fragility of us.'

(David Jones, *In Parenthesis*)

The literature of 1 July 1916 is endless. Salutary at first, a proper
corrective to the streams of propaganda clap-trap about 'laughing
heroes' and 'the Great Adventure' which had previously gushed

forth, after a time it developed into a most mischievous mythology. To concentrate so single-mindedly on one day of battle on one front in a war of many fronts lasting over 1,500 days cannot fail to be mischievous. To continue to do so when six decades have gone by is not only mischievous but morbid too. In any case, since no war has a monopoly of disaster, the day to look at is not 1 July, but 2 July; what matters, in the end, is how the disaster is taken, what the response to it is. July the 2nd, 1916, was a 'make or break' day; the British Army decided to 'make', not 'break', to its eternal honour.

Nobody, of course, on 2 July, could really assess the dimensions of the catastrophe of the previous day, but, on the other hand, nobody at or near the battle-front could escape the awareness that something awful had taken place. Nothing like those 57,000 casualties had ever happened before, and, contrary to popular mythology, nothing like it happened to the British Army again in that war. Indeed, in the army's whole history there is no other day so tragic until 15 February 1942, when 85,000 officers and men surrendered to the Japanese in Singapore, to begin a captivity fatal to many and vile for all. On 1 July 1916, British divisions sustained casualties which later in the battle they would only expect to incur in a week, a fortnight or even a month of hard fighting.[1] Certainly no single day in the whole Third Ypres ('Passchendaele') battle can begin to compare with that first day of the Somme; not even the calamity of the German break-in on 21 March 1918 produced such losses. I have said already that 1 July was a freak; one eighth of the total loss for the whole battle, with 141 more days to go; need one say more?

The reason for the disaster, unfortunately for mythology, is not to be found in any single, simple fact – such as an imprecise order (as at Balaklava), running out of ammunition at a critical moment (Isandlhwana), over-confidence (Maiwand), failure to reconnoitre (Spion Kop), or stupid generalship (popular myth). It is, as in most large affairs, rather in a complex of causes that we may find the key to the tragedy. The first of these deserving consideration, I would suggest, is one that British insularity and a certain unconscious but unpleasant arrogance have obscured and often neglected entirely; the quality of the German Army. Because the Battle of the Somme was the first great test of the Kitchener Army – the Citizen Army of Great Britain – British accounts generally dwell upon the enthusiasm and élan of these high-spirited, patriotic and physically élite volunteers. Often such accounts ignore or play down the almost complete lack of experienced officers and N.C.O.s, and the consequent low level of practical training and tactical clumsiness of these formations, contrasted with the B.E.F. of 1914 or the German Army of mid-1916. It is revealing that British units habitually used three or four times as many officers in action as their opponents used[2] – with the natural result that British officer casualties were three or four times as high, thus preventing the accretion of experience. The Germans, on the other hand, took care to preserve their officers as a precious asset (without, apparently, provoking adverse reactions from their disciplined rank and file).

The main reason why the Germans were able to economize on officers in this way was that there still remained, in the German Army, a fair proportion of those 100,000 highly trained N.C.O.s with which they began the War, to which I have already referred. It was, among other things, the training and discipline imparted, at the depôts and at the front itself, by these invaluable men that enabled the German infantry to endure the miseries and losses of the eight-day preliminary bombardment, during which they received from the British artillery no less than 1,732,873 shells of all calibres. Admittedly, owing to British inexperience in munitions production, the disgracefully high proportion of about 30 per cent of the shells turned out to be 'duds'. Nevertheless, the remainder constituted a severe and novel ordeal for the Germans, a foretaste of the *'material-schlacht'* ('battle of matériel') of the later stages. But on 1 July discipline and courage (which rarely failed them) enabled them to leave their shelters, deep or frail, man their shattered parapets and defend bitterly the ruins of their village-fortresses. Those who would truthfully seek reasons for the slaughter of the advancing British regiments should look first towards their enemies, down the steady, levelled rifle barrels of the German infantry, and note the calm purpose and cool nerves of the well-trained German machine-gunners, and the quick, accurate reactions of their artillerymen.

That said, giving credit where it is overdue, one may turn to the faults on the British side – and these were certainly many. We have remarked the shocking results of inexperience in the munitions factories. The same defect made itself apparent on the battlefield; it began with the troops themselves. A very young officer in July 1916 later wrote: '. . . enthusiastic amateurs when the fighting began, the British were soldiers at the end.'[3] He means, of course, the ones who survived – though even the dead had lessons to teach. The cruel loss of regimental officers which so appalled Lloyd George (see p. 103) was largely due to inexperience, to officers having to expose and expend themselves in attempts to compensate for the inexperience of the other ranks – in other words, by doing jobs that corporals and sergeants should have been doing,[4] with the ironical result that very soon sergeants and corporals were having to step into the shoes of dead or wounded officers. And so the errors compounded.

But inexperience stretched upwards far beyond the regiments. The level of generalship in closest contact with the front line was that of brigadier. In August 1914, the six infantry divisions formed for war contained eighteen brigadiers. The fifty-six infantry divisions of the 1916 B.E.F. required 168 (the B.E.F. as a whole, of course, required far more). Hastily promoted from all arms, it would be to ascribe to these officers superhuman qualities to pretend that their performances were not variable. Here is a portrait of one under whom it would have been better not to serve, though fortunately there were many who did not resemble him:

It must be admitted that our Brigadier was exceedingly brave, and therefore he retained our respect to a large extent, in spite of his schoolmaster's manner. Unfortunately, he could not consent to delegate authority, and he left no initiativee to his subordinates; he treated his colonels like company commanders, and they supplied him with any amount of eyewash. He had a terribly symmetrical mind, and symmetry and good organisation rarely go together; also, he loved blood, and he seemed callous as to whether the blood was German or British; danger excited him but blood intoxicated him, and his eyes would glow when a show was on. Possibly this more or less homicidal mania took the place of other vices, for both wine and women were a dead letter to him.[5]

So we come to the major-generals commanding the divisions. These were very important people; indeed, a theory developed (and won continued advocacy after the War) that the division had replaced the regiment as the Army's basic unit, which is really to misunderstand the functions of both. That apart, it is fair to say that in 1916 the most effective level of battle control was divisional;[6] this was the nearest point to the front where co-ordination of all arms took place, where reserves could be committed, held back or redirected, where plans could be significantly modified. It was also the key point for the collection and transmission of information to higher formations, corps, army, G.H.Q. Fifty-six good major-generals to command the infantry divisions (plus five for the cavalry, more for the staff, then those required for other theatres – Egypt, Mesopotamia, Salonika, East Africa, and others besides) was a lot to ask of an army which had begun its operations with only six. A year earlier, when he was commanding the First Army, and Mr Asquith had come to lunch at his headquarters, Haig had told the Prime Minister (among other things) of the 'necessity for promoting young officers to high command. To make room some of the old ones must be removed. We went through the lists of Major-Generals etc. in the Army List. I said it was important to go low down on the List and get young, capable officers. He agreed.'[7]

No doubt he did; but, as most wars show, such matters are easier to agree than to implement. When we consider the Somme on 1 July, we need to remember that of the twenty-three divisional commanders present, only three had commanded as much as a brigade before the war. Such are the penalties of making do with a small peacetime army.

Above the divisional commanders stood the eighteen commanders of army corps: lieutenant-generals, lofty potentates disposing of two, three or more divisions. Before August 1914 there was only one formed army corps in the British Army, the one at Aldershot; II and III Corps only came into existence at the outbreak of war, though their commanders were designated. Everything above that was an *ad hoc* wartime creation. Of the eighteen corps commanders in 1916, two had commanded divisions in peacetime. Yet each of these generals might now be entrusted with 60,000 men or more, powerful artillery, aircraft, and important administrative functions requiring staffs which together totalled well over 400 officers. These were in addition to the staffs of brigades, divisions, armies, G.H.Q. and the lines of communication. Such numbers of staff officers take some finding; as far back as 1902 Field-Marshal Lord Roberts had warned:

. . . it seems clear that the entire staff should be thoroughly trained; that a definite system of carrying out staff duties should be laid down; and that *we should have enough trained staff officers to supply,* in case of emergency, *a large army* . . . staff officers cannot be improvised; nor can they learn their duties, like the rank and file, in a few weeks or months, for their duties are as varied as they are important. I am decidedly of opinion that we cannot have a first-rate army, unless we have a first-rate staff, well educated, constantly practised at manoeuvres, and with wide experience.[8]

Yet in August 1914 there were only 447 officers in the entire Army List who could put 'p.s.c.' (passed Staff College) after their names;[9] the staffs did have to be improvised, after all, and, as may be supposed, their quality was correspondingly uneven.

So we come to the two British generals who actually 'fought' the Battle of the Somme (in the sense that Wellington 'fought'

Waterloo, Montgomery 'fought' the Second Battle of Alamein, or Slim 'fought' the Battle of Meiktila-Mandalay): General Sir Henry Rawlinson, commanding the Fourth Army, and General Sir Hubert Gough, commanding the Reserve (later Fifth) Army. For both, this was a first time: the awesome first experience of responsibility for hundreds of thousands of their fellow men, in circumstances completely unfamiliar, with no blueprints, no clear rules. Both these officers were to display, at various times, high qualities. It is generally agreed that Gough's dismissal in 1918 was politically inspired and most unfair; Rawlinson, in that year, was a considerable architect of the final victory. If they made mistakes on the Somme in 1916 it was certainly not because either was stupid; if they had made no mistakes they would not have been human. It was their fate that *any* mistake, in a war of such masses, very quickly becomes a dreadful affair.

Two more people were intimately concerned with the British attack on 1 July: General Sir Douglas Haig, the British Commander-in-Chief, and General Foch, commanding the French Northern Army Group, whose Sixth Army attacked alongside the British. A week before the battle opened, Haig's Advanced Headquarters came to the Somme area, to occupy a hutted camp near Amiens. The C.-in-C. himself was lodged in the Château de Valvion nearby, roughly equidistant from the headquarters of Rawlinson and Gough.

The correct position for a C.-in-C. at such a time is not easy to decide. Obviously, the great offensive, the biggest thing the British Army had ever undertaken, was going to occupy a great deal of his time and attention. However, his responsibility for the sectors of the Third, First and Second Armies, stretching up into Belgium, remained undiminished (just as General Alexander in Cairo remained responsible for the Middle East as a whole while Montgomery was fighting his battle at Alamein, and General Leese – with his headquarters in Ceylon – carried the responsibilities of South East Asia Command Land Forces Commander while Slim was advancing down Burma in 1945). Grant, in a similar situation in 1864, had chosen to establish his headquarters alongside Meade's; no doubt, in a war fought without benefit of telephone or wireless (though the electric telegraph did already exist), this was correct; for communicating with distant theatres Grant might have found Washington more convenient – but he hated the atmosphere of Washington. Joffre and his opponents, Falkenhayn and later Hindenburg and Ludendorff, were content to keep their headquarters a long way from the front, and pay visits to the armies engaged in battle.

As a national chief, Haig was rather more than just the commander of a group of armies. He could expect to have to receive and transact business with many very important people: the King, the French President, other Allied heads of state, Ministers, notabilities of the Dominions, Allied officers from Joffre (whom he regarded as in practice Generalissimo of the whole front) downwards. Hence the château – but Haig too was learning. The following year he found that a properly equipped train made a more satisfactory Advanced G.H.Q. when battles were in progress; in the next war Montgomery and others would use caravans.

Haig kept a close eye on all the planning of the Somme attack, but he suffered from certain serious inhibitions. He believed firmly in the principle of leaving decisions to the 'man on the spot', the man who would actually have to carry them out. In this particular case, this belief was reinforced by the fact that Haig himself was a cavalryman, while Rawlinson was an infantryman, and it had become perfectly clear by July 1916 that the infantry would always bear the brunt of battle in this war. Consequently, though Haig drew attention to the German probing methods at Verdun, which had impressed him, when Rawlinson and the other infantrymen settled for linear attack (in order to obtain simultaneous impact), Haig did not feel that he could override them. Later in the War he would be less diffident. And when Foch demanded an attack in broad daylight (in accordance with the French doctrine that the gunners should have the benefit of maximum visibility) instead of the dawn half-light that many British officers would have preferred, once again Haig gave way to his more experienced partner. The resulting contrast of style and performance has been harrowingly described by General Spears, watching at the junction of the two armies: '. . . my memory was seared with the picture of the French and British attacking together on the Somme on July 1st, 1916, the British rigid and slow, advancing as at an Aldershot parade in lines that were torn and ripped by the German guns, while the French tactical formations, quick and elastic, secured their objectives with trifling loss. It had been a terrible spectacle.'[10]

So at every stage, from the Commander-in-Chief himself to the humblest devoted soldier 'doing his bit', right back to the munitions workers in the factories at home and a general public which had never brought itself to consider such ghastly scenes, we see inexperience and sheer novelty playing their parts in the tragic

drama. Of course, no one and no nation is born with experience. In
1915 the French had conducted two major offensives in
Champagne and two more in Artois, buying their experience of
such matters at a price of some 1,430,000 casualties. They, too, had
attacked in lines, wearing red képis and red trousers; the 'horizon-
blue' uniforms and elastic formations of 1916 were belated after-
thoughts. In the autumn of 1914, when the Germans threw
enthusiastic but untrained volunteers into the First Battle of Ypres,
the result was what they called the '*Kindermord*' – the 'massacre of
the innocents'. Now it was Britain's turn.

Significant though this inexperience was, there were other
factors present on 1 July that were equally so. There was, above all,
technology, and in particular, at that stage of the War,
communication, urgently awaiting a technological breakthrough.
It never came; this was a problem never really overcome during the
entire War, though inroads were made into it. What was required
was apparatus which did not become available until the next war.
The result was that, from 1914 to 1918, at the moment when troops
were committed to battle, the moment when they left their
trenches to make their footings in the complex of enemy positions,
usually lost to sight behind a curtain of shell-bursts, they almost
certainly passed out of the control of their generals. Generals, in
fact, became quite impotent at the very moment when they would
expect and be expected to display their greatest proficiency; as
Haig ruefully remarked in 1918, 'This is really a platoon
commanders' war.'[11] Meanwhile, attempts were made to cure the
evil by a long list of devices; one single one, of course, would have
done the trick: the two-way portable radio set, the 'walkie-talkie'.
But it did not exist. And because it did not exist, no one, on 1 July
and many other days of murderous battle, had the slightest idea of
what was happening at the front, where the troops were, or where
the enemy was; and there was no chance at all of doing anything
about it. So one forlorn attack followed another, because no one
could stop them, and to the lines of dead and wounded from the
first sickening repulse were added line upon line of those that
followed along mile after mile of front.

The British preliminary bombardment amazed the Germans,
and as the battle continued their consternation at the ever-
increasing weight of British artillery fire grew. To the British
gunners and their commanders came a sense of luxury, after the
penury of 1914 and 1915, when guns themselves had been few and
every shell precious. Now, they believed, they had at last the power
to unlock a defensive front. In fact they had not. It seemed

prodigious, in June 1916, to fire off 1,732,873 rounds in eight days, but a year later, in June 1917 at Messines, the Second Army artillery fired off 3,258,000 rounds in the same period. And in September 1918, in the course of the assault on the Hindenburg Line, the British artillery fired off 943,847 rounds in *twenty-four hours*. It was an artillery war;[12] the British were still learning what that meant, and the failure of so much of their ammunition in 1916 did not make matters easier for them. That, like inexperience, was something that time would correct; meanwhile the infantry would bleed still more.

There was not much, then, to brag about on 2 July, in the way of success. Along a great deal of the front, no gain had ben made at all – or, if made, not held. The remains of the units in the first attack were pulled out, and replaced by divisional and corps reserves; the awful task of collecting the wounded and, where possible, doing something about the 19,240 dead, went forward. The Germans, oddly enough, made little attempt to interfere with the British activities; even their shelling, both on the British front line and on the congested rear areas, was light. No doubt they, too, had their problems. Anyway, it was, in the words of the Official History, 'an almost peaceful scene'.

On the extreme right, however, next to the French, for whom 1 July had been a day of spectacular success,[13] a different pattern established itself. There the British XIII Corps had gained almost all its objectives – and as a result became the first formation to learn what the true texture of this battle was going to be. Between 3 and 4 a.m. on the morning of 2 July, four large groups of infantry, belonging to the German *23rd Reserve, 18th Reserve, 51st Reserve Regiments* and *16th Bavarian Regiment,* counter-attacked on both sides of the captured village of Montauban and the junction of the British and French Armies. These attacks failed, as most of the British attacks had failed on the previous day; but they were a warning of things to come, a sign of what was going to make the Battle of the Somme the turning point of the War.

What modern students, misled by myth and deafened by sixty years of lamentation, often find difficult to grasp about 2 July 1916 is that despite everything that had happened during the previous twenty-four hours, nowhere does one find any hint or suggestion of not continuing the fight. It was clear that the German positions had not fallen like ripe plums – but the British Army was not in any case accustomed to a diet of ripe plums. As early as 10 p.m. on 1 July, Rawlinson was giving orders for the resumption of the battle along the whole front, and on the same evening he handed over the two left-hand corps to Gough, for easier control. The next day, as more, but still very incomplete, information came in, Haig was at Fourth Army headquarters and told Rawlinson: 'The enemy has undoubtedly been severely shaken and he has few reserves in hand. Our correct course, therefore, is to press him hard with the least possible delay . . .'[14]

Rawlinson concurred, but they disagreed about how it should be done. Apart from his insistence on the early capture of Fricourt in the centre (the hinge of the whole front, now forming a sharp and dangerous re-entrant in the British line), Haig's idea was to concentrate on exploiting the success on the right beside the French. Rawlinson, he says, 'did not seem to favour the scheme' – probably because of the awkward congestion of Franco-British communications on the north bank of the Somme. But Gough's appalled discovery of the extent of the disaster on the left put a swift end to Rawlinson's idea of a general attack. 'In one day,' says Gough, 'my thoughts and ideas had to move from consideration of a victorious pursuit to those of the rehabilitation of the shattered wing of an army.'[15] As a result, the next fortnight's operations of the Fourth Army took on a disconnected look, each of the three corps attacking strong localities (Fricourt, La Boisselle, Ovillers, etc.) with varying success. The hard grind had begun; nobody could dream how long it would continue.

What made it certain to continue, however, was the frame of mind of the enemy. The 'motor' of the War, the German Army was also the 'motor' of the Somme. On 2 July General von Falkenhayn paid a visit to General von Below, whose *Second Army* held the Somme front. Falkenhayn told von Below that 'the first principle in position warfare must be to yield not one foot of ground; and if it be lost to retake it by immediate counter-attack, even to the use of the last man.'[16] Von Below accordingly issued an Order of the Day on 3 July, saying:

The decisive issue of the war depends on the victory of the *Second Army* on the Somme. We must win this battle in spite of the enemy's temporary superiority in artillery and infantry. The important ground lost in certain places will be recaptured by our attack after the arrival of reinforcements. For the present, the important thing is to hold our present positions at any cost and to improve them by local counter-attacks.

I forbid the voluntary evacuation of trenches. The will to stand firm must be impressed on every man in the Army. I hold Commanding Officers responsible for this.

The enemy should have to carve his way over heaps of corpses . . .[17]

These were the orders that gave the Battle of the Somme its texture. It is always referred to as a 'British offensive', and quite correctly: there were few days when some British unit, large or small, was not attacking the enemy in some fashion. From time to time these assaults were undertaken on a grand scale, such as the dawn attack on 14 July (contrasting so vividly with the *débâcle* of 1 July), or the famous sub-battle of Flers-Courcelette in September, when tanks made their *début* in war. In between these big occasions there was a constant struggle for particular objectives during which the British inched their way forward over what rapidly became the landscape of a dreadful nightmare, marked by place-names which became signposts on the roads of Hell. By the end of July, at a cost reported by British G.H.Q. of 7,920 officers and 156,789 other ranks, they had won the splintered stumps of Trônes Wood, but they had not won Guillemont, less than a mile beyond, for all their trying. They had got Longueval, but they still could not claim the whole of Delville Wood, 'Devil's Wood', which seemed veritably to be the home of the Devil. They had got Bazentin-le-Petit, and they had just got Pozières; the 1st Australian Division alone suffered 5,278 casualties in a week to put that name into history. They had got Ovillers at last, but they had not got Thiepval, where the Ulstermen had lost over 5,000 on 1 July; another three and a half months were going to have to pass before they would get Beaumont Hamel, where the Newfoundland Regiment had been literally annihilated on that opening day.

That was the British record for July. The French, of course, had also been busy, as their increasing losses show. From the French point of view, however, something far more important had been gained than patches of soggy ground along the River Somme. The first of July, a 'curtain-up ' for the British that they would never forget, was, as I have already said and cannot say too often, for France the 132nd day of the Battle of Verdun, the 'mill on the Meuse' where Falkenhayn had planned to grind down the French Army. On 11 July, because of what was happening on the Somme, he had to order a 'strict defensive' at Verdun. He needed every man he could lay hands on to carry out the orders he had given to von Below.

By the end of July, responding to every British or French advance or attempt to advance, the German infantry had made not less than sixty-seven counter-attacks, large or small, that I can identify. Probably they had made a great many more, now lost in time's obscurity – possibly twice as many. This was the texture of the battle: attack, counter-attack; attack again, counter-attack again. This was why the Germans, both in the army at the front and at home, began to talk with horror about 'the bloodbath of the Somme'. This is why it is so utterly pernicious to dwell constantly on the freak of 1 July, and to associate the whole battle with the image of that day. The picture of the British infantry rising from their trenches to be mown down is only a true picture of the Battle of the Somme when set beside that of the German infantry rising from their trenches to be mown down. Those military historians of the 1930s who did not perceive this were seriously at fault; those who, like Captain Liddell Hart, preferred to lend support to the Lloyd George-Churchill version of the battle did grave disservice to the men who fought on from 2 July, to history, and thereby to a nation which would shortly have to gird itself for another war.

The texture of the battle continued unchanged through August.[18] The Official History displays it in its sketches and maps by endless thin lines like fish-hooks: they are the attack arrows, going out, curving round, and coming back again, sometimes because the thing never stood a chance, most often because of counter-attacks – each hook the outline of another tragedy. In the chronologies, based on the contemporary communiqués, the texture comes through in the endless repetition of place-names: counter-attacks at High Wood on the 1st, Delville Wood on the 2nd, Mouquet Farm on the 4th; High Wood again on the 12th, 17th, 18th and 19th; Delville Wood again on the 18th, 23rd and 24th, and then four times in one day in the big German counter-stroke on 31 August; Mouquet Farm again on the 11th, 12th, 18th and 26th. A German regimental history, writing of this period, says: 'The days on the Somme were the worst in the War.'[19] British officers with much battle experience on the Western Front said afterwards that the Germans never fought better than they did during this period on the Somme. For both sides it was, in the words of the Official History, 'a grim test of endurance'.[20] Yet such are the boundless resources of the human spirit that a young officer in the British 48th Division could write to his mother on 30 August: 'The battle is going awfully well . . .'[21]

September brought the crisis. This was not, as generally represented in British accounts, 'the month of the tank'. These were a brand-new British invention in 1916; controversy surrounded their development after the War; in the Second World War British tanks did not, on the whole, do well. So September 1916 is often written about as though a whole history of error began then; thus Lloyd George:

'So the great secret was sold for the battered ruin of a little hamlet on the Somme, which was not worth capturing.'[22]

The truth is, however, that the forty-nine Mark I tanks which appeared in battle on 15 September were no war-winners; neither were any others of First World War vintage. What made that day important was not the use of a new weapon by the British; it was that this was the only occasion in the entire war when the whole strength of the Entente was thrown into battle against Germany at the same time. On 12 September the Russians and Romanians attacked in Transylvania; on the same day the French Sixth Army also made a fresh, successful attack. On the 15th the Italians opened their Seventh Battle of the Isonzo. The British effort on that day was thus part of a concerted Allied endeavour, whose purpose was no less than to win, and so end, the War. Had this succeeded, 'saving' the tanks would have had little point indeed.

As we know, it did not succeed. One reason for this was, I suggest, the seventy-eight German counter-attacks which I have counted in the *first fortnight* of the month. They signified the last sacrificial exertion of the old German Army; High Wood attacked four times on 1 September, again on the 3rd, 8th and 15th; Mouquet Farm attacked on the 3rd, 4th, 8th, 9th, 10th, 11th and 12th; Ginchy attacked twice on the 3rd, twice on the 6th, several times on the 9th, three times on the 10th – and so on. Then came the big Allied attack on the 15th, with heavy loss to the Germans, and in the remainder of the month I can only identify forty-eight counter-attacks. Only! This massive counter-offensive effort by Germany in September 1916 seems to have escaped the notice of British historians; yet this was the very essence of the battle. This was what wore down the splendid German Army.

When at last the bastion of Thiepval fell to the British 18th Division on 27 September, a German soldier wrote:

'. . . it was absolutely crushing. According to my idea, every German soldier from the highest general to the meanest private had the feeling that now Germany had lost the first great battle.'[23]

Every indication –soldiers' letters, letters to the soldiers, reports from inside Germany – was that he was right; that the Germans were weakening at last; that the time was at hand for the Allies to reap the reward of all their effort. Now, at last, one more big heave might finish the job. But now a new enemy was in the field; in the ominous words of the Official History: 'As September wore to a close, the troops of all arms began to regard the mud as their chief enemy.'[24] By mid-October, 'the British front positions and the approaches thereto were a maze of water-logged shell-holes and flooded trenches'.[25] A British officer describes the act of physical movement on the Somme in November:

It was like walking through caramel. At every step the foot stuck fast, and was only wrenched out by a determined effort, bringing away with it several pounds of earth till legs ached in every muscle. No one could struggle through that mud for more than a few yards without rest. Terrible in its clinging consistency, it was the arbiter of destiny, the supreme enemy, paralysing and mocking English and German alike. Distances were measured not in yards but in mud.[26]

By the end of the battle conditions were indescribable – worse than 'Passchendaele', according to some survivors of both:

'Our vocabulary is not adapted to describe such an existence, because it is outside experience for which words are normally required. Mud, for the men in the line, was no mere inorganic nuisance and obstacle. It took on an aggressive, wolf-like guise, and like a wolf could pull down and swallow the lonely wanderer in the darkness.'[27]

Yet the battle continued, thanks to the unbelievable devotion of the Army, until 18 November. On the 13th, in clammy fog which no doubt hampered the defence as on many other occasions in the War, the 51st Highland Division at last took Beaumont Hamel. It is a measure of the change that had come over the battle that the 51st division, in the four days of fighting which included the capture of Beaumont Hamel, lost some 2,200 officers and men – compared with the 223 officers and 5,017 other ranks lost by the 29th Division for no gain at all, attacking the same village on 1 July.

Beaumont Hamel was the last success; five days later the battle officially ended. By that time, to my certain knowledge, the Germans had attacked the British not less than 330 times.[28] Three hundred and thirty: it was the texture of the battle created by these incessant counter-attacks that gave the Somme its real significance. Just as, after the First Battle of Ypres in 1914, according to the Official History, 'the old British Army was gone beyond recall', so, according to one German staff officer, 'the Somme was the muddy grave of the German field army'.[29] Field-Marshal Prince Rupprecht of Bavaria said: 'what still remained of the old first-class peace-trained German infantry had been expended on the battlefield.'[30] And this was what Ludendorff meant when he said (see p. 109): 'The Army had been fought to a standstill and was utterly worn out.'

This, then, was what the Somme – linked to Verdun, where the French pressed home their own successful counter-offensives in October and November, and to General Brusilov's achievement in the East – really meant in the War: the loss, once and for all, of that intrinsic superiority of quality through peacetime training which the German Army had hitherto enjoyed – irreparable damage to the 'motor' of the War. Henceforward the German Army was in decline, becoming what its leaders called a 'militia'. The British had been a militia ever since their small Regular Army vanished in 1914–15; now they were on equal terms, and, being relatively fresh late-comers, they would get better. The Somme was the turning point. The first dim harbingers of the still far-distant victories of 1918 may be discerned in the crude texture imparted to the Battle of the Somme by the German Army in 1916.

---

1 e.g.:

	1 July	2nd Tour	
4th Div.	5,752	8–28 Oct.	just over 4,000
8th Div.	5,121	23–29 Oct.	nearly 2,500
29th Div.	5,240	11–30 Oct.	1,874
etc., etc.			

2 Professor Sir Charles Oman, in his important article, 'The German Losses on the Somme', in *The Nineteenth Century and After,* May 1927, says: 'in July 1916 we were sending into the line battalions with twenty-five combatant officers or more – the German battalions with only eight or nine.' This simple fact, which seems to have entirely escaped both Lloyd George and Churchill, sufficiently accounts for the much heavier British officer casualties which upset them both so much.

This was a persistent fault in the British Army. Writing of the Battles of Arras in 1917 (i, p. 554) the Official History says: 'When British troops lost their officers, they were . . . apt to fall back, not because they were beaten but because they did not know what to do and expected to receive fresh orders. Perhaps the large numbers of officers commissioned and the fact that a sergeant rarely held command of a platoon for more than a few days lessened the prestige of the non-commissioned officer . . .'

We find the same situation in the Army of the 1930s and the Second World War: 'The British Army with its large number of Officers tended to wet nurse the men mentally with the result that the rank and file never thought for themselves and all, including warrant officers and N.C.O.s, lacked initiative.' (Brigadier John Prendergast, *Prender's Progress,* Cassell, 1979, p. 56).

3 C. E. Carrington's, *Soldier from the Wars Returning,* Hutchinson, 1965, p. 120.

4 Thus, on the night of 26–27 June 1916, the 1/4 East Yorkshires carried out a raid on the German trenches: 'Immediately prior to the raid the enemy wire where we were to enter was cut *by two subalterns,* a dangerous and difficult job which they carried out well.' (Cecil M. Slack, *Grandfather's Adventures in the Great War 1914–1918,* Arthur H. Stockwell, 1977, p. 71; my italics.) This was normal in the British Army, unthinkable in the German.

5 Neville Lytton, *The Press and the General Staff,* Collins, 1920, pp. 50–51.

6   This remained to a large extent true in the Second World War. Thus Field-Marshal
    Lord Slim, *Defeat into Victory,* Cassell, 1956, p. 447: 'To watch a highly-skilled,
    experienced, and resolute commander controlling a hard-fought battle is to see, not
    only a man triumphing over the highest mental and physical stresses, but an artist
    producing his effects in the most complicated and difficult of the arts. I thought as I
    watched what very good divisional commanders I had.' He was referring to Major-
    General D. T. ('Punch') Cowan, 17th Indian Division, at Meiktila, 1 March 1945.
7   Haig Diary, 8 July 1915; author's papers.
8   Lord Roberts: Minutes of Evidence taken before the Royal Commission on the War in
    South Africa, i, p. 441; my italics. Lord Roberts's idea of 'a large army' was '250,000
    and 300,000 men'; the B.E.F. on 30 June 1916 numbered 1,426,000.
9   See the Royal United Services Institute *Journal,* November 1938.
10 Spears, *Prelude to Victory,* p. 91.
11 Haig Diary, 29 July; see Duff Cooper, *Haig,* Faber, 1935, ii, p. 334.
12 See Table E, p. 127.
13 For the French, as well as for the British, 1 July was a freak. The Germans expected
    only a demonstration, not an attack, and were taken by surprise. Just as the British
    never again did so badly, so the French never again did so well.
14 Haig Diary, 2 July; author's papers.
15 General Sir Hubert Gough, *The Fifth Army,* Hodder and Stoughton, 1931, p. 139.
16 O.H., *1916,* ii, p. 27.
17 Author's papers; a captured copy of von Below's Order is included in the Haig Papers
    of 4 July.
18 I count not less than fifty-eight German attacks.
19 *125th Regiment,* quoted in O.H., *1916,* ii, p. 201, f.n.3.
20 Ibid., p. 174.
21 Graham H. Greenwell, *An Infant in Arms,* Allen Lane, The Penguin Press, 1972, p.
    134.
22 *War Memoirs,* Odham's, 1936, i, p. 385.
23 H. W. Wilson and J. A. Hammerton, *The Great War: The Standard History of the
    All-Europe Conflict,* Amalgamated Press, 1914–1918, viii, p. 174.
24 O.H., *1916,* ii, p. 356.
25 Ibid., p. 444.
26 Sidney Rogerson, *Twelve Days,* Arthur Barker, 1933, p. 29.
27 O.H., *1917,* i, pp. 65–6, referring to November and December 1916.
28 The reader will note my recurring use of the phrase 'not less than'. Sometimes, on a
    particular date, the source will say 'several' or simply 'attacks' in the plural. I decided to
    count all such cases as two attacks, because we know they mean more than one, but we
    do not know how many more; all my figures are therefore minimum.
29 O.H., *1916,* i, p. 494.
30 Ibid., ii, p. xii.

XIII

ANTI-MYTH

Table E

'Artillery War': A Selection of Statistics

	Officers	Other Ranks
Strength of Royal Artillery,		
1 Aug. 1914	**4,083**	**88,837**
1 Aug. 1918	**29,990**	**518,790**
B.E.F. Artillery, Aug. 1914		
(1 Cavalry, 5 Infantry Divs.):		**410 guns (all types)**
Fourth Army, 1 July 1916		
(3 Cavalry, 18 Infantry Divs.):		**1,493 guns (all types)**
B.E.F., 11 Nov. 1918		
(3 Cavalry, 61 Infantry Divs.):		**6,406 guns (all types)**
Maximum British Ammunition Expenditure in 24 Hours:		
Noon, 28 Sept.–noon, 29 Sept. 1918:		**943,847 rounds**
British Casualties Caused by		
Artillery and mortars	**58·51%**	
Machine-guns, rifles, etc.	**38·98%**	
	(O.H.) 1916, i, p. 282, f.n.)	
French Artillery, Battle of the Aisne,		
16 April 1917:	**5,350 guns**	
German Artillery, Battle of Picardy,		
21 March 1918:	**6,473 guns**	
Western Front, 11 Nov. 1918:		
Allied Artillery	**21,668 guns**	
Central Powers	**16,181 guns***	

*N.B. The Allies had captured 6,615 German guns since 8 Aug.

Comment: ' "There's too much fuckin' artillery in this bloody war," said Jakes irritably, as though they had all failed to appreciate the fact. "You don't get no sleep".'
(Frederick Manning, The Middle Parts of Fortune, Peter Davies, 1977, p. 222.)

Yet all this assembled might of gunnery was to be thoroughly eclipsed. For the final attack on Berlin, April–May 1945, the Russians brought forward 7 million rounds of artillery ammunition for the use of their 42,000 guns and mortars and their 3,155 tanks and self-propelled guns. This was on the Berlin front alone.

Table F

The Main Enemy (1):
German Divisions engaged by the B.E.F., 1916–18

Battle	German Divs. Engaged	German Total	Source
Somme, July–Nov. 1916	95½ (43½ twice, 4 three times)*		German Official Account, qu. O.H., 1916, ii, p. 555.
		175 (125 in West)	O.H. 1916, i, pp. 45–6.
Arras April Messines to Lens Nov.	131		Haig's *Despatches*, p. 135.
Third Ypres 1917		**256 (137 in West)**	Repington: *The First World War*, Constable, 1920, ii, p. 329.
Third Ypres, 31 July –Nov. 1917	73 77		German Official Account, General von Kuhl, quoted in O.H. 1917, ii, p. 362 f.n.
German Offensives, March–April	109		Haig's *Despatches*, p 235.
		248 (192 in West)	O.H. 1918, i, p.142 and f.n.
Final offensive, Aug.–Nov. 1918	99		Haig's *Despatches*, p.299.
		235 (197 in West)	O.H. 1918, iii, p.192 gives Western total 207, June-July; 10 were disbanded at end of July; p.253 gives 38 in the East.

*Professor Sir Charles Oman (see p. 105), on the basis of contemporary Intelligence, gives a total of eighty-three separate divisions, thirty-three of them twice, four three times. The German Official Account (vol. xi, pp. 103–4) gives an equivalent of 143 divisions ultimately engaged, Professor Oman's calculation gives 120. Clearly, British Intelligence was not disposed to exaggerate.

N.B. This refers to the Intelligence Branch of the General Staff at the War Office, under that most able Director of Military Intelligence, Major-General Sir George Macdonogh.

THE TEXTURE OF THE SOMME: 'the picture of the British infantry rising from their trenches to be mown down is only a true picture when set beside that of the German infantry rising from their trenches to be mown down.' Above: the British 34th Division attacks La Boisselle, 1 July 1916; below: one of the 330 German counter-attacks.

'...the bullet, spade and wire were the enemy on every front ...': (1) Confederate trenches at Petersburg, 1864.

'. . . the enemy on every front . . .'. (2) A Russian trench on the Eastern front, 1914–17.

'. . . the enemy on every front . . .'. (3) A Japanese 'bunker' at Tarawa, 1943; in the Pacific and in Burma such defences, resolutely defended, took a heavy toll of Allied attacking forces.

Table G

The Main Enemy (2):
German Divisions engaged by the British, Second World War

Comparisons with the Second World War are difficult because, except in the Western Desert, the armies of the British Empire never fought their battles against the Germans alone in that war. Moreover, as Sir Basil Liddell Hart has said, reductions in German establishments after 1942 'gave unreality in subsequent years to the tendency of the Allied Intelligence staffs to continue reckoning the number of German divisions as if they were of similar size to their own'.[1] There is also the problem of the different values at different times of Panzer and Infantry divisions. However, comparing like with like, it is not difficult to see where the German main body stood at various stages of the Second World War.

Figures in brackets in the table below show the number of *United Kingdom* divisions present; Empire forces are additional.

Campaign	German Divisions Engaged	German Total
'Dunkirk', May–June 1940 (9)	16[2]	137 (in West)[2]
El Alamein, Oct.–Nov. 1942 (7)	4[3]	200 in Russia[4] + Occupied Europe
North Africa, Nov. 1942– May 1943 (11)	9[5]	171 in Russia[6]
Italy, end 1944 (equivalent of 6)	7[7]	
Normandy, 'D-Day' 6 June 1944 (2)	3[8]	315[9]
Normandy, 25 July (break-out) (7)	11[10]	
Reichswald, Feb. 1945 (7)	7[11]	325[12]

1   *History of the Second World War*, Cassell, 1970, p. 243.

2   This is the strength of the German *Sixth Army*, which Gregory Blaxland *(Destination Dunkirk*, William Kimber, 1973, p. 66) calls the 'chief adversary of the British'; however, the *Sixth Army* was also engaged against the Belgians and the French. The German total is also from Blaxland, p. 67.

3   Peter Young, *World War 1939–45*, Arthur Barker, 1966, diagram on p. 217. Rommel also had seven Italian divisions, while Montgomery also disposed of the 9th Australian, 2nd New Zealand, 1st South African, 4th Indian, a Greek Brigade, and a Free French contingent.

4   H. A. Jacobsen and J. Rohwer (ed.), *Decisive Battles of World War II: The German View*, André Deutsch, 1965, p. 358.

5   James Lucas, *Panzer Army Africa*, Macdonald and Jane's, 1977, p. 193: Appendix II; this is the full total of German divisions employed in North Africa (including the Afrika Korps) and engaged by British, Americans and French, inextricably intermingled.

6   Major-General J. F. C. Fuller, *Decisive Battles of the Western World*, Eyre and Spottiswoode, 1954, iii, p. 520. The decrease is due to losses and disbandments after Stalingrad.

7   G. A. Shepperd, *The Italian Campaign 1943–45*, Arthur Barker, 1968, pp. 332–3. The total of German divisions in Italy was twenty-seven, of which eighteen faced the Allied 15th Army Group. The 'British' Eighth Army contained the 2nd New Zealand Division and 4th New Zealand Armoured Brigade, the 8th and 10th Indian Divisions and 43rd Lorried Gurkha Brigade, II Polish Corps (two divisions), four Italian Combat Groups (six battalions each) and a Jewish brigade. A tendency to the use of independent brigades makes precise calculations difficult.

8   Chester Wilmot, *The Struggle for Europe*, Collins, 1952, map on p. 203.

9   Ibid., total shown on map, front end-paper.

10   Ibid., map on p. 363.

11   L. F. Ellis and A. E. Warhurst, *Victory in the West*, H.M.S.O., 1968 (Official History), ii, p. 254.

12   Shelford Bidwell in *The Encyclopedia of Land Warfare in the 20th Century*, Spring Books, 1977, p. 128. Many of these divisions existed only on paper and in Hitler's imagination; all were seriously under strength.

XIV

SOMME MYTHS (1):
Machine-Guns: 'The Most Lethal Weapon'

'Tak, tak, tak, tak . . . a single sweep of the machine gun accounted for more of them than ten mothers could have borne in as many years.'

(Georg Bucker, *In the Line*)

'The war will not be understood in traditional terms: the machine gun alone makes it so special and unexampled that it simply can't be talked about as if it were one of the conventional wars of history.'

(Paul Fussell, *The Great War and Modern Memory*)

Professor Fussell does not much care for David Jones, whose famous poem, *In Parenthesis,* tells in its half-mystical, half-factual manner the familiar story of a Kitchener Army battalion (Royal Welch Fusiliers) making its way stage by stage from England to the Somme and massacre on 1 July. This is the British epic of the First World War, repeated in novels and histories without number. Being a man steeped in the accumulated consciousness of his people, David Jones invested the whole experience with affinities to ancient wars; the sweat, the pain, the fatigue, the comradeship, the pride, the jokes, the sudden deaths of past generations of soldiers are all present with his Welshmen in 1916:

My fathers were with the Black Prinse of Wales
at the passion of
the blind Bohemian king.
They served in these fields,
it is in the histories that you can read it, Corporal . . .[1]

Then the passage continues:

> I was with Abel when his brother found him,
> under the green tree.
> I built a shit-house for Artaxerxes.

This last line has a footnote; David Jones reports a 'front-area conversation':

'He was carrying two full latrine-buckets. I said: "Hallo, Evan, you've got a pretty bloody job." He said: "Bloody job, what do you mean?" I said it wasn't the kind of work I was particularly keen on myself. He said: "Bloody job – bloody job indeed, the army of Artaxerxes was utterly destroyed for lack of sanitation".'

I once remarked to a colleague that while nearly every young Welshman of the period was likely to be familiar with Genesis iv, surely the misfortunes of a Persian king in the fourth century B.C. constituted a somewhat esoteric piece of knowledge for a private soldier, even in the Citizen Army. My colleague reminded me that the first decades of the century were the heyday of the penny libraries, the flowering of evening classes, Workers' Education, and the belief that the acquisition of knowledge was a virtue as well as being a powerful charm.

Professor Fussell will have none of it:

by placing the suffering of ordinary British soldiers in such contexts as these, Jones produces a document which is curiously ambiguous and indecisive . . . It even implies that, once conceived to be in the tradition, the war can be understood. The tradition to which the poem points holds suffering to be close to sacrifice and individual effort to end in heroism (sic); it contains, unfortunately, no precedent for an understanding of war as a shambles and its participants as victims.[2]
We feel that Jones's formula is wrong, all wrong . . .[3]
Jones has attempted in 'In Parenthesis' to elevate the new Matter of Flanders and Picardy to the status of the old Matter of Britain. That it refuses to be so elevated, that it resists being subsumed into the heroic myth, is less Jones's fault than the war's . . .[4]

And that brings Professor Fussell straight to the machine-gun, which 'alone' makes the war 'so special and unexampled that it simply can't be talked about as if it were one of the conventional wars of history'. This is the 'machine-gun myth', as it has entered legend and literature, in just about its purest form.

Hard facts, as usual, make sad havoc of this myth, as so many others; what it ignores is the 'artillery war' – revealed in the statistic which shows that while bullets (whether fired by machine-guns, rifles or revolvers) accounted for 38.98 per cent of British casualties during the War, shells and bombs accounted for 58.51 per cent (see Table E, p. 127). General Spears's description of the attack on 1 July which I have quoted on p. 111 is a description of slaughter by shell-fire: 'explosions a mile long . . . gaps of hundreds of yards where there had been men before . . .' Artillery was the killer; artillery was the terrifier. Artillery followed the soldier to the rear, sought him out in his billet, found him on the march:

Sustained shell-fire was the most trying and terrifying thing to be feared by all. Many of us were naturally prepared to face up to rifle or even machine gun fire without much trepidation, as one felt there was a sort of sporting chance, and even an opportunity to hit back, as also with hand grenades. Shell-fire, however, was something devilish and beyond comprehension.[5]
One had to try and shut everything from one's mind and to become oblivious to what was going on around. There was a feeling of having a tight violin string in one's head which was due to snap at any instant and drive one insane.[6]
I lost all count of the shells and all count of time. There was no past to remember or future to think about. Only the present. The present agony of waiting, waiting for the shell that was coming to destroy us, waiting to die.[7]

The idea of the machine-gun as a supreme killer is literary, not historical. Soldiers in trench warfare were only exposed to machine-gun fire from time to time – when carrying out attacks or daylight raids, or working in the open; they were exposed to artillery fire the whole time they were in the front zone, often right back to their rest billets. Machine-guns, like other weapons in that and other wars, were effective when they were unexpected, and when no drill yet existed for dealing with them. In 1914 they badly shocked the French. In July 1916 the German Army possessed some 11,000 machine-guns, and these took a heavy toll of the inexperienced (and inadequately equipped) Kitchener divisions. By 1918, the Germans had 32,000 of the heavy (Maxim 1908) type, and in addition 37,000 light, sling-carried Bergmann models (developed in answer to the British Lewis gun). When the Allies passed to the counter-offensive in July, machine-guns soon became recognized as the 'hard core' of the German defence; yet they were never able to halt the Allied advance, and the British Armies alone captured over 29,000 of them from the Germans in battle. Tactics and technology had caught up with them; smoke-shells (which did not exist in 1916) blinded them, accurate artillery fire crushed them; concentrated British machine-gun and Lewis gun fire neutralized them and sometimes tanks rolled over them. Professor Fussell was looking at the wrong year. History does, after all, 'subsume' its wars.

Subsuming the myths is, of course, something else again. It is another part of the machine-gun myth that the same obtuseness which exposed British youth to machine-gun fire also deprived it of the support of these useful weapons. Thus Lloyd George (who, like Professor Fussell, considered the machine-gun 'the most lethal weapon of the war'):

'the military direction completely failed to appreciate the important part this arm would play in the war.'[8]

He continues: 'It took our generals many months of terrible loss to realise the worth of the machine-gun . . .'

This point of view disregards the fact that in 1914 the British establishment of two machine-guns per infantry battalion was the same as the German;[9] that this establishment was doubled as early as February 1915; and that the heavy, belt-fed, tripod-mounted gun is primarily a defensive weapon, whereas the British Army was continuously on the offensive from March 1915 to March 1918. During that time, infantry battalions acquired thirty-two Lewis guns each. The Machine-gun Corps, founded in October 1915, evolved offensive techniques for the heavy guns (e.g. indirect barrage fire) in advance of German practice; it also, in conjunction with the R.A.F., pioneered air supply to a battlefield with the dropping of 100,000 rounds of ammunition to the Australian machine-guns at Le Hamel on 4 July 1918. By the Armistice the strength of the Corps was 6,432 officers and 124,920 other ranks. Between 1914 and 1918 the three firms of Vickers, Lewis and Hotchkiss manufactured 239,840 machine-guns for the British Army. *Pace* the myths, *someone* must have appreciated them!

How did the myth of the British generals' blindness to the value of machine-guns come about? How has it persisted to this day in the teeth of all the evidence? A small amount of personal history helps to answer these questions. When my book, *Douglas Haig: The Educated Soldier,* came out in 1963, Sir Basil Liddell Hart took a deep dislike to it (for obvious reasons). As was his custom, he industriously circularized a number of people, prompting them to attack it (though he never did this publicly himself); I know of at least eight whom he approached in this way, or supplied with critical material, including the actor who played the part of Haig in the musical *Oh! What a Lovely War!* and who was invited to review my book for *Tribune*. One of these people was kind enough to send me an extract from the 'brief' that Liddell Hart had given him:

In case what I told you over the telephone about the source of the statement about Haig's 1915 verdict on machine-guns was not quite clear on that bad telephone line, it may be useful to repeat it here –

Edmonds (the Official Historian) wrote me on the 25th Feb. 1930 recommending me to read Brig.-Gen. Baker-Carr's forthcoming book *From Chauffeur to Brigadier* which he had vetted – as an 'account of the struggle of a specialist with the General Staff'. He said it was 'truthful about the things with which he was actually connected', viz. machine-guns and tanks. I found on p. 87 the account of how Baker-Carr was instructed in 1915 'to put down on paper the reasons for my proposed increase in the numbers of machine-guns'. He summarised the comments written on the file by the Army and Corps Commanders, and states that 'One Army Commander gave his opinion that "the machine-gun was a much over-rated weapon and two per battalion were more than sufficient".' On reading this I asked Baker-Carr who this Army Commander was (there were only two) and he told me that it was Haig. I gather that Baker-Carr was quoting from the Minute which he still had in his files. I subsequently checked it with Edmonds, who confirmed it. [10]

Since Haig was soon to become Commander-in-Chief, if this really was his '1915 verdict on machine-guns' it was a serious matter. Certainly this little essay by Brigadier-General Baker-Carr, and the subsequent use made of it by Liddell Hart and many others, have been the source of a positive torrent of mythology.

Before we plunge deeper into the subject we need to know who Baker-Carr was. In 1914 he was a retired Rifle Brigade Officer who knew how to drive a car – not a usual skill in those early days of motoring – and he registered himself as a driver for the B.E.F. He had some startling experiences driving iron-nerved generals about during the retreat from Mons, and he ended the War as a tank brigadier. What was his connection with machine-guns? It was this: the gruelling First Battle of Ypres, which absorbed all the energies of the B.E.F. while it was in progress, ended on 12 November 1914. Precisely ten days later – 22 November – a B.E.F. Machine-gun School was set up, and Baker-Carr, who had once served on the staff of the School of Musketry at Hythe, was appointed its first Commandant. The reader may consider that this procedure was reasonably expeditious; it certainly seems at odds with Lloyd George's strictures quoted earlier.

Now let us turn to Baker-Carr's narrative. It has to be said at once that it has a serious defect for the historian: one searches in vain for actual dates – the nearest one comes to such a thing is the phrase 'Christmas came and went'; generally the brigadier prefers to leave us with vaguer concepts, like 'already' or 'soon'. Fortunately, there are other sources for such tiresome but necessary details. Right from the beginning, says Baker-Carr, he encountered 'widespread resistance . . . when striving to secure the recognition of the machine-gun as one of the most important weapons of the foot-soldier'.[11] Nevertheless, from his own account it is apparent that all his requirements (demonstration guns, instructors, accommodation, cooking facilities, etc., etc.) were promptly met. 'At last the great day arrived';[12] the school was in business. At this stage Baker-Carr confined his instruction to the mechanism of the gun, with a little shooting practice; the course lasted fourteen days. He made no attempt, in these early days, to instruct on tactical handling, 'about which little or nothing was laid down officially. At that time, the sole mention of machine-guns was confined to a dozen lines in the *Infantry Training Manual*. Nobody in authority concerned himself with this weapon of enormous potential importance, and battalion commanders, before the War, frankly and cordially disliked it.'[13] It is difficult to tell, at this distance, whether Baker-Carr took his mythology with him to the Machine-gun School, or whether he grew it after he arrived there. The above passage is quite simply untrue, as Sir James Edmonds must have known, and Liddell Hart should have known.

The British Army had used 315 machine-guns in the South African War; against a normally invisible enemy like the Boers, usually fighting on the defensive, they were not a particularly useful weapon. However, both during and after that war there was considerable debate about how they ought to be used; *Field Service Regulations* (Part II) in 1900 concluded that they should be deployed in pairs because, if massed, they would attract hostile artillery fire. *Cavalry Training* in 1907, on the other hand, said 'they will usually be massed under one commander' (which turned out to be correct). *Infantry Training*, 1911, however, continued to deprecate the massing of guns. In 1909 Lieutenant-Colonel R. V. K. Applin, D.S.O., M.P., produced a handbook entitled *Machine-Gun Tactics*, many of whose recommendations were adopted in the course of the War. If Baker-Carr did not know of all these, that was his fault and no one else's. Among those who had been staunch defenders of the machine-gun before the War were General Sir Horace Smith-Dorrien, commanding II Corps in 1914 and soon to command the Second Army, Major-General C. C. Monro, who had been Commandant of the School of Musketry from 1903 to 1907, and now commanded the 2nd Division in Haig's I Corps (he would later rise to Army Commander and Commander-in-Chief, India), and Brigadier-General W. N. Congreve, V.C., who had been Commandant of the Musketry School from 1909 to 1911, and would later command an army corps. Baker-Carr presents his entire story as a constant battle of wits between himself and his loyal assistants on the one hand, and the 'General Staff' and 'commanders of larger units, such as armies and army corps' ('the enemy at the gate') on the other. This also has to be dismissed as mythology.

At some point after Christmas 1914 Baker-Carr was 'urging the advisability of doubling the number of machine-guns per battalion, i.e. raising it from two to four'.[14] 'After much striving and after enduring many snubs' he was 'at last' instructed to put his proposal down formally on paper, which he did, and 'after allowing a decent interval to elapse, I forwarded it to G.H.Q.'. His account here takes on the tone of tragic drama:

'Week after week went by and nothing happened. We were beginning to feel almost desperate when at length the file, containing my proposals, was returned with the comments of Army and Corps Commanders. Eagerly we opened it and scanned the views expressed. When we read them, we nearly wept.'[15]

This was where he found the comment that 'the machine-gun was a much over-rated weapon and two per battalion were more than sufficient'. 'It seemed,' he says,

as though the High Command did not *want* to see . . . Nothing stands still in this world except the Military Mind, which steadfastly refuses to look ahead, until it suddenly finds itself involved in a new conflict, having learned nothing, having forgotten nothing . . . This is not the fault of the individual; it is the fault of the whole system. Nothing is more discouraged in the Army than a departure from the well-worn path of tradition. The 'good soldier' is one who does what he is told without thinking . . . The chief trouble at G.H.Q. was that there was no one there who had time to listen to any new idea. Everybody was so busy writing 'Passed to you', 'Noted and returned', or 'For your information' etc., etc., on piles and piles of 'jackets', that no one had a moment to consider any proposal for altering the existing condition of affairs.[16]

It seems slightly indecent to interrupt this heart-rending eloquence with the observation that this same purblind High Command did actually authorize the doubling of the machine-gun establishment per infantry battalion in February 1915 – which may be thought, in the circumstances, rather fast work.[17]

'In the circumstances'; mythology flourishes by ignoring circumstances. It is an important circumstance of 1914 that the machine-gun then on issue was the Maxim, an obsolete pattern which was in process of being replaced by the Vickers (which remained in use until 1968, a half-century of usefulness which no doubt also illustrates the inability of the Military Mind to think ahead). One week after the outbreak of war (and twelve days before the Army even saw a German soldier) the War Office ordered 192 guns from Vickers – sufficient for ninety-six units. That is just about the size of the six-division B.E.F. originally planned, so this order has to be regarded as a re-equipment programme, not an expansion. In September, however, the War Office order was stepped up to 1,792, which definitely did mean expansion, and Vickers were asked to deliver these by July 1915 at a rate of fifty per week. We have it on the authority of Lloyd George that at the outbreak of war Vickers' maximum output was ten to twelve guns a week,[18] so this War Office order meant quadrupling the maximum.

In November – the month that G.H.Q. set up Baker-Carr's Machine-gun School – the War Office went much further. Impressed, no doubt, by the grim lessons of Ypres, which Baker-Carr was convinced had gone unnoticed by almost everyone in authority except himself, the War Office asked Vickers to step up production to 200 per week – sixteen times the original maximum. Then came the doubling of the establishment in February, and in that same month the War Office placed an order for 2,000 machine-guns in America. That is a total order for nearly 4,000 guns; to understand the significance of the figure we need a little more circumstance – the circumstance that in 1914 the mighty German Army possessed 4,500 machine-guns and the French Army possessed 2,500.[19] Not a bad performance by the Military Mind, one might say!

Brigadier Baker-Carr's mythology, however, has no time for such perspectives. A particularly entertaining passage in his book tells of his encounters with Lord Kitchener, who ruled over the War Office and the Army in his capacity as Secretary of State for War;

Lord Kitchener, in common with almost all other soldiers in high position, failed to realise the importance of the automatic weapon. He had definitely laid down that 2 machine-guns per battalion were a minimum, four per battalion a maximum, and anything in excess of four a luxury. When informed of Lord Kitchener's decision, Mr Lloyd George, on his own initiative, laid down a figure of 64 per battalion and it was on this basis that orders for manufacture were placed. Thus wars are won.[20]

It is here that we enter a veritable Wonderland of myth. Lloyd George himself tells us how this figure of sixty-four was arrived at. In May 1915 the Ministry of Munitions was created, with Lloyd George at its head and Sir Eric Geddes in charge of machine-gun and rifle production. It was Geddes who reported Kitchener's dictum to Lloyd George, who says, 'According to Geddes I said to him: "Take Kitchener's maximum (4 per battalion); square it; multiply that result by 2; and when you are in sight of that, double it again for good luck".'[21] Hence the sixty-four. This version of events was endorsed not only by Baker-Carr in 1930, but also by Major-General Sir Ernest Swinton (protagonist of the tanks) in 1933, and a similar version was propagated by Liddell Hart in his book *The Real War* in 1930,[22] so its place in mythology has been secure. But two important points are regrettably obscured. First, there is the circumstance that *whatever* the orders, and no matter where they came from, Vickers were going to be unable to fulfil them until new productive capacity had been created. Out of the 1,792 guns ordered by the War Office in September 1914 for delivery by July 1915, Vickers were only able to deliver 1,022. It was not 'vision' in the War Office or at G.H.Q. that was needed, it was new factories, and until these were built and working it did not greatly matter who ordered what. The simple fact, which wrecks the myth, is that the War Office had placed orders well beyond Vickers's capacity long before the Ministry of Munitions was born.

Secondly, we need to look again at that magical figure of sixty-four. Lloyd George says that what this was intended to mean was thirty-two guns per battalion with thirty-two more in reserve, but Baker-Carr treats it as a real establishment of sixty-four guns. And so indeed it was, later in the war. But they were Machine-gun Battalions. We have noted the formation of the Machine-gun Corps in October 1915; the heavy (Vickers) machine-guns were concentrated in its hands, and in due course one battalion was provided for each infantry division. These battalions actually had sixty-four guns. With the 13-infantry-battalion division of 1915–18, that works out at a proportion of just under five guns per infantry battalion. So the difference between Lord Kitchener's dull lack of vision and Lloyd George's war-winning perspicacity turns out to be slightly less than one gun per battalion.

Of course, something else is missing, too: the Lewis gun, which began to replace the heavy machine-gun in infantry units in 1915. And mention of the Lewis gun brings us conveniently to Haig, and his real 'verdict' on machine-guns. I fear that we shall never know what he actually wrote on Baker-Carr's paper, because as far as I can discover the records of the Machine-gun Corps (and presumably the school out of which it was born) became a casualty of the Second World War. When I asked a member of the Baker-Carr family whether the general had left any papers, I was told that either he had destroyed them himself, or they were destroyed after his death. So if we really wish to know Haig's mind, we have to look elsewhere; fortunately, we do not have to look far.

General E. K. G. Sixsmith, in his book *Douglas Haig*,[23] supplies the interesting information that as far back as 1898 Haig gave up two days of his embarkation leave on the way to the Sudan to look at the Enfield factory, and study the manufacture and mechanics of machine-guns. Duff Cooper, in his biography, quotes a letter that Haig wrote to Sir Evelyn Wood from the Sudan, describing his first action and saying, 'we felt the want of machine-guns.' If that was so in 1898 it seems, *prima facie,* unlikely that he would have scorned them in 1915.

Haig, as I have indicated, was not the only British officer to form an early appreciation of machine-guns. Colonel Huguet, the French Military Attaché in 1905 (who was certainly no Anglophile) remarked on the British Army's awareness of machine-guns at that date. In 1909 the School of Musketry (Colonel W. N. Congreve being Commandant) recommended that the establishment should be six per battalion. This was turned down for financial reasons, and as the Army Estimates were shortly to be reduced the idea was dropped. The Chancellor of the Exchequer at the time was Mr Lloyd George.

To return to Haig, we have to wait for our next piece of direct evidence on his 'verdict' until 20 August 1914. The B.E.F. was now in France, the enemy was coming close (the Battle of Mons was three days off), and Haig held a conference of senior officers of I Corps. Point 4 on the agenda was the information which Haig imparted that 'German machine-guns are said to be well commanded; the French are believed to have lost heavily by attacking them with infantry', and he gave instructions that they should always (if possible) be attacked by artillery. There follows a long silence on the subject in his papers. The truth is that that

splendidly trained B.E.F. of 1914, with its famous 'mad minute'
musketry (developed after 1909, when the request for six machine-
guns was turned down), managed to do extremely well without
them, even (at Ypres) persuading the Germans that they faced a
'machine-gun army'. So there was not a great deal to say. But on 6
November, as the Battle of Ypres approached its climax, we do find
another important piece of evidence. Haig wrote a letter to his
nephew, Colonel Oliver Haig, who commanded the 3rd County of
London Yeomanry;[24] Colonel Haig was anxious to get his regiment
to France, and obviously had been trying to persuade his important
uncle to use some 'pull'. Haig's reply was: 'You must not fret
because you are not out here. There is a great want of troops, and
numbers are wanted. So I expect you will *all* soon be in the field.
Meantime train your machine-guns. It will repay you.'[25]

After that there is another long silence (people do not normally
harp on the obvious in their diaries). On 20 May 1915, however,
Haig records a meeting with the Commanding Officer of the newly-
arrived 51st (Territorial) Division, Major-General R. Bannatine-
Allason. General Allason complained that his men were not yet
fully trained (some of his battalions had gone to Gallipoli, and had
been replaced by 'second-line' battalions): 'I replied that infantry
peace training was little use in teaching a company how to capture a
house occupied by half a dozen machine-guns . . . He should urge
his men to operate at wide intervals, and use cover and try to bring
a converging fire on the locality attacked. We should also use our
machine-guns as much as possible.'[26]

So the true 'verdict' begins to emerge. It was about a month
later, when representatives of Lloyd George's new Ministry of
Munitions were touring the front to find out the Army's needs, that
Haig revealed his real thinking; he told them: 'A lighter machine-
gun, with tripod and gun in one part, is a necessity. Mobility is most
important.'[27] Haig, with the experience of Neuve Chapelle behind
him, was looking ahead to fresh offensive battles and what the
Army would need in order to fight them. The gun it received was
the Lewis, which began to arrive in pitifully small numbers in July
1915; a year later each infantry battalion had sixteen of these guns,
and Haig had taken steps to ensure that the best use was made of
them. At one of his weekly Army Commanders' conferences in
March,

we discussed the use of Lewis guns in an advance. A few of these guns can
develop as great a volume of fire as a considerable number of infantry.
They are far less vulnerable and can find cover more easily. I emphasised
the necessity for company and platoon commanders being trained in the

use of these guns in tactical situations. At present only a comparatively few officers of infantry realise the great addition of fire-power which has been given them by the formation of machine-gun companies and Lewis gun detachments.[28]

It was during the winter of 1913 that the Royal Flying Corps conducted tests in order to find a suitable machine-gun for use in aeroplanes. The air-cooled Lewis, weighing 26 lb. (compared with the 38½ lb. of the water-cooled Vickers) found favour with the airmen, who placed an order. Production plant therefore existed in 1914, and the Army profited by this. The War Office did not rush to place orders with Lewis because, frankly, the gun was far from perfect for land warfare conditions; the open ammunition pans were awkward to carry and easily clogged in mud, as did the firing mechanism. But the plant existed, and that settled the matter, given all the shortages of 1915. Ultimately 133,104 Lewis guns were manufactured during the War – far more than any other type. No doubt if Haig had been offered a Bren gun, he would have jumped at it; but Brens, like so much else, were for another war. So he gratefully received the Lewis and became its warm advocate. By 1918, with all its defects, it had so much become the right arm of the infantry that the Australian General Monash, when his battalions were becoming very weak, remarked, 'so long as they have 30 Lewis guns per battalion it doesn't much matter what else they have.'[29]

So much for the machine-gun myth. In its creation and perpetuation we see the baleful influence of a mendacious politician, a silly, conceited brigadier who thought he was so clever, and a renowned military commentator who could have taken more care to inform himself correctly – a formidable and disastrous combination.

One last question remains: why did Sir James Edmonds, who clearly knew the truth, choose to point Liddell Hart in such a profitless wrong direction? What imp of mischief or malice prompted him to feed this myth? I suppose we shall never know.

---

1   David Jones, *In Parenthesis*, Faber, 1937, Part 4.
2   Paul Fussell, *The Great War and Modern Memory*, O.U.P., 1975, pp. 146–7.
3   Ibid., p. 152.
4   Ibid., p. 153.
5   John F. Tucker, *Johnny Get Your Gun: A Personal Narrative of the Somme, Ypres and Arras*, William Kimber, 1978, p. 130.
6   Ibid., p. 72.

7   P. J. Campbell, *In the Cannon's Mouth,* Hamish Hamilton, 1979, p. 80.
8   Lloyd George, *War Memoirs,* Odham's, 1936, i, p. 357.
9   The Germans, however, had the advantage of a more sensible organization for continental war than the British. The British Army in 1914 (and long after) remained an imperial service army, with the 'linked battalion' system devised by Mr Cardwell in the 1870s – each regiment (in theory) maintaining a battalion overseas, fed by a battalion at home. Thus the British Army always had to fight by battalions, using what was available. The Germans, like all other continentals, fought by regiments: each regiment consisted of three battalions, which gave it six machine-guns (like three British battalions), but it also had a regimental reserve of six guns for replacements. Naturally, if things became difficult, these would not be left behind in the transport. So in effect a German division really had forty-eight guns compared with the British twenty-four.
10 Author's papers; the person who kindly allowed me to see this was a friend of Sir Basil Liddell Hart, and continues to think warmly of him. He should remain nameless because he would not wish to be drawn into this discussion.
11 Brigadier-General C. D. Baker-Carr, *From Chauffeur to Brigadier,* Ernest Benn, 1930, p. 72.
12 'At last': here, as usual with Baker-Carr's narrative, it is difficult to fix a timespan, but not utterly impossible. The first beginning of Baker-Carr's connection with machine-gun instruction was, he tells us, a visit to Major-General T. Capper's 7th Division which 'had at last been withdrawn from the line', gravely weakened by heavy fighting. According to the Official History, the 7th Division came out of the line on 5 November. It is unlikely that Baker-Carr would be visiting it that day, or the next; I should say that the earliest date for his visit would be 7 November. The Machine-gun School, as I have said above, was formally set up on 22 November – just fifteen days later. Surely some phrase like 'almost at once' would be more suitable here than 'at last'?
13 Baker-Carr, op. cit., pp. 79–80. To illustrate the prevailing contempt for machine-guns in the pre-war army, Baker-Carr offers this little dialogue: "What should I do with the machine-guns today, sir?" would be a question frequently asked by the officer in charge, on a field-day. "Take the damned things to a flank and hide 'em!" was the usual reply.' Considered quite objectively, it is, of course, the correct reply. As Baker-Carr himself says (and his school taught), 'the greatest value is obtained from a machine-gun when it enfilades its target' – so, clearly, the flank was the right place for them. And, once there, would it have been a good idea *not* to hide them? I cannot help thinking that if such a dialogue ever did take place, and the commanding officer sounded short, it may well have been because he thought the officer who asked the question was being rather wet.
14 Baker-Carr, op. cit., pp. 84–5.
15 Ibid., p. 87.
16 Ibid., pp. 88–9.
17 O.H., *1915,* i, p. 11.
18 Lloyd George, op. cit., i, p. 363.
19 Paul-Marie de la Gorce, *The French Army,* Weidenfeld and Nicolson, 1963, p. 83.
20 Baker-Carr, op. cit., p. 123.
21 Lloyd George, op. cit., i, p. 360.
22 This was re-published in 1934 under the title, *A History of the World War 1914–1918,* and again in 1970 as *History of the First World War,* Cassell, p. 193.
23 Weidenfeld and Nicolson, 1976, p. 20.
24 The 3rd County of London Yeomanry were the 'Sharpshooters'; this was my father's regiment in 1914.
25 I have a photocopy of this letter in my files.
26 Haig Diary; author's papers.
27 Ibid.
28 Duff Cooper, *Haig,* i, pp. 309–10.
29 Monash, 8 September, quoted in the *Official History of Australia in the Great War 1914–18* by Dr C. E. W. Bean, Angus and Robertson, 1942, vi, p. 936.

XV

SOMME MYTHS (2):
'Physically Impossible'

In the Preface to Volume I of the Official History for 1916, Sir James Edmonds says:

It may be that there would have been complete victory everywhere on the 1st July had the infantry been ordered to cross No Man's Land at the fastest speed possible, instead of at 'a steady pace', although there was no creeping barrage to help then. in this first stage. An officer, who rose from the rank of captain to that of major-general during the war on the Western Front, has said that the Battle of the Somme was lost by three minutes.[1]

It is perhaps as well that that officer remains nameless, because his remark must have been uttered in an unthinking moment and has contributed largely to more myth. The Battle of the Somme lasted four and a half months. Its object was to overthrow the German Empire, which suggests that it would have taken at least four and a half months in any circumstances. In 1918, even after the shattering losses of the unsuccessful German offensives earlier in the year, it took a hard three-month campaign to make the German Empire sue for peace. In 1865, as the year opened, the Confederacy was in the direst straits; yet it did not surrender until the fourth month. In 1945, the Third Reich began the year in a hopeless position, but it did not give in until May. Obviously, Germany in the pride of her strength in 1916 would not easily or quickly accept defeat. How a 4½-month battle can be lost in three minutes is not clear to me; if Sir James Edmonds understood, I think he should have explained.

There is, I need hardly add, rather more to all this than the Official Historian discloses in his Preface. Later on we read:

Every infantryman – the officers in most units were dressed like the men – wore 'fighting order', viz. the normal equipment, including steel helmet and entrenching tool, less the pack and greatcoat; with rolled groundsheet, water-bottle, and haversack in place of the pack on the back. In the haversack were small things, mess tin, towel, shaving kit, extra socks, message book, 'the unconsumed portion of the day's ration', extra cheese, one preserved ration, and one iron ration. Two gas helmets and tear goggles were carried, also wire-cutters, field dressing and iodine. Officers and N.C.O.s carried 4 flares. Moving on from dump to dump, the men picked up, besides, 220 rounds of S.A.A. [small arms ammunition] (partly in cotton bandoliers), two sandbags and two Mills grenades, these last only to be thrown by trained bombers. Each leading company also took 10 picks and 50 shovels, and wire-cutters were distributed to the leading sections. Consolidating companies took additional tools and sandbags. The total weight carried per man was about 66 lbs., which made it difficult to get out of a trench, impossible to move much quicker than a slow walk, or to rise and lie down quickly.[2]

In a footnote Sir James Edmonds adds: 'This overloading of the men is by many infantry officers regarded as one of the principal reasons of the heavy losses and failure of their battalions; for their men could not get through the machine-gun zone with sufficient speed.' And so another myth was born. Captain Liddell Hart, in *The Real War,* seized upon Edmonds's words with relish:

The question that remained was whether the British infantry could cross no-man's-land before the barrage lifted. It was a race with death – the greatest of such races – run by nearly sixty thousand men in the first heat. They were hopelessly handicapped. The whole mass, made up of closely-packed waves of men, was to be launched together, without discovering whether the bombardment had really paralysed the resistance. Under the Fourth Army's instructions, those waves were to advance at 'a steady pace', symmetrically aligned like rows of ninepins ready to be knocked over. 'The necessity of crossing no-man's-land at a good pace, so as to reach the parapet before the enemy could reach it, was not mentioned.'[3] But *to do so would have been physically impossible,* for the heaviest handicap of all was that 'the infantryman was so heavily laden that he could not move faster than a walk'. Each man carried about 66 lbs., over half his own body weight, 'which made it difficult to get out of a trench, impossible to move much quicker than a slow walk, or to rise and lie down quickly'. Even an army mule, the proverbial and natural beast of burden, is only expected to carry a third of his own weight! The 'race' was lost before it started, and the battle soon after.'[4]

Let no one say that the late Sir Basil Liddell Hart was not a master of pejorative prose; alas, that verification made such small appeal to him. He clung to this view (repeating it in his *Memoirs* in 1965) and propagated it far and wide, to be received by many so-called historians as uncritically as he had received it himself. Yet, certainly by 1965, the facts of the matter were not by any means in short supply. Before I set them out, I must say one thing: I do not question for one moment that it would have been correct for the British infantry, on 1 July 1916, to cross No Man's Land as quickly as possible, and it was clearly a most serious error on the part of the Fourth Army, in its tactical instructions, not to emphasize this. The chief reason for this error was, as I have indicated above (pp. 118-19), misplaced confidence in the power of the British artillery to overcome the German defences.

That said, let us now reconsider 1 July. It was *not* – and this can hardly be stressed too much – a Fourth Army Sports Day. 'Racing' analogies are entirely misleading; the men who tried to cross No Man's Land that day were not competing in a sprint, they were entering a battle of uncertain duration. There was no doubt (whatever Sir James Edmonds's 'infantry officer' witnesses may have told him) that they would have to carry a considerable weight with them; if they managed to reach the enemy position, they would need every item of it. The only real question was, what constitutes the 'physically impossible'? Did their 66-lb. burden really make it impossible to 'move quicker than a slow walk'?

We need some comparisons. Here is one, from a famous regiment created in 1831 for service under very arduous conditions of terrain and climate, the French Foreign Legion:

The legionnaire can march. Forty kilometres a day is the *fixed minimum performance*. He must be able to do that, day by day, without interruption, without a day of rest, for weeks on end . . . Inseparable from the march of the Legion is the baggage of the legionnaire . . . Knapsack, rifle and equipment altogether weigh *almost fifty kilogrammes;* no soldier of any other army carries such a load. With this kit he marches over sand under a burning sun . . .[5]

Forty kilometres, day by day, with nearly 100 lb. on his back; the legionnaire surely offers us one useful touchstone by which to judge the task of the British infantry on 1 July. No Man's Land, we should remember, was nowhere much more than 500 yards wide,[6] and the 'going' was firm, dry and reasonably level (in sharp contrast with the later stages of the battle, or Third Ypres).

The British Army itself, however, gives us even more direct comparisons. John Masters, who commanded a Chindit column in Burma in 1944, recorded: 'The No. 1 of a Bren-gun team, when carrying the gun, and just after a supply drop had put five days' K rations in his pack, toted a load of 86 pounds. For a Gurkha with a total body weight of about 130 pounds, this was a lot.'[7] Liddell

Hart's army mule, 'the proverbial and natural beast of burden', would seem to have lived a life of indolent ease by comparison! Brigadier Shelford Bidwell, in his book *The Chindit War,* fills in more detail:

> . . . the infantryman carried seventy pounds on his back; fifty pounds of equipment, including weapons, clothing, a full water bottle and ammunition, with another eighteen pounds of rations immediately after a supply drop . . . The whole weighed even more after crossing a river or in monsoon rain since the webbing packs absorbed water. This was the monstrous load every Chindit from brigadier to private had to carry, throwing it off only to fight or to snatch a few hours of uneasy sleep on the ground . . . [8]

The men of the Chindit columns were thus burdened, not for one assault on level dry ground, but for the whole of a campaign which lasted longer than the entire Battle of the Somme (162 days) in some of the most difficult country in the world, a considerable part of the time being within the period of the monsoon.[9]

Finally, as regards military evidence of what is and is not possible for soldiers to carry, there is the simple fact which I gleaned from my daily newspaper some time in 1964: a Commando Brigade on an exercise marched thirty miles in six hours carrying 80-lb. packs. It passes belief that the 'physical élite' which filled the ranks of the Fourth Army in 1916 was not capable of a similar speed with 66-lb. packs for at least six *minutes.*[10] It seems extraordinary that two military writers of such eminence as Sir James Edmonds and Liddell Hart should not have taken these significant comparisons into account. Sir James Edmonds may perhaps be forgiven, because he was a Royal Engineer, with less direct experience of march loads; but Liddell Hart was an infantryman. Between them, they manufactured a myth of remarkable tenacity.

Readers may find it helpful to reflect on this further comparison from civilian life, which I discovered in a third (or fourth) leader in *The Times* on 14 July 1965:

> Air travellers will not have been alone in responding to the news that has come from a panel of twelve experts – experts in what, one wonders? – convened by the International Labour Organization. But more than others they may have found themselves involuntarily flexing their muscles. These experts have decided that a man's load is 88 lb. or, to let the decision flow through the channels of official prose, that 40 kilogrammes should be the maximum permissible load to be carried by an adult male worker. Twice, that is to say, the tourist air traveller's ration,

and a third as much again as that of the first-class traveller – assuming this rare bird has also had the experience of having sometimes to hump his own 30 kilogrammes [66 lb.] . . .

We are not told how long the experts have been deliberating or, as one would prefer to think, testing a carefully chosen cross-section of adult male workers in this search for a standard. It has been divulged that the question was first broached in 1914 on behalf of dockers for whom a maximum of 60 kilogrammes [132 lb.] was then sought . . .

Were there any ex-dockers in the Fourth Army, I wonder?

———————

1   O.H., *1916*, i, pp. viii-ix.
2   Ibid., pp. 313–4.
3   Ibid., p. 293.
4   Now titled *History of the First World War,* Cassell, 1970, p. 314; my italics.
5   T. H. McGuffie, *Rank and File: The Common Soldier at Peace and War 1642–1914,* Hutchinson, 1964.
6   O.H., *1916,* i, p. 487.
7   John Masters, *The Road Past Mandalay,* Four Square edition, 1964, p. 158.
8   Shelford Bidwell, *The Chindit War: The Campaign in Burma 1944,* Hodder and Stoughton, 1979, p. 53.
9   North Burma is the wettest country in the world. The rain falls during the period of the north-west monsoon, May-October; as much as 800 inches has been recorded in a year.
10 30 miles in 6 hours=5 m.p.h.=1 mile in 12 minutes=½ mile in 6 minutes. Half a mile was the maximum width of No Man's Land.

XVI

SOMME MYTHS (3):
Tanks: 'The War-Winning Weapon'

'A Tank is walking up the High Street of Flers with the British Army cheering behind.'

(Airman's message, 15 September 1916)

'. . . tanks, which were to play a decisive part in 1918 . . .'

(Winston Churchill, 1939)

'Tanks are a life-saving weapon.'

(General Guderian, 1939)

Closely linked to the machine-gun myth is the tank myth – for obvious reasons. As General Swinton, to whom I have already referred (p. 138), informs us, it was reflection on the deadly combination of German machine-guns and barbed-wire entanglements that finally crystallized, in October 1914,

'in the form of a power-driven, bullet-proof, armed engine, capable of destroying machine guns, of crossing country and trenches, of breaking through entanglements, and of climbing earthworks.'[1]

Out of Swinton's vision, with the aid of Churchill and others, came the tanks which made their début on 15 September 1916, and which Churchill in 1918 called 'invincible',[2] believing them to be a 'decisive' factor in the Allied victory. This myth has its devotees to this day; it was Lord Beaverbrook, in 1956, who wrote of 'the wonderful war-winning weapon, the tank',[3] and many have echoed that thought.

Churchill, fixed in his belief that the 1916–18 tanks were war-winners, also firmly believed that '[their] use was not comprehended either by the British or French High Command'.[4] In 1918, as Minister of Munitions, he outlined a scheme for attack by 10,000 fighting tanks, backed by 10,000 tracked support vehicles. It must have been irritating to watch the Allied High Commands succeeding in winning the War without invoking this stirring vision (which, incidentally, even 1939–45 production was never able to realize on one battlefield). Churchill remained convinced that the generals of the First World War (and, indeed, much of the Second World War) 'threw away' the advantages of tanks by misunderstanding and mishandling. This belief became the foundation of adamantine myth.

The truth – for those who care – is, as usual, somewhat different. As I have said above and been at some pains to elaborate in my book *To Win a War, all* tanks of that vintage were clumsy, slow, vulnerable weapons. The maximum (road) speed of a 1918 Mark V (the basic British heavy tank) was 4.6 m.p.h.; the Medium Mark A ('Whippet') had a road speed of 8.3 m.p.h. Across a cratered battlefield, either was lucky to exceed 1.5 or 2 m.p.h., which makes any resemblance to dogs of the greyhound breed very tenuous. At such speeds it was going to be a long, long way to the Rhine. But mythologists and critics generally prefer to ignore such tedious details as the characteristics of the tanks themselves – their weak armour (only just bullet-proof and quite incapable of resisting artillery fire), lack of springs, bad ventilation, etc. It spoils the myth to learn, for example, that in the Mark V Star infantry-carrier (capable of lifting twenty to twenty-five men) a design defect had lodged the radiator inside the vehicle without compensating ventilation. Fumes, heat and carbon monoxide meant that any infantry lifted in this manner 'required a considerable time for recovery'.[5] Tank crews themselves suffered in the same way; the late Sir Basil Henriques commanded a tank on the Somme in September 1916, and recorded:

'The nervous strain in this first battle of tanks for officers and crew alike was ghastly. Of my company, one officer went mad and shot his engine to make it go faster; another shot himself because he thought he had failed to do as well as he ought; two others had what I suppose could be called a nervous breakdown.'[6]

It is so much easier, of course, to ignore mechanical and human weaknesses such as these, and blame the 'High Commands' for failing to perceive the potential of the wonder-weapons, and wastefully using them in 'penny packets'. The prosaic truth is that the 'uncomprehending' French High Command ordered 400 of the heavy Schneider tanks straight off the drawing board in February 1916, and shortly afterwards another 400, equally untested, from

Saint Chamond. Later the French switched their allegiance to the light Renault M-17s, and no less than 4,000 of these were manufactured. In the British Army, the Commander-in-Chief, Sir Douglas Haig, without even having seen a tank, was anticipating the 'surprise and demoralizing effect which they seem likely to produce'[7] five months before they made their début in battle. On 11 August 1916 he was 'looking forward to obtaining decisive results from the use of these "Tanks" at an early date'.[8] On 19 September, four days after their first action (which many considered a somewhat equivocal occasion) he sent his Deputy Chief of Staff to London to press for 1,000 tanks.

The mythologists prefer not to notice that no such number was available to him for any single battle of the War. Tanks were not used in penny packets because the generals were blind or stupid; they were used in penny packets because only penny packets existed. Forty-nine tanks were available for the great attack on 15 September 1916 (see pp. 122–3), of which thirty-two actually reached their starting points and took part in the action. Six months later, at the end of March 1917, despite all Haig's requests,[9] only sixty tanks were available for the Battle of Arras, and 'most of these were machines that had been repaired after the Somme',[10] This was an extraordinary state of affairs which tendentious historiography (e.g. Liddell Hart's history of the Royal Tank Regiment) has entirely obscured. It is therefore worth examining it more closely.

What was later to become the Royal Tank Corps was, in 1916–17, known as the Heavy Branch of the Machine-gun Corps (H.B.M.G.C.). Lieutenant-Colonel H. Elles · (R.E.) was appointed to command it on 24 September. 'Warmed by the sun of official approval',[11] the H.B.M.G.C. expanded rapidly until by February 1917 it was 'about 9,000 strong', with a projected organization of three brigades, each of three battalions, each battalion to consist of seventy-two tanks with Headquarters Section and Workshop. There was also to be a Central Depot and Repair Shop. All that was missing was the actual tanks. Needless to say, this was a matter of some concern to Colonel Elles, to G.H.Q., and also to the Government. The War Cabinet discussed it on 22 March:

The Minister of Munitions [Dr Christopher Addison] reported that considerable delays had occurred in the completion of the original estimate for the output of Tanks. A serious miscalculation had been made in the original estimate. Tanks had been first used in September 1916. The final design, however, had not been approved until the 23rd

November, and the drawings had not been ready until the 7th January, 1917. According to the latest estimates, Dr Addison hoped that the programme would only be a month or six weeks in arrears of the original estimate. Having regard to the labour difficulties realised in the construction of Tanks, this would be a good engineering performance. Lieutenant-Colonel Stern (secretary of the Tank Supply Committee) gave the War Cabinet particulars of the various new types, including a small high-speed Tank and a heavy gun-carrier.

The Minister of Munitions further stated that he was not satisfied with the tank [production] organisation and was taking steps to improve the same, and that everything was being done to speed up the supply as much as possible.

The Master-General of the Ordnance informed the War Cabinet that only about sixty Tanks were in France, although Dr Addison stated the total deliveries amounted to 250. This discrepancy was explained by Lieutenant-Colonel Stern as due partly to losses on the Somme, partly to the difficulty of supplying sufficient spare parts, and partly to the heavy wastage, particularly among those retained in this country for instructional and experimental purposes. Lieutenant-Colonel Stern stated also that some of those lost in France had already been salved, and that further steps were being taken in that direction.

The War Cabinet observed with concern that the number of Tanks available in the immediate future for offensive operations on the Western Front is less than the number available last September. They took note of Lieutenant-Colonel Stern's anticipations that when deliveries commenced they would take place in considerable quantities, so that during the summer months, which were most favourable for the employment of these machines, large numbers would be available.

The Minister of Munitions, however, wished it to be clearly understood that if the rate of wastage and the requirements for spares in respect of the 1,000 Mark IV Tanks on order should prove to be on the same scale as for those already supplied, it would be quite impossible to keep anything like that number available for service.[12]

This is a most revealing document, and it has to be said that the Ministry of Munitions does not appear in it in a particularly favourable light. Making every allowance for the still embryonic stage of development – only fifty each of Marks II and III were manufactured; Mark IV was already on order – the statements of Dr Addison and Colonel Stern do not impress one with a sense of grip. The latter's explanation of the discrepancy between Dr Addison's 250 and the B.E.F.'s sixty is not very helpful; neither is the Minister's final lament about the rate of wastage, which by this stage must surely have become a manifest characteristic of the weapon. Nor did matters much improve as the year went on. By July, for the Third Battle of Ypres, when according to Colonel

Stern 'large numbers would be available', the number actually present for duty was still only 136. Planned production for the first nine months of 1917 was 1,460 tanks, of which 1,000 were to be the new, supposedly bullet-proof Mark IVs, and after August there were to be some of the even better Mark Vs. None of the latter, however, actually appeared until March 1918, and of the promised Mark IVs only 378 were available for the Battle of Cambrai on 20 November 1917.

However, there were other problems besides numbers. Churchill, who had replaced Dr Addison as Minister of Munitions in July, quickly became aware of most of them, and of their causes. His old department, the Admiralty, was considerably to blame, keeping a stranglehold on supplies of steel plate for reasons that seemed to him less and less convincing. Furthermore, there were disappointments with the new Mark IVs, though these were undoubtedly a great advance on the Mark Is and Mark IIs. Lord Robert Cecil, Assistant Secretary of State for Foreign Affairs, wrote to Churchill on 9 October:

'My Dear Churchill,
    When I was over in France last week I was taken to the Headquarters of the Tanks & found the people there in a rather critical frame of mind. They complain that the tanks now being sent out to them are too short to be useful. The new German trenches are so wide that the tank cannot get out of them. They represent that weeks or even months ago they put forward six requirements – including greater length – none of which have been complied with. In despair they are beginning with very inadequate equipment to try to lengthen a tank experimentally for themselves . . .'[13]

Replying to this the next day, Churchill made the admission: 'Broadly speaking, I consider a year has been lost in Tank development, and the most strenuous efforts will now be made to repair this melancholy state of affairs.'

'A year lost in Tank development': it is here, and not in any foolish predilection of the 'High Command', that the reason for the 'penny packets' may be found. But of course these problems are bound to arise in the very early days of any technical advance. A natural desire to do the best possible thing compounds the difficulties. In August the Tank Supply Committee became the Mechanical Warfare Supply Department (M.W.S.D.) under Colonel (later Sir Albert) Stern. The tank designers came under this department, but of course had to lend an attentive ear to the specifications demanded by the 'fighting side' in France.

Both constantly asked for small alterations in design. Often these alterations were necessary; frequently they were more or less frivolous, even when they came from what might be considered the best source, that is, from those who fought the Tanks.

If the M.W.S.D. was sometimes accused of adopting an academic attitude towards the results of the 'acid test' of battle, it may as truly be said of the Fighting Side that they often underrated the difficulties and problems of manufacture and failed to appreciate how often quality could only be obtained by a disproportionate sacrifice of quantity.[14]

It is against the background of these realities that we must view the Battle of Cambrai. This was the first time that anything better than a penny packet was actually at the disposal of the High Command. It threw the entire strength of the Royal Tank Corps into the action: all three brigades, all nine battalions. This meant 324 fighting tanks (Mark IV) with fifty-four more (six per battalion) in reserve, supported by supply tanks, tanks fitted with grapnels to pull away the German wire, two bridging tanks, wireless tanks and a telephone cable tank. Clearly, a fair degree of sophistication was already present. On 20 November 1917 this array proved beyond the doubt of any sceptic (and there were quite a number, both in France and in England) that tanks were most useful for economically breaking *into* even very powerful enemy defences. A year later it had become equally clear that breaking *through* was something else again.

There are other aspects of the Battle of Cambrai that mythologists tend to ignore or play down. Even entirely reputable writers credit the Mark IV with steel plate capable of resisting the German armour-piercing bullet; according to the Official History, this was not the case – it quotes reports coming in after 21 November saying: 'The present armour plate is either bad material or the enemy is using a better A.-P. bullet.'[15] Of even more sinister omen for the future was the exploit of a German field gun at Flesquières; served single-handed by a devoted artillery officer, this gun knocked out sixteen tanks one by one as they came over the skyline. The German officer was killed at his gun, having won the admiration of all who witnessed his deed; Sir Douglas Haig awarded him the unique distinction of a mention in British Despatches, thus giving rise to another minor myth. His magnanimous gesture was held to 'have encouraged what the Tank crews considered a most undesirable spirit in enemy gunners'.[16] This overlooks the fact that Haig's Cambrai Despatch was not published until 1 March 1918, by which time German preparations for their own offensive were nearly complete. It was some nine

months after Cambrai before British tanks renewed acquaintance
with German field artillery to any notable extent; one feels that in
that time the German tacticians could well have evolved their
anti-tank methods without instruction from the British C.-in-C.

What mythologists also overlook – and this is serious indeed – is
the cost of the big tank battles. On 20 November 1917 this
amounted to 179 (sixty-five by enemy fire) destroyed or
immobilised (56 per cent) and many more damaged. One historian
says: 'Even though a considerable number were still mechanically
fit for action, their crews were dead tired.'[17] Another tells us that at
the end of a week the tank crews 'were almost fought to a
standstill'.[18] In other words, it was the Somme over again; physical
and nervous exhaustion set the limits of tank warfare.

The only other occasion in the War when a large number of tanks
was available all at once on the British front was the Battle of
Amiens, 8 August 1918. On that day 342 Mark Vs (a great
improvement on the Mark IV, but still with a serious ventilation
defect) and seventy-two 'Whippets' took part. Once more they
made a big contribution to a spectacular victory; once more there
was a price. On 9 August, 145 remained fit for action; on 10
August, eighty-five; on 11 August, thirty-eight ('the crews were
completely exhausted'). By 12 August, only six tanks were able to
fight; as I said in *To Win a War,* 'The German Empire was not going
to be overthrown by six tanks.'

Never again were more than about 150 available for one battle –
it was very rare to have so many. Meanwhile German anti-tank
methods were improving all the time. During the last victorious
'Hundred Days' Campaign' of 1918, no less than 2,000 tanks
(including supply tanks, gun-carriers, personnel-carriers, special
duty tanks and armoured cars) were engaged at one time or
another. Of these many were destroyed by enemy action; 887 went
to salvage; one third of the Tank Corps officers and men became
casualties. By 4 November, for the last setpiece attack of the War,
only thirty-seven tanks were available. These are the brutal facts
that the mythologists – the believers in the 'wonderful war-
winning weapon', 'ending the war at a stroke', playing a 'decisive
part in 1918' – prefer to set aside.

The actual ending of the war, as I have said above, even seems to
annoy the tank mythologists; certainly one detects a note of
disappointment. It was not merely Winston Churchill, with his
grand scheme for 10,000 tanks and 10,000 supporting vehicles
(10,000 fighting tanks, at 1918 manning levels, would have meant a
Tank Corps of well over 200,000[19] at a time of acute manpower

difficulties); there was another frustrated prophet of some significance – Major-General J. F. C. Fuller. In 1918 Fuller was G.S.O.1. at Tank Corps Headquarters with the rank of Lieutenant-Colonel; in May of that year he presented what his latest biographer, Brigadier A. J. Trythall,[20] has called 'his greatest idea, one that was to have . . . far-reaching consequences'. According to Fuller himself, he conceived the idea while sitting on Mont St Quentin, outside Peronne, watching British troops retreating before the great German March offensive. He embodied it in a paper ultimately entitled 'Plan 1919', 'a proposal for winning the war with tanks in 1919 by using them in mass and in new tactical and strategic ways'.[21]

The basic concept of 'Plan 1919', says Brigadier Trythall,

was derived from the question, 'Why were our troops retreating?' and the answer 'Because our command was paralysed.' The concept was 'strategic paralysis', to be brought about by attacking and cutting off the enemy's brains, in other words his field headquarters, from his fighting troops. 'Plan 1919' was originally called 'The Tactics of the Medium D Tank', but before becoming 'Plan 1919' became 'Strategical Paralysis as the Object of the Attack'. According to Fuller himself the idea was 'a psycho-tactical one', but he used 'strategical' rather than 'tactical' in conjunction with 'paralysis' because 'the primary aim of the attack was to paralyse the enemy's command and not his fighting forces . . . that is his strategical brain and not his fighting body.'

It will be readily apparent from what I have already said that with the tanks currently in use in 1918 this was a very far-fetched idea indeed. It was, in fact, firmly based on the existence of a new piece of hardware: the Medium D tank. Only one experimental model of this new tank was actually built in 1918, but there was no doubt that by the standards of the time it was a wonderful weapon. The Medium D had a maximum speed of 18 m.p.h. (compared with 8.3 for the Medium A 'Whippet') and a range of 200 miles; it was capable of crossing a 13- to 14-foot gap. Its armament was carried in a revolving turret at the rear of the hull, giving it a distinct look of the future by comparison with the existing heavy Marks I–V, or even the new Medium C. To carry out 'Plan 1919' Fuller asked for some 1,600 of these (plus 400 Medium Cs) – which was at least a lot more realistic than Churchill's proposition – and with them he proposed to attack German brigade, divisional, corps and even army headquarters, thus paralysing the German front by the elimination of its brain cells.

Such was the essence of 'Plan 1919'. While deeply impressing
military theorists down the years, it is bound to impress military
historians somewhat less because the War in fact ended in 1918.
Fuller's plan was never put into effect; it has no history.
Furthermore, the actual military history of 1918, on careful
analysis, calls the futuristic quality of Fuller's thinking severely into
question.

Let us consider, very briefly, what that history was. It amounts to
this: by mid-July four attacks in great strength by the Germans, first
against the British, then against the French, had brought them
enormous losses and *no strategic gain whatever* – a demoralizing
situation in itself. The French were seriously weakened, but the
British had by now made a remarkable recovery, and the
Americans were becoming more formidable every day. On 15 July
the Germans attacked again in Champagne; this was intended to be
only the preliminary to the coup de grâce against the British in
Flanders, but by the very next day it was already clear that the
attack had failed. On 17 July the German offensive died away –
their last offensive of the War. On 18 July Foch struck back in the
Second Battle of the Marne, the turning point. By 19 July
Ludendorff, effectively the commander-in-chief of the most
centralized army in the War, was, in Correlli Barnett's graphic
phrase, reduced to the condition of 'a beetle on its back, waving
and wriggling furiously to no effect'.[22] Thus, at the head of the
German Army, he says, there was 'fundamental panic, paralysis of
command.' He further speaks of Ludendorff being 'in a state of
intellectual dislocation' and 'a gruesome state of nerves'. Fuller's
'revolutionary' concept of 'brain warfare', in other words, had
advanced far beyond theory; it was now a fact of military history –
only it was not the minor brain cells of the German Army that were
paralysed, it was the very central directing element, which
henceforward proved incapable of real strategic grip. And this
result was certainly not due to the Medium D tank or to any other
single weapon; it was, as usual, due to the judicious and balanced
co-operation of all arms which the Allied counter-offensive of 1918
increasingly displayed.

Mythology, unfortunately, in the famous words of one of its
chief practitioners, is an 'expanding torrent'. The 1914–18 tank
myth begat the belief that armour and mechanization would
replace manpower in future wars, and so reduce casualties. So we
find even so able a military writer as the late John Connell saying in
1965: 'tanks . . . halved the casualty lists of my generation as
compared with my father and my uncles.'[23] Entirely respectable

historians have quoted with approval General Guderian's reply
when Hitler, in amazement, asked the reason for the low number
of German casualties in Poland in 1939;[24] this, said the general,
'was primarily due to the effectiveness of our tanks. Tanks are a
life-saving weapon.'[25] He was wrong. It was not German tanks that
saved German lives, it was the absence of Polish tanks and anti-
tank weapons. When the German tanks found their match, in
Russia from 1942 onwards, German casualties mounted
astronomically. As we have seen, the most armoured, the most
mechanized war in history was also the greatest manpower war,
with the greatest human losses. Tanks or no tanks, strong,
determined, equally-matched opponents will always inflict terrible
damage on each other.

Footnote

It has been the fate of the tank to be the victim of mythology
from the moment of its first public appearance. As Sir Philip Gibb
says:

They caused a sensation, a sense of excitement, laughter which shook the
nation, because of the comicality, the grotesque surprise, the possibility
of quicker victory which caught hold of the imagination of people who
heard for the first time of those new engines of war, so beast-like in
appearance and performance. The vagueness of our descriptions was due
to the censorship, which forbade, wisely enough, any technical and exact
definition, so that we had to compare them to giant toads, mammoths and
prehistoric animals of all kinds.[26]

General Swinton tells us more: 'Public excitement naturally did not
die down for some time, and for days many lurid stories about the
tanks were current. Amongst other "real truths" were the
following:- That the tanks carried a crew of 400 men, were armed
with 12-inch guns, had a speed of 30 m.p.h., were constructed in
Japan by Swedes, and – dire insult to the Heavy Section – were
officered by airmen who had lost their nerve.'[27]
   Philip Gibbs was one of the many who reported the airman's
message: 'A Tank is walking up the High Street of Flers with the
British Army cheering behind.' In one of his subsequent
despatches to The *Daily Chronicle*, Gibbs wrote:

The officer who did what the soldiers call the great 'stunt' in Flers told me
his story today, and I found him to be as modest a fellow as any naval
officer on a light cruiser, and of the same fine type. He went into Flers

before the infantry and followed by them, cheering in high spirits, and knocked out a machine-gun which began to play on him. The town was not much damaged by shell-fire so that the Tank could walk about real streets, and the garrison, which was hiding in dug-outs, surrendered in small scared groups. Then the other Tanks came into Flers, and together they lolloped around the town in a free and easy manner before going farther afield.[28]

It is scarcely to be wondered at that the First World War is saturated with myth when we see how this was perpetrated from the very beginning. In 1956 I received a letter from Mr J. W. Staddon, who had served in a Kitchener battalion of the East Surrey Regiment. He said:

The legendary exploits of the Flers tank have never been disputed because there were too few survivors of the *leading waves* to contradict the story composed by the newspapermen who were not there, from scraps of information largely fanciful, which filtered back.

The section of the German line which included the High Street of the village, of which few walls were more than shoulder-high, came within the objective of the battalion of which I was a junior officer. All other officers of the battalion were either hit before reaching the wire belt or perished in it. A solitary tank made its way through the rubble and its commander opened his little trap and asked me to direct him to the fourth objective, Flers being the third, approximately 3,000 yards, I think, from the jumping-off point. I was emphatic that further infantry progress was unlikely since both flanks seemed behind us. And he went gaily on towards the hamlet of Gueudecourt in splendid isolation. 'C'est magnifique, mais ce n'est pas la guerre.'

The other ranks of my battalion were extremely sparse and were occupied in nervously ferreting out Germans from dugouts and cellars. The observer biplanes were slow-moving and low-flying, the day was brilliant, and good observation could have been made, helped by our red flares, had it not been for the columns of black smoke from the bursting heavies and the dust and flying débris. The cheering army behind the Tank I personally attribute to the small column of fours which I was mobilising of the gathering prisoners in the street, for despatch to the rear under a signals corporal. The Germans were in some cases shivering with fear, not I thought at the Tank (which indeed they had probably not seen) but at the bursting of the heavies. The situation was in fact much too grim for joyful singing.[29]

Returning to the subject of the tanks at Flers in a later letter, Mr Staddon said: 'I personally don't believe anybody was frightened of them, nor indeed interested in them – they were too thin on the ground. It would have been different if they had been field kitchens.'

Then, in 1963, Mr Staddon had a remarkable experience; he actually tracked down and corresponded with the officer who commanded that tank in Flers: Lieutenant Stuart Hastie, then seventy-four years old. Mr Hastie wrote to him:

D. 17 Dinnaken was my tank and I took it into Flers on the morning of Sept. 15th 1916. Owing to having to force the engine due to steering being carried out by using brakes alternately on the tracks (the steering wheels in rear were hit early and out of action) the bearings were 'run' in the big ends and when we entered Flers the old Daimler was in a sorry state.

Eventually I withdrew to Flers trench on our end of Flers main street and I distinctly remember discussing the situation with an Infantry officer. I never knew his name and I have forgotten his regiment at this distance of time, so what you have told me in your letter is very interesting to me as you must have been that officer.

Owing to the mechanical condition of the tank in Flers (I expected the engine to pack up at any time) I eventually withdrew and struggled very slowly back up the Flers/Delville Wood road for a short distance, when I left what was left of the road, swung left-handed and I had just reached the edge of a hillock about 200 yards from the road when our engine packed up for good. That was Sept. 15th for me.

Could this be the man that Philip Gibbs had talked to? Could he? What had become of the 'cheering army'? What had happened to the jolly 'lolloping'? Yet Sir Philip Gibbs was a conscientious reporter, no willing purveyor of imbecilities. Truly war does have thick enough fogs without mythology adding to them.

---

1   Major-General Sir Ernest Swinton, *Eyewitness*, Hodder and Stoughton, 1932, p. 79.
2   Martin Gilbert, *Winston S. Churchill*, iv, Companion Part I, Heinemann, 1977, p. 369: Churchill to Lady Churchill, 10 August 1918.
3   Lord Beaverbrook, *Men and Power*, Hutchinson, 1956, p. 186.
4   Introduction to *Prelude to Victory* by Sir Edward Spears, Jonathan Cape, 1939.
5   Colonel H. C. B. Rogers, *Tanks in Battle*, Seeley Service, 1965, p. 69.
6   *The Times*, 16 September 1976; letter.
7   Haig Diary, 5 and 7 April 1916; author's papers.
8   Haig Diary, 11 August; author's papers.
9   On 18 September, only three days after their début, Haig was discussing the use of tanks amphibiously, landing them on beaches from flat-bottomed boats. On 24 September he was hoping to receive sufficient reinforcements to use fifty to sixty in line, with no preliminary bombardment (the tactic carried out at Cambrai fourteen months later). On 23 November he told Mr Montagu of the Ministry of Munitions and Colonel Stern, 'I would like as many tanks as possible by 1st May.' On 10 February, discussing plans for the projected Ypres offensive with General Rawlinson, he urged 'an attack by surprise in the centre with Tanks, and without artillery preparation'. But 1917 was, in this respect as in so many others, a year of disappointment.

10 C. and A. Williams-Ellis, *The Tank Corps,* 'Country Life', 1919, p. 43.
11 Ibid., p. 41.
12 War Cabinet No. 102; CAB 23/2.
13 Gilbert, op. cit., pp. 173–4.
14 Williams-Ellis, op. cit., p. 44.
15 O.H., *1917*, iii.
16 Williams-Ellis, op. cit., p. 111.
17 Rogers, op. cit., p. 60.
18 Williams-Ellis, op. cit., p. 116.
19 In 1918 there were five Tank Brigades, seventeen battalions (the seventeenth was an Armoured Car Battalion), with a strength of 11,150 officers and men on 1 July. The maximum 'battle effectiveness' of the Tank Corps was 415 tanks (8 August); this gives a ratio of personnel to tanks of 27:1. By comparison with the Royal Air Force, where, as Churchill said, 'anything from 50–100 men are required . . . for every one man fighting in the air' (Gilbert, op. cit., p. 388), this was economical. Churchill also tells us that an increase of Tank Corps strength to 55,000 had been agreed; 'This is only about half what will be needed for the Tanks I shall actually have ready by the summer of next year.' For an army whose infantry battalions were generally down to about 350 or less, this represents a massive investment of manpower. The infantry, after all, was engaged in winning the war, and it was in little doubt as to where its most effective help was coming from: the Royal Artillery, as usual.
20 Anthony John Trythall, *'Boney' Fuller: The Intellectual General 1878–1966,* Cassell, 1977, p. 60.
21 Ibid.
22 Correlli Barnett, *The Swordbearers,* Eyre and Spottiswoode, 1963, pp. 341–2.
23 In the Royal United Services Institute *Journal,* August 1965, p. 224.
24 10,572 killed, 30,322 wounded, 5,029 missing (presumed killed). 'For this price the Germans conquered a nation of 33 million people.' (Philip Warner, *Panzer,* Weidenfeld and Nicolson, 1977, p. 40.)
25 From Heinz Guderian, *Panzer Leader,* Michael Joseph, 1952.
26 Philip Gibbs, *Realities of War,* Heinemann, 1920, p. 315.
27 Swinton, op. cit., p. 291, f.n.
28 Gibbs, *The Battles of the Somme,* (collected despatches), Heinemann, 1917.
29 Author's papers.

'. . . the wonderful, war-winning weapon . . .': the Medium D of 1918 (see p. 155), which was the basis of General Fuller's 'Plan 1919'; the type was never developed.

'. . . a good, sound "work-horse" tank . . .': Germany's *Panzer IV* of World War II. Armed with a 75-mm. gun and with a speed of 25 m.p.h., this was the backbone of the armoured divisions; a total of some 9,000 were built.

'FUTILITY' (1): this photograph displays the 1st Tennessee Coloured Battery in 1864; during the Civil War some 180–200,000 Negroes served in the Union Army, of whom probably 66% had been slaves when war broke out. Emancipation 'was enough to justify that war'.

'FUTILITY' (2): this Corpus Christi procession in Warsaw in 1919 illustrates the beginning of the brief twenty-year span during which Poles could worship in their own way and march under their own flags in their own uniforms —a consequence of the 'great surge of national liberation', which was a result of the First World War.

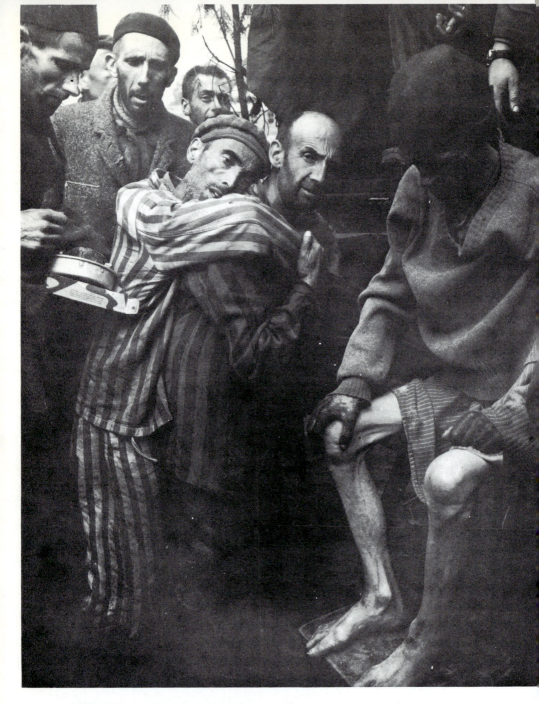

'FUTILITY' (3): 'the unforgettable faces'—concentration camp survivors being evacuated for medical treatment after liberation by the 82nd U.S. Airborne Division. 'Without the war those soldiers would never have come.'

XVII

SOMME MYTHS (4):
Cavalry Generals and the 'Gee' in Gap

'The Army Chiefs were mostly horsemen . . .'
(Lloyd George, *War Memoirs*, i, p. 76)

'. . . most British generals were cavalry men.'
(A. J. P. Taylor, *The First World War*, Hamish Hamilton, 1963,
p. 20)

'All our generals were cavalrymen . . .'
(Robert Graves in *Promise of Greatness: The War of 1914–18*
ed. George A. Panichas, Cassell, 1968, p. 6)

Myths about casualties, myths about weapons – the mythology of the First World War does indeed extend to virtually every part of it. There are two more particularly British specimens which deserve attention, both of them deriving much force from the grim spectacles of the Somme. They are the 'Donkey Myth' – the myth of the 'stupid' British generals – and the 'Futility' Myth; the remainder of this book will be taken up with considering them, and their aftermath. Let us begin, however, with an aspect of the first, a convenient 'explanation' of the supposed neglect of the 'war-winning weapons' and the dreadful sight of the swathes of mown down infantry. The three quotations offered above express it in succinct form; it encapsulates the view that British generals had no tactical ideas beyond searching for a non-existent gap, which infantry and artillery would make for them, so that they could pour their cavalry ('gee-gees') through it.

It may, perhaps, be as well, before investigating the background and thoughts of the generals, to look briefly at the Cavalry itself. From some accounts of the War one might suppose that the cavalry arm was a uniquely British phenomenon, or, at the very least, that the British Army had an unduly large number of cavalry. Thus one singularly bad book on the Battle of the Somme, written in 1961, discussing the 1914 Army, says: 'No one thought, apparently, about the effectiveness of a large force of cavalry, such as Britain proudly possessed, against a handful of machine-guns.'[1]

What was this 'large force'? In August 1914 the Regular Army contained thirty-one regiments of cavalry (see Table I, p. 169) numbering at full establishment 21,830 officers and men out of a total strength on 1 August of 232,763. The war strength of the whole thirty-one regiments, however, was 17,081.[2] In the B.E.F. of August 1914 there were 9,918 cavalry (five brigades, plus divisional and army troops) compared with 66,000 infantry (five divisions, plus six extra battalions).Nevertheless this percentage (6.6), low though it may seem (and the actual numbers were certainly low by European standards as Table I shows), was high by comparison with the rest of the War. In 1916 there were five cavalry divisions in the B.E.F. (two Indian); in September of that year this represented 2.5 per cent of its total strength. In 1918 the Indian cavalry divisions departed, leaving only three; these supplied 1.3 per cent of the strength of the B.E.F. in June. By 11 November the percentage had fallen to 1.01.

It is against this quantitative background that we have to assess what Lloyd George called the 'ridiculous cavalry obsession'[3] of the British generals. And it must be said at once that Sir James Edmonds, the Official Historian, must bear a considerable amount of blame for the myth which Lloyd George and many others have perpetuated; it was Edmonds who wrote:

Both British Commanders-in-Chief were cavalrymen. They each in the first instance had an infantry officer as Chief of the General Staff, whom they replaced by a cavalryman, so that in 1915 and 1918 both Commander-in-Chief and Chief of Staff were cavalrymen. Further, two of the five Army Commanders, Generals Byng (who succeeded Allenby, another cavalryman, in the Third Army) and Gough (who was superseded in the Fifth Army by another cavalryman, Birdwood) were cavalrymen. In all, of the nine generals who commanded Armies, five were cavalrymen, three infantrymen, and one was a gunner. What the Army called the 'cavalry spirit' led to pressure for haste and to expectation of gain of ground incompatible with siege warfare in the field by men who had to struggle over shell-pocked ground and through deep mud.[4]

With that to feed upon, it is scarcely surprising if less well-disposed people have found myth easy to manufacture; and so we arrive at 'all our generals were cavalrymen'.

Unfortunately, there is a document called the Army List, which identifies every commissioned officer. This tells us, for example, that in July 1914 the Army contained (excluding royalty) eight field-marshals, of whom two were cavalrymen; eighteen generals, of whom one was a cavalryman; twenty-seven lieutenant-generals, of whom three were cavalrymen; 114 major-generals, of whom eight were cavalrymen. If we look a little beyond the thirteen appointments selected for scrutiny by Sir James Edmonds, we find a distinctly different picture: a list of twenty-seven top appointments during the War reveals that the highest post held by any soldier – Secretary of State for War – was occupied by a Royal Engineer. The professional head of the Army was the Chief of the Imperial General Staff; five men successively held that office, only one of them a cavalryman. Out of twelve Commanders-in-Chief in different theatres of war, three were cavalrymen. In the British Expeditionary Force, out of four Chiefs of Staff, two were cavalrymen, and out of ten Army Commanders (at different times) five were cavalrymen (see Table H p. 168). Similar investigation reveals that in 1918, out of seventeen corps commanders, only one was a cavalryman, and out of fifty-one divisional commanders, only five. The fact that the B.E.F.'s Commanders-in-Chief were both cavalrymen is thus seen to be a most unusual circumstance. The overwhelming majority of the generals actually handling troops in battle came, as one might expect, from the arm which produced the overwhelming majority of those troops: the infantry.

All this Sir James Edmonds must have known quite well. Perhaps, on the day he wrote the passage quoted above, he was bitten by a horse. He certainly raised a fine herd of donkeys.

Before leaving the subject of cavalry, a short summary of its performance on the Western Front may be appropriate. In 1914 the Germans deployed 10 cavalry divisions in the West (one in the East), as did the French; the Belgians had one division; the British one large division (4 brigades) plus an extra brigade. According to one distinguished officer, the British cavalry under Major-General E. H. H. Allenby was

a fine and well-mounted command, and its fighting value was probably much greater than that of any force of its size in the Allied or enemy armies. It was well trained not only to shock but to fire tactics (the results of long experience in colonial warfare) and while our horse-mastership

was good, that of the Germans was inferior and that of the French (who . . .
never got off) was bad. The British cavalryman walked nearly as much as
he rode, with the consequence that his horse whom he regarded as a
friend and comrade kept condition remarkably well.[5]

As another distinguished officer remarked, the British horsemen
'were easily first of the cavalries of Europe in dismounted work'.[6]

Neither the French nor the German cavalry performed with
much distinction in 1914, though the French did establish an
ascendancy over their enemies in purely mounted actions (of which
there were few). The British cavalry did its work well during the
retreat from Mons, was disappointing in the advance to the Aisne,
and invaluable (dismounted) at First Ypres. In 1915 the trench
deadlock ossified; generals continued to hope for a breakthrough
which would give their cavalry an opportunity, but except on the
Eastern Front none offered. 'An opportunity'; what does the
phrase mean? To judge by some critics, it only means 'an
opportunity to show their paces', to 'show what they could do'. It
does not mean that at all. The hard fact is that between 1914 and
1918 cavalry was the *only* arm of exploitation that any general
possessed. I hope that what I have already said about tanks has
made it clear that, whatever their merits or demerits, they were
never an arm of exploitation. That cavalry proved to be an
ineffective exploiting arm does not alter the fact that that is what it
was. A general who launches what he hopes will be a decisive
offensive without an arm of exploitation (as Ludendorff did in
1918) strikes me as criminally culpable. It was in the hope that
infantry lives might thereby not be vainly expended that British and
French generals brought cavalry up behind their offensive fronts.

In 1916 no opportunities for exploitation offered; on 14 July on
the Somme an erroneous report suggested that the moment might
have come, and the 2nd Indian Cavalry Division was moved up.
One squadron each of the 7th Dragoon Guards and 20th Deccan
Horse went into action with some success near High Wood, but
night found them fighting dismounted as usual and soon they were
withdrawn. It was during 1916 that the Germans began
dismounting whole units for use as infantry; henceforth almost all
their mounted troops would be in the East. In April 1917, during
the Battle of Arras, there were spirited scenes at Monchy, where
the British 6th and 8th Brigades charged through driving snow.
Once more, however, they soon had to dismount. Blood-curdling
reports of mounds of dead horses and riders should be discounted;
the two brigades lost just under 600 officers and men between them
(397 in the 8th Brigade). On the Aisne, where the great

breakthrough was to take place, the French cavalry was once again frustrated.

The long-awaited opportunity seemed to have come at last in November, at Cambrai. If the tanks could break into the German defences (which they splendidly did) surely the cavalry could break through to roll up the German lines and turn defeat into rout. No such thing occurred. The advancing infantry and tanks, aware of wonderful opportunities of a kind rarely seen during the War, looked in vain over their shoulders for the mass of horsemen who should have been exploiting them. The cavalry did not appear; as an eminent historian says, 'the inaction of the . . . cavalry divisions has never yet been intelligibly explained.'[7] By the next day, of course, the opportunity had gone.

I would suggest three explanations of this lamentable failure: first, the normal difficulty of quick communication which haunted every battle of the First World War; second, staleness – long waiting for a big event does not improve efficiency or morale (as D-Day would show again in 1944); third, the quality of the commander of the Cavalry Corps. Amid all the condemnations of British cavalry generals of that war, the name of the actual cavalry commander is rarely heard: Lieutenant-General C. T. McM. Kavanagh. It is difficult to detect, on the part of General Kavanagh at Cambrai, any of that thrusting leadership which one associates with cavalry commanders, and for which others (Sir Hubert Gough, for example) have been copiously though unjustly blamed. I would hesitate to blame General Kavanagh (not having experienced his responsibilities and difficulties) had not the same pattern manifested itself so clearly in 1918 also.

In 1918 cavalry appeared in sharply contrasting guise. As I have said, Ludendorff produced no cavalry for the great offensive by which he hoped to win the War; as a British infantry officer remarked:

'It was a crowning mercy that [the Germans] had no cavalry. How many times during the retreat did we thank heaven for this! The sight of a few mounted men in the distance would at once start a ripple of anxiety . . . Cavalry was the one factor which would have smashed the morale of the defence in a twinkling.'[8]

The British cavalry divisions, on the other hand, used as 'putty' to fill the cracks in the defence, and profiting by their mobility in so doing, proved as invaluable as they had been at First Ypres in 1914.[9]

When the time came for a counter-offensive, however, as I have said in *To Win a War*, the cavalry performance was once again disappointing; in particular, co-operation between cavalry and tanks proved to be an idle dream. In Mesopotamia and above all Palestine, on the other hand, the cavalry found, in the words of Captain Cyril Falls, 'a magnificent opportunity to wind up its career in success and glory'.[10] Indian regulars, Yeomen, Australians, New Zealanders, French Chasseurs d'Afrique, all seized their chance and left their (somewhat deceptive) mark on history. It is Captain Falls who also reminds us that 'a hard-bitten, hard-drinking Frenchman with an immortal name, General Jouinot-Gambetta' performed a similar deed at the head of a brigade of Spahis and Chasseurs d'Afrique in the final stages of the Salonika campaign.

As the War ended, the soldier on horseback was still the only available instrument of swift exploitation; these Eastern campaigns, followed by the Polish-Soviet War of 1919–20, and the Greek-Turkish War of 1919–22, suggested that he would remain so. The internal combustion engine was about to make great strides, but for the time being few were interested in its military possibilities. It took a long time for the message to penetrate that what mattered was horsepower, not the horse.

---

1   Brian Gardner, *The Big Push,* Cassell, 1961, p. 5.
2   David Woodward, *Armies of the World 1854–1914* (Sidgwick and Jackson, 1978, p. 117) says: 'The three regiments of Household Cavalry had a strength of 24 officers and 430 other ranks,* while the establishment of line cavalry regiments was 26 officers and 696 men.' This gives the total of 22,382. Captain A. H. Atteridge, *The British Army of Today,* (T. C. and E. C. Jack, a useful little handbook published in 1915, p. 56) tells us that 'the total war strength of a regiment is 25 officers and 526 men'. The normal 'establishment' was four squadrons; the 'war establishment' was three squadrons.

    *Normally, the Household Cavalry would furnish a composite regiment for overseas service. This it did in 1914, but so rich was it in reservists that each regiment was able to form a depôt, and in October the 7th Cavalry Brigade was formed with three full Household regiments.
3   Lloyd George, *War Memoirs,* Odham's, 1936, ii, p. 2038.
4   O.H., *1918,* v, p. 605, f.n.3.
5   Lieutenant-General Sir Tom Bridges, *Alarms and Excursions,* Longmans Green and Co., 1938, p. 81.
6   Major-General Sir F. Maurice, *Forty Days in 1914,* Constable, 1919, p. 72.

7   C. R. M. F. Cruttwell, *A History of the Great War 1914–1918*, O.U.P., 1934, p. 473.
8   Sidney Rogerson, *The Last of the Ebb*, Arthur Barker, 1937, p. 112.
9   It must always be remembered that, dismounted, 'the rifle strength of a cavalry division was approximately equal to that of an infantry brigade' (O.H., *1918*, i, p. 116). A cavalry division lacked all heavy weapons for defensive fighting.
10 Cyril Falls, *Armageddon 1918*, Weidenfeld and Nicolson, 1964, p. 34.

XVIII

ANTI-MYTH
Table H
The 'Top Twenty-seven', 1914–18

Post	Artillery	Cavalry	Infantry	Engineers
Secretary of State				Kitchener
C.I.G.S.	Wolfe-Murray	Robertson	Douglas A. Murray Wilson	
C.-in-C.s	Milne (Salonika) Beauchamp-Duff (India)	French (B.E.F.) Haig (B.E.F.) Allenby (Egypt)	Hamilton (Gallipoli) Cavan (Italy) Nixon (Mesopotamia) Lake (Mesopotamia) Maxwell (Egypt) Monro (India) Maude (Mesopotamia)	
C.G.S. (B.E.F.)		[Robertson]* Lawrence	[A. Murray] Kiggell	
Army Commanders (B.E.F.)	Horne (1)†	[Haig] (1) Gough (5) Byng (3) [Allenby] (3) Birdwood (5)	[Monro] (1, 3, 1) Smith-Dorrien (2) Plumer (2) Rawlinson (4)	
Totals	4	8	14	1

*Square brackets indicate second appearance in the table.
†Numbers in brackets signify the army commanded; e.g. (1) means First Army.

Table I

Cavalry in European Armies, 1914; Regiments by Types

Type	Germany*	France	Britain†
Cuirassiers	10	13	3 (Household Cavalry)
Heavy Cavalry	4 (2 Bavarian, 2 Saxon)	—	7 (Dragoon Guards)
Dragoons	28	31	3
Chasseurs à Cheval	13 (Jäger zu Pferde)	21	—
Chevaulégers	8 (Bavarian)	—	—
Hussars	21	14	12
Lancers	26 (Uhlans)	—	6
Chasseurs d'Afrique	—	6	—
Spahis	—	4	—
Totals	**110**	**89**	**31**

*The Germans formed thirty-nine Reserve cavalry regiments during the War.

†The British Army had in addition fifty-five Yeomanry (Territorial Army) regiments in various states of efficiency. The first to go overseas were the Oxfordshire Hussars, 22 September 1914. A Yeomanry Division (in which the author's father served) fought dismounted on Gallipoli in 1915; in 1916 the 35th Division was reconstituted chiefly with Yeomanry (see p. 42); Yeomanry formed the bulk of the mounted troops in Egypt and Palestine until 1918, when nine regiments were brought back to France and converted to infantry to form the 74th Division.

According to David Woodward (*Armies of the World 1854–1914*, Sidgwick and Jackson, 1978, p. 75) the Russian cavalry consisted of sixty-nine regiments (Guard and line) plus an indeterminate number of Cossacks. H. W. Wilson and J. A. Hammerton (*The Great War: The Standard History of the All-Europe Conflict*, Amalgamated Press, 1914–18, i, p. 306) say: 'The regular cavalry is organised in twenty divisions (two of the Guard, fifteen of the line, two mixed divisions of Cossacks and line cavalry, and a Cossack division). This makes a force of about 80,000 sabres. Besides this there is the general levy of Cossack cavalry.' Sir James Edmonds, in his *Short History of World War I*, O.U.P., 1951, says the Russians had thirty-six cavalry divisions.

Woodward and other authorities state that the Austro-Hungarian Army contained fifteen Dragoon regiments, sixteen (Hungarian) Hussar regiments and eleven Uhlan regiments, a total of forty-two. Sir James Edmonds, however, credits it with eleven cavalry *divisions*, which alone would require more than forty-two regiments, besides all the other demands for cavalry. Dr Norman Stone, in *The Eastern Front 1914–1917*, Hodder and Stoughton, 1975), places ten cavalry divisions in Galicia, which supports Edmonds. It should be noted that the French, with eighty-nine regiments, only put ten cavalry divisions in the field.

In the German, French and British Armies, as well as true Lancers, a proportion of the units of each of the other types also carried the lance.

XIX

SOMME MYTHS (5):
'The Donkeys' (British Generals)

' "Good-morning, good-morning!" the General said,
When we met him last week on our way to the Line.
Now the soldiers he smiled at are most of 'em dead,
And we're cursing his staff for incompetent swine.
"He's a cheery old card," grunted Harry to Jack,
As they slogged up to Arras with rifle and pack.

*   *   *   *   *

But he did for them both by his plan of attack.'
(Siegfried Sassoon: 'The General', 1917)

'Ludendorff: "The English soldiers fight like lions."
Hoffman: "True. But don't we know that they are lions led by
donkeys." (Falkenhayn, *Memoirs)'*
(From front-papers of Alan Clark, The Donkeys,
Hutchinson, 1961)

'I have been sufficiently curious to inquire further into the source
of this quotation. Assuming that Falkenhayn, Hoffman and
Ludendorff were the German generals of those names in World
War I, I have sought the assistance of the librarians of the
Imperial War Museum and of the Library for Contemporary
World War literature in Stuttgart, and I have received replies
from both, to the effect that the reported conversation could not
be traced in any books connected with those names which had
been examined.

An inquiry to the publishers of *The Donkeys* could be met only
by a reference back to the printed statement in the book . . . A
letter addressed to the author which the publishers'
representative undertook to forward to him remains
unacknowledged.'

(J. C. Sharp Esq., Birmingham: letter in *The Daily Telegraph*,
16 July 1963)

'In Francisque Sarcey's *Le Siège de Paris,* published by Nelson in
1871, on page 57, is quoted the words of the London *Times* about

the French soldiers who had been completely defeated by the
Prussians in 1870: "Vous êtes des lions conduits par des ânes!" '
(D. G. Libby Esq., London S.W.15, letter in *The Daily
Telegraph,* 19 July 1963.)
'There is no need for your son to go into the Army: he is really
quite intelligent.'
(The Headmaster of Winchester to Field-Marshal Wavell's
father)'

It is characteristic of a basically unmilitary population that a freak
occasion – 1 July 1916 – should have been permitted to put the
brand of Cain on a whole generation of British generals. It is that
hugging of the whole War as a private British sorrow – the 'dense
and impenetrable insular mythology' to which I have referred on
(p. 108) – that is responsible for the calumny, and, as one might
suppose, a chief instigator was Lloyd George. This arch-
calumniator of the British generals says:

It is not too much to say that when the Great War broke out our Generals
had the most important lessons of their art to learn. Before they began
they had much to unlearn. Their brains were cluttered with useless
lumber, packed in every niche and corner. Some of it was never cleared
out to the end of the War . . . They knew nothing except by hearsay about
the actual fighting of a battle under modern conditions. Haig ordered
many bloody battles in this War. He only took part in two . . . He never
even saw the ground on which his greatest battles were fought, either
before or during the fight. Robertson never saw a battle . . . In the most
crucial matters relating to their own profession our leading soldiers had to
be helped out by the politician . . . [Here follows an impressive but quite
mendacious list of the generals' blind spots.] . . . Politicians were the first
to seize upon the real character of the problem in all these respects and it
was they who insisted on the necessary measures being taken – and taken
promptly – in order adequately to cope with it.[1]

A little further on the Welsh wizard strikes his lyre with really
savage force:

'The distance between the châteaux and the dugouts was as great as that
from the fixed stars to the caverns of the earth.'[2]

Lloyd George was, of course, by no means alone in heaping
scorn on the 'Military Mind' – even soldiers joined him, like
General Baker-Carr, whose strictures I have quoted on p. 136, and,
needless to say, Liddell Hart and Fuller. Academics also joined the

chorus; their habitual contempt for the military has never been better expressed than by Professor Llewellyn Woodward in his book *Great Britain and the War of 1914–1918*. Connoisseurs of mythology may find in his pp. xviii-xx as densely compacted a sample as they could desire. It includes this gem: in 1919 Woodward was complaining to an Oxford colleague of the 'low mental level of our military leadership', which he held responsible for his own distressing experience of the soldier's life. His colleague had a ready explanation: 'the army "was run by pass men".' Loftily Professor Woodward adds that

'the English could not complain of the consequences when they had left the fate of a generation in the hands of a custom-bound clique which would never have been permitted to take over the management of any other important department of state or of a great business.'[3]

Such ideas are now as firmly entrenched in the mythology of the War as the armies themselves were on the Western Front.

What spoils this myth, whether in the form presented by Lloyd George, or by Professor Woodward, or anyone else, is the Professor's *sotto voce* admission that 'the enemy generals were equally obtuse'. Since he does not specifically exempt them (and there is nothing in the record to suggest that he should) we must assume that he includes the generals of the Allies as well. And so we arrive at the truly Oxbridge (or Westminster) proposition that a whole generation of generals right across the globe – the highly trained professionals of the German Great General Staff, the unpredictable but sometimes very successful officers of the Imperial Russian Army,[4] the republican products of St Cyr, the Polytechnique and West Point, as well as those of Sandhurst and the shires – were *all* (since their performance was similar) 'pass men'. Such a proposition must surely be mythology unadulterated.

It seems, indeed, almost impolite to interrupt the flow of denunciatory rhetoric with the suggestion that a phenomenon so strikingly universal must have an equally universal, more credible (and fundamental) *raison d'être* than that suggested by the arrogant and thoughtless assumptions of politicians, academics and journalists. Yet it is necessary to intrude upon their fantasies by considering just what it was that the 'custom-bound clique' was confronting. When Lloyd George says that 'our Generals had the most important lessons of their art to learn' he states no less than the truth; they had indeed. What that generation of naval and military leaders, no longer young, brought up in Victorian society and accustomed to a leisurely process of technical and social change, had to face was this:

the first war of aviation, with all the implications of that;
the first real under-sea war, entirely altering the nature of naval power;
the first war of the internal combustion engine, therefore also the first war of the mechanics, a new breed of men in uniform;
the first war of wireless telegraphy;
the first of the two great artillery wars, with all *their* destructive implications;
the first chemical war, using (among other things) poison gas and napalm (flame-throwers, petroleum-based);
the first war of modern mass production, mass logistics and mass administration (by 1916 British G.H.Q. in France was administering a population bigger than any single unit of control in England, except Greater London);
and much else besides.

All in all, the 'custom-bound clique' had a good deal to think about; its experience was in fact unique; never before or since has so much innovation been packed into such a short space of time. The imagination of that generation (in every country) had no option but to work overtime; those who were short of imagination had to develop it rather fast. The truth is that those ruddy-cheeked, bristling-moustached, heavy-jawed, frequently inarticulate generals rose to challenge after challenge, absorbed weapon after weapon into their battle systems, adapted themselves to constant change with astonishing address. But no one cared to make a legend out of that.

The arrows of the mythologists come from all sides. I have just mentioned G.H.Q., and earlier I mentioned Haig's positioning of his Advanced G.H.Q. for the Battle of the Somme, and his use of a specially fitted train in 1917 and 1918 (p. 117). There should be no mystery about such matters. The existence and location of Advanced G.H.Q. is referred to in the Official History and elsewhere; descriptions of the train have been public property for sixty years – there are photographs of it, even clips of film. Yet as recently as 1967, in a book by a Canadian officer, Colonel Fairlie Wood, described by Liddell Hart as 'one of the most outstanding recent reappraisals of World War I' (and Colonel Wood in turn pays pleasing tribute to Liddell Hart), we find:

'Haig's headquarters at the time of Vimy was the comfortable Château de

Beaurepaire. He and his staff moved there in March 1916, and remained there until after the war, isolated from reality.'[5]

I fear that this particular piece of nonsense is due to inaccurate wording by Haig's loyal and admiring biographer, Duff Cooper, who wrote: 'On April 1st General Headquarters were transferred to Château Beaurepaire, a commodious and comfortable house two and a half miles south-east of Montreuil, which was to remain the home of Haig and his immediate Staff for the rest of the war.'[6] Home, yes – but it is the lot of soldiers to be much away from home, as Duff Cooper knew quite well, since a little later on he refers to Advanced G.H.Q. at Beauquesne and later still quotes Haig's enthusiastic description of his H.Q. train. Little did he know what malevolent use would be made of his careless words.

Duff Cooper was not merely misleading about Haig and his 'immediate Staff', he was also incorrect about G.H.Q. This august body was too large for any château; it was lodged in the little walled town of Montreuil itself. A staff officer who served there tells us:

Montreuil was chosen as G.H.Q. for a wide variety of reasons. It was on a main road from London to Paris – the two chief centres of the campaign – though not on a main railway line, which would have been an inconvenience. It was not an industrial town and so avoided the complications alike of noise and of a possibly troublesome civil population. (The population of Montreuil in 1906 was 2,883). It was from a telephone and motor transit point of view in a very central situation to serve the needs of a Force which was based on Dunkirk, Calais, Boulogne, Dieppe, and Havre, and had its front stretching from the Somme to beyond the Belgian frontier . . . The great Ecole Militaire offered accommodation for the chief offices. There was sufficient billeting accommodation in the town houses and the neighbouring châteaux.[7]

The same source tells us that 300 staff officers worked in Montreuil, and 240 in outlying directorates.

Advanced G.H.Q., of course, was a much smaller affair; Haig himself, his Chief of Staff (the Deputy would generally remain at Montreuil), the Heads of 'O' (Operations) Section and the 'I' (Intelligence) Section, and such other senior staff officers, as the C.-in-C. might from time to time wish to consult, together with liaison officers, clerks and orderlies. In March 1917 Advanced G.H.Q. was still at Beauquesne, badly placed for the forthcoming Battle of Arras (9 April); on 14 April we find Haig complaining:

'It is necessary for me and the Operations Section to be in close touch with the Hqrs of Armies, and for me to be able to visit corps and divisions without wasting time on the road.'[8]

Very soon afterwards he moved Advanced G.H.Q. to Bavincourt, ten miles south-west of Arras, where it remained for the rest of that battle. In June he took up residence in the train, which stood in a siding at Godewaersvelde, six miles north-north-east of Hazebrouck, for the Third Battle of Ypres. In October, following the transfer of control of that battle from Fifth Army to Second Army, Haig moved into a house in Cassel, where General Plumer's headquarters were located. For Cambrai he returned to Bavincourt. In March 1918 he centred on Dury, in the Somme area; for the final offensive he used the train up and down the front. Small wonder that the officer whom I have quoted above should add: 'one rarely saw the Chief . . . when Haig did appear at Montreuil all felt they had the right to go to the window to catch a glimpse of him.'[9]

This, naturally, is no use to mythologists; Sir Philip Gibbs visited Montreuil, where he found 'the pageantry of war still maintained its old and dead tradition'. He tells us:

An 'open Sesame' by means of a special pass was needed to enter this City of Beautiful Nonsense. Below the gateway, up the steep hillside, sentries stood at a white post across the road, which lifted up on pulleys when the pass had been examined by a military policeman in a red cap. Then the sentries slapped their hands on their rifles to the occupants of any motor-car, sure that more staff-officers were going in to perform those duties which no private soldier could attempt to understand, believing they belonged to such mysteries as those of God. Through the narrow streets walked elderly generals, middle-aged colonels and majors, youthful subalterns all wearing red hat-bands, red tabs, and the blue-and-red armlet of G.H.Q., so that colour went with them on their way. Often one saw the Commander-in-Chief starting for an afternoon ride, a fine figure, nobly mounted, with two A.D.C.s and an escort of Lancers. A pretty sight, with fluttering pennons on all their lances, and horses groomed to the last hair. It was prettier than the real thing up in the Salient or beyond the Somme, where dead bodies lay in upheaved earth among ruins and slaughtered trees. War at Montreuil was quite a pleasant occupation for elderly generals who liked their little stroll after lunch, and for young Regular officers, released from the painful necessity of dying for their country . . .[10]

It is a clever piece of writing, building up a picture of pompous and absurd activity, similar to Sassoon's 'Base Details':

If I were fierce and bald and short of breath,
I'd live with scarlet majors at the Base,
And speed glum heroes up the line to death . . .[11]

Gibbs must have had very long sight indeed if he 'often' saw the Commander-in-Chief; his description of Haig and his escort, however, is quite stereotyped – it would do for all sorts of occasions in all sorts of places. And there is a nasty insinuation in his reference to young Regular officers enjoying themselves at Montreuil, the implication being that the New Army was doing the dying while they relaxed. The staff officer whom I have quoted tells a different story: 'Put to the test of getting a post at G.H.Q., which was supposed to be the crowning test of efficiency, the New Army Officers did not do badly. I made a rough poll one night at the club dinner. More than half the officers present were "New Army" men. In what may be called "specialist" branches New Army men predominated.'[12]

It is one of the facts of the War that deep antipathy existed towards G.H.Q. on the part of men who were otherwise entirely reasonable. Colonel R. S. Stafford, who commanded the 1/King's Royal Rifle Corps in 1918, and corresponded with me to my great profit in 1964, said: 'G.H.Q. was simply loathed. Partly because we thought with some justification that they were completely out of touch with conditions in the front line. They lived in luxury while we certainly did not. A particular grievance was the matter of return leave-boats . . .'[13]

Once more, the view from inside is different:

At G.H.Q., in my time, in my branch, no officer who wished to stay was later than 9 a.m. at his desk; most of the eager men were at work before then. We left at 10.30 p.m. if possible, more often later. On Saturday and Sunday exactly the same hours were kept. 'An hour for exercise' in the afternoon was supposed to be reserved, in addition to meal-hours; but it was not by any means always possible. During the worst of the German offensive in the spring of 1918 Staff officers toiled from 8.30 a.m. to midnight, with half-hour intervals for meals. I have seen a Staff officer faint at table from sheer pressure of work, and dozens of men, come fresh from regimental work, wilt away under the fierce pressure of work at G.H.Q.

The extreme character of the strain at G.H.Q. used to be recognised by a special allowance of leave. A short leave every three months was, for a long time, the rule. With pressure of work, that rule fell into abeyance, and a G.H.Q. Staff Officer was lucky to get a leave within six months. In the case of the big men at the head of the departments leave was something to be talked of, dreamt of, but never realised. Compared with conditions at G.H.Q. regimental work was care-free and pleasant.[14]

Despite its distinctive (and somewhat garish) arm-band, G.H.Q. undoubtedly attracted odium which sometimes properly belonged elsewhere. The staff of General Gough's Fifth Army was very unpopular, despite the geniality of the general himself. His Chief of Staff was Major-General Neil Malcolm, an intellectual soldier of considerable ability with an abrasive tongue which caused him to be heartily disliked by high and low alike. A visitor to Fifth Army H.Q. in October 1917 remarked:

I have come to the conclusion that the chief fault of the people who do staff work out in France is that they have morbid consciences, do too much themselves, and work far too long hours. Malcolm, for instance, is often up at 5 o'clock to go and see some outlying division; then he is in his office for an hour before breakfast, and returns to it shortly after 9 o'clock. He is working all day, either in the office or among the divisions, and goes back after dinner, remaining there till midnight or later. I don't believe that any man can work his brain safely for as long hours as this.'[15]

It can hardly be doubted that errors and breakdowns in staff work were far more likely to be due to fatigue through over-work than to the blithe incompetence for which the staffs were universally blamed. Nothing could persuade the average 'line soldier', especially the infantryman, that staff officers were not a breed apart, a privileged caste of *embusqués*, who knew nothing and cared less about conditions at the front. This table, showing the distribution of staff officers in 1918, may help dispose of this myth.

Location	Number	Source
War Office (London)	1,725	*Statistics, p. 565.* *
G.H.Q. (Montreuil)	300	G.S.O., *G.H.Q.*, Philip Allan, 1920,
('outlying')	240	p. 35.
Army H.Q.s	225	Calculated on the basis of a group photograph of Fourth Army H.Q. taken in July: 45 officers, including two French. Five Armies in the field.
Corps H.Q.s	504	O.H. *1916*, i, p. 58, says corps establishment was raised from 19 to 24 in that year. (Possibly it was even higher in 1918.) 21 army corps, including cavalry, Australian and Canadian.
Divisional H.Q.s	1,386	*The Guards Division in the Great War* by C. Headlam, John Murray, 1924, Appendix II, gives a full and clear breakdown: 22 Officers; 63 divisions including cavalry.
Brigade H.Q.s	1,134	Calculated on the basis of a group photograph showing 6 officers. 189 brigades.
5,514		

This does not take into account staff officers on lines of communication, at base camps, schools, etc., who must have comprised a very large number. Nor does it include Home Forces, India, or the other expeditionary forces outside France.

*The proportion of fit to unfit among these officers was 2:5.

The full total of staff officers in the British Army in 1918 may well have been in the region of 10,000. This represents a staggering increase from the 447 Staff College graduates of 1914 (see p. 115). Where did they all come from? Clearly a number of 'specialists' were recruited for expertise, but the overwhelming majority of these officers can only have come from the regiments, batteries and field companies themselves. They would be seconded for staff duties because of skills or wounds or meritorious service; in all cases they would be perfectly cognisant of fighting conditions. This would not automatically make them good staff officers; their manners – their approach to line officers and soldiers – would obviously vary from individual to individual. No doubt there were swollen heads; Captain Nolans are not confined to Balaklava. Personally, I am convinced that the practice of issuing red tabs to *every* staff officer, even the most junior (and there were no less than sixty-two different arm-bands to be seen) was very considerably responsible for the sense of apartness of Staff and Line. In the Second World War no one below the rank of full colonel was permitted to wear red hat-bands or tabs.

So much for the staffs; let us return now to the generals. It is not wonderful that two pairs of eyes perceive the same object in somewhat different ways. Thus the Liberal Philip Gibbs says of the British generals: 'One had to talk to them on the lines of leading articles in the *Morning Post*. Their patriotism, their knowledge of human nature, their idealism, and their imagination, were restricted to the traditional views of English country gentlemen of the Tory school. Anything outside that range of thought was to them heresy, treason, or wishy-washy sentiment.'[16]

An officer who was in later years to become a general himself recalls his old divisional commander, General Fanshawe (48th Division) – 'a dear old boy'. He remarks on a widespread belief that generals have to be 'loud-voiced, blustering bullies':

This false impression seems to me to be derived from political propaganda, based on military dictators in other countries. Britain was ruled by major-generals under the Commonwealth, 1649–1660, and was determined never to repeat the experience. As a result, she preferred that her army be commanded by rich members of society, who would have no inducement to carry out *coups d'état* and seize political power – or even to take any interest in politics at all . . . This country gentleman corps of officers have always, it is true, been slightly amateurish generals, but the country could not have it both ways. The really tough, selfmade military commander is always liable to be tempted by the lust for ruthless power. Not so the usual kind-old-gentleman British commander.[17]

'Amateurish', 'country gentlemen' or 'hard-looking, determined men'[18] – it was a daunting task that faced them all. Not only did they have to deal with that formidable flood of innovations which I have just listed; there were also certain grievous lacks. That failure of the cavalry as an arm of exploitation which we have already considered was but one of them; in 1918 its significance became apparent. As one soldier-historian wisely says, 'Foch was caught by a hiatus in the mobile arm: horsed cavalry had become obsolete and the *blitzkrieg* tank had not yet been developed.'[19] It is not agreeable to be caught in 'a hiatus' of technology; yet that was the fate of that entire generation. It was their evil luck to be presented with the poisons of the new technology, well in advance of the antidotes.

The tragedy of the generals, as I have already remarked (p. 118) – and it really has to be seen in tragic terms – was that they 'became quite impotent at the very moment when they would expect and be expected to display their greatest proficiency'. There is a very simple reason for this, ignored by almost all historians, and definitely ignored by all 'clever' ones. It was expressed to me in deadly clear terms by the late General Sir Alan Bourne (Royal Marine Artillery, G.S.O. 1, 8th Division, 1918) in a letter written in 1966, quoting Lieutenant-Colonel C. F. Jerram (Royal Marine Light Infantry and G.S.O. 1, 46th Division), who agreed that some recent writer

ignores or simply hasn't noticed the *only* thing that matters and without which you cannot begin to criticise, i.e., the fact that it was the *only* war ever fought without voice control; which came back in World War II with Walkie-Talkie and without which the modern soldier is as completely lost as we were. Nobody recognises that once troops were committed to the attack, *all* control was over. Why didn't you and I and our generals go up and take charge? – See for ourselves and give the necessary orders? – What the hell use would we have been? The ONLY place where it was possible to know what was going on was at the end of a wire, with its antennae to Brigades and Artillery.[20]

At Cambrai in 1917, Brigadier-General Hugh Elles, commanding the Tank Corps, proclaimed his intention of leading the corps into battle; which he did, in the tank 'Hilda', flying the Tank Corps flag. It was an admirable gesture, but no more than that. General Elles soon discovered that his only command capacity inside 'Hilda' was to kick the driver's right shoulder if he wanted to turn right, or kick his left shoulder if he wanted to turn left. After quite a short time General Elles realized that, if he wanted to influence the battle at all, he had better leave 'Hilda'; so he got out and walked back to his headquarters, and started being a general again, at the end of several telephone lines. One of the most fire-eating, forward-position generals of the whole war, General Charles Mangin, faced this truth gloomily in 1916, remarking: '*Si j'allais me promener en première ligne, je ne commanderais plus qu'une ou deux compagnies.*'[21] ('If I went marching about the front line I would be commanding no more than one or two companies.') This was the hiatus, the real hiatus of command; as Colonel Jerram said, 'the *only* war ever fought without voice control'. I would like to know what the critics would have done in such circumstances. Neither Lee nor Grant ever faced such problems. Even on the disconcerting 'empty battlefields' of South Africa, generals seemed able to transmit orders; we hear no complaints on this score. In the Second World War, there were the 'walkie-talkies' – and when they broke down, what laments! Only in the First World War were generals prevented from giving commands in battle. It is worth thinking about.

The politicians suffered from different handicaps. As Lord Esher says:

Twenty very able gentlemen in England, and about an equal number in France of similar age and habits, are trying to do something which long life, sedentary occupation, leisurely habits of mind render ludicrously impossible. I was educated, brought up and have lived all my life among these people. I know them. And I say that hardly one of them, except possibly in sobriety of temper and judgment, can be compared with what he was twenty years ago. They may be qualified to discuss and settle questions of domestic policy in peaceful times, but this very fact condemns them in war, so different are the qualities required in war from those desirable in peace.[22]

He was writing in 1915; the Government of that day, said Lord Esher, consisted 'of men whose training and mental equipment unfit them for carrying on a struggle with the Emperor and the German Great General Staff'.[23] It is hard to resist the conclusion that this remained the case throughout the War.

As regards the generals, perhaps the last word here should be spoken by one who served under them: Captain Stair Gillon, King's Own Scottish Borderers, editor (actually author) of *The Story of the 29th Division*:

'The editor has never discovered that there exists any other point of view than that of the Higher Command. Broadly speaking, commanders and commanded have seen eye to eye.'[24]

1   Lloyd George, *War Memoirs,* Odham's, 1936, ii, pp. 2038–*9.*
2   Ibid., p. 2040.
3   Sir Llewellyn Woodward, *Great Britain and the War of 1914–1918,* Methuen, 1967, pp. xviii-xx.
4   Only two major events of the First World War are known by the names of the generals responsible for them: the disastrous 'Nivelle Offensive' of 1917, and the brilliant 'Brusilov Offensive' of 1916.
5   Herbert Fairlie Wood, *Vimy,* Macdonald, 1967, p. 63.
6   Duff Cooper, *Haig,* Faber, 1935, i, p. 310.
7   *G.H.Q. (Montreuil-sur-Mer)* by 'G.S.O.', Philip Allan, 1920, pp. 14–15.
8   Haig Diary, author's papers.
9   G.S.O., *G.H.Q.,* p. 37.
10 Philip Gibbs, *Realities of War,* Heinemann, 1920, pp. 25–6.
11 Siegfried Sassoon, *Selected Poems,* Heinemann, 1925.
12 G.S.O., *G.H.Q.,* p. 177.
13 Author's papers.
14 G.S.O., *G.H.Q.,* pp. 35–6.
15 F.S.Oliver, *The Anvil of War,* Macmillan, 1936, p. 225.
16 Gibbs, op. cit., p. 46.
17 Sir John Glubb, *Into Battle,* Cassell, 1977, pp. 105–6.
18 Haig Diary, 20 July 1917 (author's papers). Haig had been visiting the Fifth Army and was referring to the corps and divisional commanders he had seen.
19 Brigadier C. N. Barclay, *Armistice 1918,* Dent, 1968, p. 90.
20 Author's papers.
21 *General Charles Mangin, Lettres de Guerre 1914–1918,* Librairie Arthème Fayard, 1950, p. 120.
22 Lord Esher, *Journals and Letters,* Nicolson and Watson, iii, p. 249.
23 Ibid., p. 239.
24 Captain Stair Gillon, *The Story of the 29th Division,* Nelson, 1925, pp. xi-xii.

XX
ANTI-MYTH
Table J
Surprises of the War (Strategic, Tactical, Technical), 1914–18

	Effected by THE ALLIES	*Effected by* THE CENTRAL POWERS
1914	Arrival of the B.E.F. The Heligoland Raid The Marne counter-stroke Battle-cruisers at the Falkland Islands	Scope of the Schlieffen Plan, use of Reserve formations Large use of heavy artillery in the field The Tannenberg encirclement
1915	The short bombardment at Neuve Chapelle The Anzac Landing (Gallipoli) The Suvla Bay Landing Shooting through propellor blades (Roland Garros)	Gas at 'Second Ypres' The U-boat campaign The overthrow of Serbia
1916	The dawn attack of 14 July (Somme) First use of tanks, 15 Sept. (Somme) The Brusilov Offensive Recapture of Fort Douaumont	The first attack at Verdun (French surprised by weight of attack, especially artillery, and unprepared) Conquest of Romania
1917	Use of Arras cellars for covered assembly The Messines mines Massed tanks at Cambrai French attack at Verdun (August)	Retreat to Hindenburg Line (seriously dislocating Allied plans) The Gotha raids Wide use of ferro-concrete (Aisne, Flanders) Caporetto
1918	The second Marne counter- stroke on 18 July; 8 August, 'the black day of the German Army'	Weight of German artillery, Picardy 21 March Chemin des Dames, 27 May
Totals	**18** (12 British, 7 under Haig)	**14** (all German except one)

Table K

GREAT COMMANDERS
1914–18

German
Field-Marshal von Hindenburg
Chief of the General Staff,* 1916–18. His stable temperament and great authority provided a 'leader-image' for the German Army and people which proved invaluable in the difficult stages of the war.

Field-Marshal von Mackensen
A first-class practitioner of battle on the Eastern Front. Conducted the quick, victorious campaign against Romania in 1916.

General von Hutier
Also a first-class practitioner of battle. The 'Hutier Tactics' employed against the Russians at Riga in 1917 were the model for Caporetto, and von Hutier himself used them again with success against the British in March 1918.

Major-General Hoffmann
Chief of Staff of the German Eighth Army in East Prussia in 1914, his plans for the encirclement of the Russians at Tannenberg were already issued when Ludendorff arrived. From 1917, as Chief of Staff to Prince Leopold of Bavaria, he was virtually Commander-in-Chief of the German forces on the Eastern Front.

---

*In the Imperial German Army, the Commander-in-Chief was the Kaiser, and the title was reserved for him. The commander-in-chief in the field was called the Chief of Staff, and his own chief of staff was called the Quartermaster-General. To mark his special position under Hindenburg, General Erich Ludendorff was designated 'First Quartermaster-General'.

Major-General von Lettow-Vorbeck

German commander in East Africa. With exiguous forces in a remote theatre he kept the field against a greatly superior enemy, only laying down his arms twelve days after the Armistice.

French

Marshal Joffre

French Commander-in-Chief, 1914-16. Unquestionably responsible for the decisive victory of the First Battle of the Marne in 1914. Throughout his tenure of command he displayed great tact and understanding as a coalition general, and great authority inside the French Army.

Marshal Foch

He embodied the best aspects of French enthusiasm and determination. He learned by his earlier mistakes, and in 1918 was chiefly responsible for the victory of the Second Battle of the Marne which marked the beginning of the end. He, also, proved to be a sensible and tactful coalition commander.

General Franchet D'Esperey

He took over a largely demoralized French Fifth Army in September 1914 and swiftly transformed it to play a vital part in the Battle of the Marne. Subsequently commanded a group of armies; 'disgraced' after the French collapse on the Aisne in 1918 and sent to Salonika. He launched a brilliantly successful campaign on the Danube in the closing stages of the war.

General Pétain

French Commander-in-Chief, 1917-18. Always a first-class practitioner of battle. He was held in affection by the ordinary soldier, and so was able to restore the Army to its duty after the 1917 mutinies. His pessimistic temperament reduced his role in 1918, but it is unlikely that anyone else could have held the French Army together as he did.

General Mangin

Army commander. He was the exact opposite of Pétain, always aggressive, eager to attack. He was also highly professional, and in 1918 the combination of these qualities made the Tenth Army the most effective in the French Order of Battle.

General Gouraud

Army commander. Although it was his personal courage and dauntless spirit that most inspired, he was also a skilful tactician with an understanding of defence in depth which few French commanders possessed. In 1918 he was considered as a possible replacement for Pétain after the Aisne disaster.

British

Field-Marshal Lord Kitchener

Secretary of State for War 1914–16. The experiment of appointing a soldier as Secretary of State was not a success. Kitchener himself, however, holds a unique place as one who not merely foresaw a long war from the very beginning, but at once set about raising and equipping the forces necessary for it.

Field-Marshal Lord Haig

Commander-in-Chief, France and Flanders, 1915–18. He was one of the very first to foresee a long, continental war. Under Lord Haldane, Haig was one of the creators of the Citizen Army for that very purpose. When war came he displayed an unequalled grasp of the disciplines of a Coalition war. In 1918 he was the first to sense imminent victory, and prompt to grasp it.

Admiral of the Fleet Lord Jellicoe

Commander-in-Chief, Grand Fleet; First Sea Lord. Jellicoe was, in Churchill's phrase, 'the only man who could lose the war in an afternoon'. He was the first British admiral to handle a great modern fleet, and brought to the task a fund of cool, level-headed judgment.

General Sir William Robertson

Chief of the Imperial General Staff, 1915–18. Robertson was the only man in the Army's entire history to go all the way from Private to Field-Marshal. The strength of character which enabled him to do this upheld him, as C.I.G.S., in his long struggle for correct military principle against all opportunism and against ferocious political pressures.

General Sir Herbert Plumer

Army Commander. He was a first-class practitioner of battle who cared deeply for his soldiers; they, in turn, held him in much affection.

Major-General Sir Hugh Trenchard

First Chief of the Air Staff in the newly born Royal Air Force; later Commander of the Independent Air Force and thus the originator of strategic air offensives. He provided precisely the strong, far-sighted leadership required by the Air Arm in its infant days.

Russian

General Brusilov

Army Group Commander, 1916; Commander-in-Chief, 1917. Only two men gave their names to a large operation of war between 1914 and 1918, one of them being Brusilov. His great victorious offensive in 1916 had a classic quality, befitting the last incandescence of the Russian Empire.

Turkish

Mustapha Kemal Pasha

As a relatively junior officer at Gallipoli in 1915 he showed admirable sang-froid and tactical grasp in defeating the Anzac and Suvla landings. His organizational skill and power of leadership were well displayed in Syria in 1918; he quickly emerged as Turkey's 'strong man' after the war.

XXI

MYTHS AND ANTI-MYTH:
'The Greatest Strategist in the Army'

Mythologists need not merely 'villains' but 'heroes' – they have to have an example to point to, to show how things might have been, had not, alas! . . . alas! . . . The man selected by the mythologists to play the rôle of Principal Boy in their First World War pantomime, if he is not Lawrence of Arabia, is generally Lieutenant-General John Monash, commander of the Australian Corps in 1918. He was, indeed, a very fine soldier.

The Australian Army Corps came into existence officially on 1 November 1917. Nine months would elapse before the formality burgeoned fully into fact; not until the Battle of Amiens, in August 1918, did the five Australian divisions in France fight on the same battlefield under their own commander. By that time, that commander was Monash, and four days after the opening of the battle he was knighted by King George V, in the field amid his victorious soldiers and the trophies they had captured. The King made a little speech, commending Monash's work, and commendation has continued ever since. Virtually alone amid the military leaders of the First World War, Monash's reputation among his own people never declined; it found notable recognition in 1961, with the naming of Monash University in his birthplace, Melbourne. If the man in the street in Britain knew little about him – displaying that unlovable characteristic of ignoring or despising 'colonials' – historians and students of war have steadily appreciated his qualities.

Indeed, Monash's fame risks turning into yet another mythology. Thus Mr A. J. P. Taylor has described him as 'the only general of creative originality produced by the First World War'.[1] Liddell Hart considered that 'he probably had the greatest capacity for command in modern war' of all those who held command during that war. I myself wrote, in the *Journal* of the Royal United

Services Institute: 'General Monash is one British commander of the First World War who leaves one in no doubt that he would have been equally at home in the Second.'[2] But the widest claim of all, the most significant, because it is probably from this that most of the others stem, was made by Lloyd George, with all his authority as ex-wartime Prime Minister.

Lloyd George's views on the generalship of the First World War need no further elaboration; the long section in his *War Memoirs* on Third Ypres ('Passchendaele') called 'The Campaign of the Mud', with which he was so pleased that he published it separately as a pamphlet, contains some of his most venomous verdicts on the British leaders, Haig and Robertson. He follows these with a significant reference to Monash.

After 'Passchendaele', Lloyd George determined upon big changes in the British Command. There was a great turning out at G.H.Q. at the end of 1917: Haig's Chief of Staff, General Kiggell, went; his Head of Intelligence, the much disliked but able Brigadier Charteris, went; his Quartermaster-General, his Engineer-in-Chief, and his Director-General of Medical Services went. But Lloyd George wanted much more than that; the scalp he was after was Haig's. In January 1918 he sent General Smuts (a member of the War Cabinet) and Colonel Hankey (its Secretary) on a confidential mission to the B.E.F. in France to find and recommend a successor to Haig. They were unable to do so. 'They came back with a very disappointing report,' says Lloyd George, and he adds:

Since the War I have been told by men whose judgment I value that the only soldier thrown up by the War on the British side who possessed the necessary qualities for the position was a Dominion General. Competent professional soldiers whom I have consulted[3] have all agreed that this man might and probably would have risen to the height of the great occasion. But I knew nothing of this at the time. No report ever reached me either as War Secretary or Prime Minister, which attributed any special merit to this distinguished soldier. The fact that he was a civilian soldier when the War broke out may have had something to do with the tardiness in recognising his exceptional abilities and achievements.[4]

This was Monash. 'No doubt,' says Lloyd George elsewhere, 'Monash would, if the opportunity had been given him, have risen to the height of it.'[5] And he repeats his suggestion of a conspiracy of silence: 'Professional soldiers could hardly be expected to advertise the fact that the *greatest strategist in the Army* was a civilian when the War began, and that they were being surpassed by a man who had not received any of their advantages in training and teaching.'[6]

So there we have it: approval of Monash is not simply a matter of acknowledging a fine corps commander, with evident further potential. It is a matter of canvassing an alternative Commander-in-Chief, with (presumably) an alternative system of war – 'the greatest strategist in the Army', or, elsewhere, 'the most resourceful General in the whole of the British Army'.[7] This is the proposition which has to be tested out as mythology or otherwise.

Monash was born in 1865. He was a Jew. His brain power was formidable: at Melbourne University he graduated in engineering, law and arts, and studied in his spare time medicine, history and archaeology. He played the piano; he sketched well; he could speak French and German. The breadth of his interest was almost his undoing as a student: he cut too many lectures, and failed the examination at the end of the first year of his arts course. 'When the result became known at home there was great mourning, and I soon felt fit to drown myself.'[8] But he easily passed the supplementary examination, and there were no more academic failures. It was at this period of his life that he established what was to become his normal working day: 6.30 in the morning until, perhaps, 1.30 the next morning. And while he was still a student he took another step of formative significance. He wrote in his diary on 6 March 1887: 'The undercurrent of my thoughts has been running strongly on military matters. Yesterday things came to a finality . . . A combination of military and engineering professions is a possibility that is before me.' He had applied for a commission in the Garrison Artillery of Australia's Citizen Forces.

The 'combination of military and engineering professions' prospered. As a civil engineer, Monash had much to do with the development of Australia's railways and bridges; he specialized in construction with reinforced concrete. In 1912 he was elected President of the Victorian Institute of Engineers, and a member of the Council of Melbourne University. In 1913 he was a full colonel in the Citizen Forces, commanding an infantry brigade. At the age of fifty he underwent his baptism of fire, commanding the 4th Brigade at Gallipoli. In 1916 the Australian Imperial Force (A.I.F.) was brought to France, expanded and reorganized: the I and II Anzac Corps were formed (four Australian divisions and the New Zealand) as part of the B.E.F. A new division (numbered 3rd) was raised in England; Monash was given the command. The division went to France at the end of November and saw its first large action at Messines in June 1917; it took a notable part in the fighting of the Third Battle of Ypres in the late summer and autumn, and was engaged with distinction in the great battles of

March-April 1918. On 31 May 1918 Monash was appointed commander of the Australian Corps, when General Sir William Birdwood was promoted to command the re-forming Fifth Army.

It is necessary to consider this synopsis of Monash's career, to understand just where he stood in the B.E.F. hierarchy. It is not surprising if Lloyd George heard nothing about him, while Secretary of State for War; Monash had only arrived in France about a fortnight before Lloyd George resigned from that post. Even by the time of the Smuts-Hankey mission to find a new C.-in-C. in January 1918, Monash was still a relatively new divisional commander, with a good but not sensational record in that capacity. There were sixty infantry divisional commanders in the B.E.F.; there were nineteen corps commanders in lofty array above them; there were four army commanders. Monash was not even particularly well known in the Australian Corps.[9] Survivors of Gallipoli would remember 'Monash Valley' – but by 1918 there were not that many Gallipoli survivors left in the A.I.F. And survivors of 'Quinn's Post' might not necessarily remember Monash with affection. Moreover, among promising officers from the Dominions, there was already a corps commander of distinction, outranking Monash: Lieutenant-General Sir Arthur Currie had held command of the Canadian Corps since June 1917. At Hill 70 and at 'Passchendaele' Currie and his Canadians had done great things. Anyone tempted, in January 1918, to look outside the ranks of the British Regular army for a new Chief would certainly have looked first at Currie.

The fact is that Monash was not a serious candidate for sensational promotion at the time that Lloyd George was so keenly desirous of parting with Haig. His complaints of 'not being told' about Monash (even when he was Prime Minister) are nonsensical; there was not very much to tell. Monash's great achievements came later, in the last three months of the War, when his army corps became, to all intents and purposes, the spearhead of the B.E.F. – indeed, of the Allied armies. But by then Haig, having mastered the most powerful German offensive of the whole War, had passed to the counter-attack, and was in the process of winning the nine successive, decisive victories which Lloyd George called, at the time, 'the greatest chapter in our military history'.[10] The urgency of dismissing the Commander-in-Chief had thus become very much less pressing.

It is worth considering, nevertheless, what sort of contribution Monash might have made, over and above the very substantial contribution that he did make – what 'alternative' he might have offered to the accepted mode of waging war. This involves setting aside the absurdities: forgetting his relative obscurity; forgetting that the Army was about to pass through a period when it would have its 'backs to the wall' – i.e. when a change of command would be most perilous; forgetting that inter-Allied relations, of which Monash had no experience at all, and into which he would have stepped as an unknown, were shortly to meet a succession of fearful crises; forgetting that war is much compounded of human factors, and that almost all the human factors (mistrust of the unfamiliar, condescension towards 'colonials', sheer jealousy) would have been against him at that elevation. Perhaps the only fair way to reach an assessment is to look at Monash at the height of his powers, during those last three months, when everything he touched seemed to turn to gold. But first we should ask how he came by this opportunity, how he became commander of the Australian Army Corps. It is an illuminating story.

The Dominion of Canada placed four divisions in the field in France during the First World War. In September 1915, when there were still only two, they were formed into a Canadian Corps under a British general, with the understanding that they should always fight together as a unit. Canada found the corps troops and administration, added two more divisions and, as we have seen, provided a Canadian commander from June 1917. From the point of view of morale, the arrangement worked excellently; the Canadians were unquestionably a *corps d'élite*. From the point of view of practical soldiering the arrangement also worked well, but it did have a serious disadvantage: an 'unbreakable' unit of four divisions (about 100,000 men all told, at peak strength) was not always the handiest tactical instrument. It was for that reason that, in the long sustained crisis of the Army in the spring of 1918, the Canadians played little part. Yet, evidently, the Canadian example was something that Australia could not disregard. (It must also be remembered, in this connection, that the third great Dominion, South Africa, was conducting her own campaigns, and both the Prime Minister, General Louis Botha, and General Jan Smuts enhanced their reputations in independent command.)

The pressure on the British Government and G.H.Q. to permit the formation of what was then called 'an Australian Army' began as soon as the Australians assembled in France in 1916. Already there were four divisions of them, bringing a high fighting reputation from Gallipoli, and linked to a splendid division of New Zealanders which was also to become a *corps d'élite*. The first organizational solution to the problem of their pride and self-

respect was a fairly happy compromise: the two Anzac Corps
referred to above, both under British officers, Lieutenant-General
Sir W. Birdwood (1st and 2nd Australian, N.Z. Division) and
Lieutenant-General Sir A. J. Godley (4th and 5th Australian).
These were practical units for battle; they raised morale by keeping
the men from the Antipodes generally together; they avoided the
rasp of incompatibility which constantly cropped up between
'Imperial' and 'Colonial' troops. But they were not quite what
Australia wanted. On 1 June 1916 the Australian Prime Minister,
the redoubtable Mr W. M. Hughes, was at G.H.Q. Haig wrote in
his diary:

Mr Hughes is very deaf, but quick and most intelligent. He suffers from
nerves, sleeps badly and did not come down to breakfast at 8.30 a.m. . . .
He asked me a few questions about the organisation and administration
of the Australians. I told him I had no intention of breaking up the
Australian Corps, but even if they put six divisions into the field that force
was not large enough to admit of 'an Australian Army' being formed. He
said he had the most thorough confidence in me and would do all he could
to help me in my difficult task.[11]

Mr Hughes was as good as his word. The Australian government
never lost sight of its object, but it did not nag. It was a satisfaction
to all Australia when at last, in November 1917, after many epics,
their (now five) divisions were formed into a corps. By common
consent, this was commanded by Birdwood; the Australian
Government trusted and admired him; the Australian people had
come to accept him with affection; the soldiers liked him very
much; Haig was not so struck with him. But Birdwood had a flair
for handling the often outrageous individualists of the A.I.F. which
Haig had to accept (but we shall note his further views shortly). He
also had to accept that Birdwood, as well as being a corps
commander in the field, was the military representative of the
Australian Government; the fact that this duality worked out
without noticeable friction is a tribute to the loyalty of that
Government, the good sense of Birdwood, and the understanding
of Haig.

The loyalty was heavily strained indeed. It was hard, having
waited so long for an all-Australian unit, to see it apparently
demolished very soon after its creation. The great battles of March
and April 1918, on the Somme and on the Lys, and the grave
manpower shortage of the B.E.F., were the cause of this. One by
one, as the climaxes of action occurred, the Australian divisions
entered the battle to fill a gap or counter-attack, doing what they

could wherever they were needed. The unselfish gesture was not lost on Haig, who had had some serious misgivings about the Australian soldiers earlier in the year. It is interesting to see how his mind changed, as he made a comparison at different dates. He wrote to his wife on 28 February:

I spent some time today with the Canadians. They are really fine disciplined soldiers now and so smart and clean. I am sorry to say that the Australians are not nearly so efficient. I put this down to Birdwood, who, instead of facing the problem, has gone in for the easier way of saying everything is perfect and making himself as popular as possible. We have had to separate the Australians into Convalescent Camps of their own, because they were giving so much trouble when along with our men and put such revolutionary ideas into their heads.[12]

This was before the battles started. On 18 April, when they had been raging for four weeks, Haig saw matters somewhat differently. He was visiting General Horne's First Army:

Currie is suffering from a swollen head, Horne thinks. He lodged a complaint when I ordered the Canadian division to be brought out of the line in order to support the front and take part in the battle elsewhere. He wishes to fight only as a 'Canadian Corps' and get his Canadian representative in London to write and urge me to arrange it. As a result, the Canadians are holding a wide front near Arras, *but they have not yet been in the battle*. The Australians on the other hand have been used by divisions and are now spread out from Albert to Amiens and one is in front of Hazebrouck.[13]

It was against this background of events and ideas that Birdwood left the Australian Corps in May, and the question of his successor had to be settled. Two authorities would have the final decision: the Australian Government, and the C.-in-C. What was Haig's thinking? We need to go back some distance in time to understand it properly – to 1909, in fact, when Haig was reaching the end of his work with Lord Haldane on army reform, and the year of a most important Imperial Defence Conference. This was when Haldane rounded off his work by laying the firm foundations of an Imperial General Staff – a first step towards practical unification of the military effort of the British Empire. 'Haig worked out the details of the plan,' wrote Haldane,[14] and this concept of imperial military unity, of each part of the machine lending strength to each other part, remained with Haig thereafter. He, at any rate, was clear about one thing – that the Australian Corps in 1918 must have an

Australian commander; in fact he was clearer on this than the Australian Government itself, which would have liked to hold on to Birdwood.

One reason for this was the difficulty of choosing among the available Australian officers. There was the administrative question to consider, with the complication that the senior claimant from that point of view would be Major-General M'Cay, commanding the Australian depôts on Salisbury Plain. The Army Corps would not have cared for M'Cay. There was Monash, of course, whose talents could not possibly be overlooked. There was Major-General Talbot Hobbs of the 5th Division, whom Birdwood for one considered fit for a corps command. But above all there was Birdwood's Chief of Staff, Major-General Sir C. B. Brudenell White, whom Monash himself had described in 1916 as 'far and away the ablest soldier Australia had ever turned out'.[15] This view was widely shared; although White had been a staff officer throughout, it was well known that he had often actually commanded in Birdwood's absence, and nobody doubted his ability to command in the future. Haig was well aware of White's qualities; as early as July 1916, when he was feeling distinctly impatient with some of the Australian commanders, who were new to the Western Front and somewhat brash in their approach to it, Haig singled White out as 'a very sound capable fellow'. A year later, shortly after Currie's appointment to the Canadian Corps, Haig said to White:

'Why don't you have a Corps commander of your own? You know, *you* ought to be commanding this Corps.'

White said, 'God forbid. General Birdwood has a position among Australians which is far too valuable to lose.'

Haig said he knew all that; but Birdwood could have an administrative command. White replied that Birdwood's great reputation in Australia depended on his being the fighting commander of their troops . . . Haig turned away impatiently and since then has been very short with White.[16]

From that moment forward, Monash was Haig's man. He had, in truth, been moving in this direction for some time. Soon after Monash's 3rd Division arrived in France at the end of 1916, Haig came to inspect it. The Battle of the Somme had just drawn to its equivocal end, and Monash wrote: 'Douglas Haig looked grey and old. On parting he put his arm around my shoulders (as I rode beside him) and with much feeling and warmth he said – 'You have a very fine division. I wish you all sorts of good luck, old man.'[17] It was a moment of unusual emotion, indicative of a lasting impression. In late May 1917, just before the Battle of Messines,

Haig was with the 3rd Australian Division again: 'The commander is General Monash. I believe an auctioneer by profession, but in my opinion a clear-headed, determined commander. Every detail had been thought of. His brigadiers are equally thorough. I was much struck with their whole arrangements. Every suggestion I made was most carefully noted for consideration. Their C.R.A. (Grimwade) struck me as a thoughtful man.'[18]

The 3rd Division had a good battle at Messines; two days after the opening (7 June) Haig referred to Monash again: '... (evidently of Jewish descent) and by trade head of a ferro-concrete firm. He is a most practical and capable commander, and had done well.'[19] In July Haig held the conversation with White quoted above; his thoughts thereafter turned more and more to Monash, who recorded in August:

'Birdwood told me that the Commander-in-Chief had a very high opinion of my division and of me personally and had gone out of his way to express himself in terms of praise of my work. Birdwood added that it was rare for the Chief to do this. White entirely confirmed these statements.'[20]

On 22 September Haig reviewed the 3rd Australian Division, as it was about to enter the successful but hard middle period of Third Ypres: 'Every detail connected with the parade had been carefully thought out beforehand, hence the parade was so successful. I think Monash a good head and commands his division well.'[21] That night Monash dined at Advanced G.H.Q. with Haig, Kiggell and Major-General Butler, the Deputy Chief of Staff:

There were only the four of us present. After each course was served, the mess stewards went out of the room and the doors were locked from inside, until the Chief gave a sign for the next course. So you may imagine that some very important and confidential matters were discussed.... Nothing could have been more charming than the affability and camaraderie of these three great soldiers, upon whom rests the whole burden of the British Western Front.[22]

The Anzacs played a great part in Third Ypres, their climax being the Battle of Broodseinde on 4 October, called by the Germans 'a black day'. Lloyd George belittled the occasion later: 'Who remembers the name now? (Try it on one of your friends.)'[23] He should have consulted Monash, who had no doubts about Broodseinde at the time:

Great happenings are possible in the very near future, as the enemy is terribly disorganised, and it is doubtful if his railway facilities are good enough to enable him to re-establish himself before our next two blows, which will follow very shortly and be very severe . . . Our success was complete and unqualified. Over 1,050 prisoners and much material and guns. Well over 1,000 dead enemy counted, and many hundreds buried out of reach. We got absolutely astride the main ridge.[24]

And then, of course, the rains came down and washed all hope away. But it is worth noting that 'the greatest strategist in the Army', 'the only general with creative originality', the man with 'the greatest capacity for command', entirely shared the G.H.Q. view of Third Ypres possibilities, at a level of much closer practical concern. This is not a surprising fact, if one looks for the real truth about Monash. The Australian Official Account quotes a reliable private diary which illuminates Monash's views of his relationship to G.H.Q. in 1918: 'Monash is very full of the idea that he is absolutely under G.H.Q. – he must not consider Australian demands – once he is under G.H.Q., G.H.Q. is all that he has to consider; a simple rule . . .' Small wonder, then, that he was Haig's candidate for command of the Australian Corps; small wonder that Haig's backing should have been strong enough to be decisive.

So we return to the question whether Monash ever really offered any 'alternative' to G.H.Q.'s system of war. And straight away it must be remarked that the word 'strategist' is utterly misleading. A corps commander on a continuous front does not have a strategy, he merely implements one; even an army commander must conform; even the Commander-in-Chief of an expeditionary force fighting beside a numerically stronger ally (on that ally's own soil) can only have a strategy that is agreed between them. Evidently, it is only fair to look for Monash's distinctive contribution at a somewhat lower level: it will be found in the fields of tactics and organization. The search for evidence of 'creative originality' will prove largely unrewarding; Monash himself confessed to being 'not strong on invention'. Only three significant innovations (one of them extremely embryonic) in a war full of innovations can be traced to him: the use of tanks much closer to the barrage line than was generally thought possible (I shall return to this further on); close cooperation, based on intensive training, between tanks and infantry (but this was really a question of degree – other formations did the same); and air-lifting supplies to troops in battle (this was the embryo; the greatly improved weight-lifting abilities of Second World War aircraft were required for useful effect).

Monash's achievements during his three months of battle command were nevertheless most striking. He tells us:

During the advance, from 8th August to 5th October, the Australian Corps recaptured and released no less than 116 towns and villages. Every one of these was defended more or less stoutly . . . The total number of enemy divisions engaged was 39. Of these, 20 were engaged once only, 12 were engaged twice, 6 three times and 1 four times . . . at least six of these enemy divisions had been entirely disbanded.

From 8th August to 5th October the total battle casualties were:

Killed	3,556
Died of wounds	1,432
Wounded	16,166
Missing	79
	21,243[25]

Under 5,000 dead in two months of constant attack – this is an unfamilar image of a First World War offensive. It suggests remarkable commanders and remarkable soldiers; the Australian Corps had both.

Indeed, the last word on the successes of Monash and his corps in 1918 should be that here, *par excellence,* we find a man and his instrument at one. It was Monash's deep respect for his often wayward troops that bred their respect for him; they knew their general cared for them, and they responded. Of course, there were English commanders who also respected and cared for their men, inspiring the same response (General Plumer and his Chief of Staff, Sir Charles Harington, were conspicuous examples), but whereas the British Army might function without this quality, in Dominion formations it was an absolute necessity. 'The Australian soldier,' said Monash, 'had the political sense highly developed, and was always a keen critic of the way in which his battalion or battery was "run", and of the policies which guided his destinies from day to day.'[26]

In a letter to a friend in Melbourne a few weeks before he took up his high command, Monash expressed the essence of his philosophy of war:

It is because we do not consider psychology enough that we are taking so long to win the war. Personally I have always found it pay well closely to consider the psychology not only of the enemy, but also of my own troops . . . to study the methods of keeping up the moral[e] and fighting spirit of my own soldiers. Indeed, it is psychology all along the line. As for myself, it did not take me long to learn that the only ways to carry out the responsibilities of command were, firstly, to erect optimism into a creed for myself and for all my brigades, arms and departments, and secondly to try and deal with every task and every situation on the basis of simple business propositions, differing in no way from the problems of civil life, except that they are governed by a special technique. The main thing is always to have a plan; if it is not the best plan, it is at least better than no plan at all.[27]

Monash was, above all, a planner; this was the true secret of his tactical successes in a war which threw unparalleled burdens on the Staff (Sir Ian Hamilton's 'General Staff War') and usually made improvisation downright dangerous. He wrote:

Although complete written orders were invariably prepared and issued by a general staff whose skill and industry left nothing to be desired, very great importance was attached to the holding of conferences, at which were assembled every one of the senior commanders and heads of departments concerned in the impending operation. At these I personally explained every detail of the plan, and assured myself that all present applied an identical interpretation to all orders that had been issued . . . The battle plan having been thus crystallised, *no subsequent alterations were permissible, under any circumstances, however tempting*. This fixity of plan engendered a confidence throughout the whole command which facilitated the work of every commander and staff officer.[28]

Monash believed that:

In a well-planned battle . . . nothing happens, nothing can happen, except the regular progress of the advance according to the plan arranged. The whole battle sweeps relentlessly and methodically across the ground until it reaches the line laid down as the final objective . . . It is for this reason that no stirring accounts exist of the more intimate details of such great set-pieces as Messines, Vimy, Hamel and many others. They will never be written, for there is no material on which to base them. The story of what did take place on the day of battle would be a mere paraphrase of the battle orders prescribing all that was to take place.[29]

At lower altitudes, there were those who might have disputed this, even in his own corps at the peak of its form; Dr Bean, indeed, remarks that 'Monash often lacked knowledge of what had happened in battle'.[30] But there can be no doubt that this meticulous preparation was the only antidote to costly failure in the First World War.[31]

As Monash was about to begin his spectacular run of victories in July 1918, Haig visited him, and they went through the plan for the Battle of Le Hamel together: 'M. is a most thorough and capable commander who thinks out every detail of any operation and *leaves nothing to chance.'*[32] On the one occasion when Monash did have to improvise, he wrote: 'For the first time I had to gamble on a chance. It was contrary to the policy which governed all my previous battle plans, in which *nothing had been left to chance.'*[33]

Haig and Monash, one perceives, were birds of a feather. It is mere mythology to assert that Monash was in any sense an 'alternative'; he was one of Haig's most trusted and admired subordinates, and it is no accident at all that Haig played a crucial part in giving him the opportunity of winning his well-deserved and lasting reputation.

Footnote

In 1976 Field-Marshal Lord Carver edited a book on military commanders of the twentieth century entitled *The War Lords*. It contained a chapter on Monash by Mr Malcolm Falkus which illustrates the dangers of allowing mythology to elevate people to the status of super-men. Quite correctly Mr Falkus says that 'Monash's first big test came at the important battle of Hamel on July 4 1918', but he is less correct when he adds: 'His careful battle plans included a new rôle for tanks, Monash insisting that they should advance with the infantry instead of ahead. The plans showed fully his characteristic attention to detail and incorporated the procedure (subsequently widely adopted by the British Army for the rest of the war) of ensuring that each participant knew exactly what rôle and objectives were expected of him.'[34] It will be convenient to unravel this passage backwards.

First, it is quite incorrect to say that careful briefing on rôles and objectives was 'subsequently' adopted by the British Army (i.e. only in the last four months of the War). Such briefing had been part of normal battle training since 1916, and was already well established by the time Monash took his division into battle at Messines in June 1917. Application of the method would naturally be better or worse according to the qualities of local commanders. The Second Army, under General Sir Herbert Plumer, was famous for its careful, detailed briefings. In XVIII Corps, application would normally be very good indeed, since this unit was commanded in 1917 by Lieutenant-General Sir Ivor Maxse, a famous trainer of troops who subsequently became Inspector-General of Training for the whole B.E.F. Judging by its performance throughout the Third Battle of Ypres, under most testing conditions, Lord Cavan's XIV Corps was also very well instructed, Lord Cavan himself rising to army commander level in 1918. II Corps under Lieutenant-General Sir Claud Jacob also had a good reputation for instruction. At the divisional level, the Guards (Major-General G. P. T. Feilding) and New Zealand (Major-General Sir Andrew Russell) both had splendid performance records based on excellent (but different) training preparations, while among Line divisions the 23rd (Major-General J. M. Babington) was one that received high praise both in Flanders and Italy for similar reasons.

Mr Falkus, like many others, is trapped by the myth that 'Monash's conception of command and generalship was fundamentally different from that of many British commanders, who continued to regard battles with the 'cavalry charge' romanticism of their predecessors'.[35] Such generalizations rarely survive inspection; even that 'attention to detail' which Monash undoubtedly displayed was not confined to him (General Currie certainly shared it, as did others), though it was carried by him to a very high pitch. Indeed, Professor C. E. Carrington says that 'the difference between Monash and others was only that he excelled them in thoroughness of preparation'.[36]

The 'new rôle for tanks', with which Mr Falkus credits him, deserves a closer look, however. I have already emphasized that tanks were not able to carry out the exploitation rôles of cavalry, as performed in *Blitzkrieg;* they were invented for a different purpose – to overcome the lethal combination of barbed wire and machine-guns which caused such appalling losses to unprotected advancing infantry. Naturally, 'progressive thinking' and the *amour-propre* of a new arm looked forward to more dramatic rôles. Already, by Cambrai in November 1917, the Tank Corps was experimenting with 'advanced guard tanks' as well as 'infantry tanks'; at that stage this only meant similar machines with different tasks, but soon it would mean different types for different tasks.

Monash's method at Le Hamel had nothing to do with such novelties; in his own words: 'Firstly, each tank was, for tactical purposes, to be treated as an infantry weapon; from the moment that it entered the battle until the objective had been gained it was to be under the exclusive orders of the infantry commander to whom it had been assigned. Secondly, the deployed line of tanks was to advance level with the infantry, and pressing close up to the barrage.'[37]

What this means is, quite simply, that Monash was insisting on a complete reversion to the infantry support rôle of tanks, their *old,* original rôle with no frills, the opposite, in fact, of the tank doctrine of the future as advocated by General Fuller, Liddell Hart, General Guderian and others.

Monash's problem at Le Hamel (and it was his own problems in 1918 that concerned him, not those of another generation in a later war) was all too familiar. Artillery was the battle-winner, and remained so for the rest of that war and the next. By 1918 it had been amply proven that if infantry were to be really protected by their supporting artillery barrage they needed to advance very close to it, almost *in* it, in fact. (Some divisions took special pride in this; the British 5th in 1918 made it a principle 'to be in the enemy trenches before the barrage lifted'.) This meant that tanks, if they, too, were going to give the infantry proper support, must also advance right up to the barrage. Now, the Mark V tank stood 8 feet 8 inches high; tank experts said that it would infallibly be hit by low-trajectory British shells. But Monash persisted, and was proved right. (That the experts were not just being silly is shown by the fact that one of the sixty tanks at Le Hamel actually *was* hit by a British shell. Thanks to the proficiency of the Royal Artillery, it was the only one.)

The purpose of this footnote is to show that it was not Monash's precise tactics (his 'resource') that mattered, but his *approach* to tactical problems, not his practice but his principles. His principles certainly taught him to dismiss what still remained of the romantic or 'inspirational' attitude to war, the attitude which found so much to admire in men like Murat or J. E. B. Stuart, which adulated Jackson for a brilliant campaign in the Shenandoah Valley in 1862 but generally ignored one even more effective by Sheridan in the same place in 1864, which placed Lee above Grant although Grant beat Lee, and Napoleon above Wellington although Napoleon's career was studded with disasters and he was finally beaten by Wellington, and which found embodiment between 1914 and 1918 in such men as General de Castelnau. Castelnau was an able officer, but he was undoubtedly a romantic; when Lloyd George mentioned Napoleon to him in 1914, 'His answer was a kind of soliloquy. "Ah, Napoleon, Napoleon. If he were here now, he'd have thought of the 'something else'." '[38]

Monash was not looking for 'something else'; he was making the best possible use of what he had. He did not find war romantic or 'inspiring'; indeed, he hated it. He was never a front-line leader, but he did give command his entire attention. One of his staff, Sir Keith Officer, told the author in 1958: 'I don't believe he thought about anything during the War except winning the War.' He was not a theorist, he was not trying to prove anything; he was trying to evolve a science of war which would be as exact as the science of engineering. He wanted to be able to rely on a battle in the same way as he would rely on a bridge. Of course, even bridges do occasionally fall down.

I still believe that Monash was a general (but by no means the only one) who would have been at home in the Second World War. I think his approach to war was more common between 1939 and 1945 than it was between 1914 and 1918 – for obvious reasons. It is not that, for example, Sir Alan Brooke was a 'better' C.I.G.S. than Sir William Robertson; both had a firm grasp of the principles of war, but Brooke's views were more likely to meet with widespread understanding in a generation educated by previous experience. All this seems worth putting down because it illustrates how important principles are in military studies. He would be an ass who tried to proffer Monash's practice in the First World War as a blueprint for the Second World War. But careful analysis of Monash's practice, untrammelled by theory or mythology, will reveal the principles on which it was founded – principles as valid in the next war as in his own.

---

1   A. J. P. Taylor, *The First World War,* Hamish Hamilton, 1963, p. 179.
2   August 1959.
3   Who? one wonders. Could it be that one of them was Captain Liddell Hart?
4   Lloyd George, *War Memoirs,* Odham's, 1936, ii, p. 1367.
5   Ibid., p. 2016.
6   Ibid., my italics.
7   Ibid., p. 2042.
8   Quoted by Dr C. E. W. Bean in *Official History of Australia in the Great War, 1914–18,* Angus and Robertson, vi, 1942.
9   Ibid., p. 194: 'to most of the troops outside his own division Monash was then merely a name . . .'
10 See John Terraine, *To Win a War,* Sidgwick and Jackson, 1978, pp. 200–1.
11 Author's papers.
12 Robert Blake (ed.), *The Private Papers of Douglas Haig,* Eyre and Spottiswoode, 1952, p. 290.
13 Ibid., p. 303; Haig's italics.
14 Richard Burdon Haldane, *An Autobiography,* Hodder and Stoughton, 1919, p. 200.
15 Lieutenant-General Sir John Monash, *War Letters,* Angus and Robertson, 1925.
16 Bean, op. cit., p. 187.
17 Monash, op. cit.
18 Author's papers. Haig must have misheard 'auctioneer' for 'engineer'.
19 C.R.A.: Chief of Royal Artillery Haig, 9 June; author's papers. He is still not clear about Monash's peacetime profession, but getting warmer.
20 Monash, op. cit.
21 Author's papers.

22 *War Letters of General Monash*. Monash, op. cit.
23 Lloyd George, op. cit., *War Memoirs*, ii, p. 1319.
24 From Monash, op. cit., 7 October; the figures of German prisoners, casualties, etc., refer to the achievement of the 3rd Australian Division only.
25 Monash, *The Australian Victories in France in 1918*, Angus and Robertson, 1936, pp. 284–9.
26 Ibid., p. 291.
27 Monash, *War Letters*, 3 April, 1918.
28 Monash, *Australian Victories in France*, p. 51; my italics.
29 Ibid., p. 227.
30 Bean, op. cit., p. 594.
31 For more on this see John Terraine, *The Road to Passchendaele*, Leo Cooper, 1977, pp. 223–4.
32 Haig, 1 July; Blake, op. cit., p. 316; my italics.
33 Monash, *Australian Victories in France*, p. 251; my italics.
34 Field-Marshal Lord Carver (ed.), *The War Lords*, Weidenfeld and Nicolson, 1976, p. 140.
35 Ibid., pp. 139–40.
36 Letter to the author, 1964.
37 Monash, *Australian Victories in France*, p, 50.
38 Lloyd George, op. cit., i, p. 93.

XXII

THE FUTILE MYTH:
'Futility' (1)

'. . . the monstrous futility of the war itself . . .'
(*Sunday Times* review of Richard Aldington's *Death of a Hero*,
22 September 1929)

'. . . the deep indignation with which he saw men uselessly
slaughtered . . .'
(*Time and Tide* review of Siegfried Sassoon's *Memoirs of an
Infantry Officer*, 1 November 1930)

'. . . an abiding sense of the futility of the grim struggle . . . the
folly of war . . .'
(*Sunday Despatch* review of same, 21 September 1930)

'. . . the futility of the nightmare through which he and his fellow
soldiers had passed.'
(*Daily Mirror* review of same, 22 September 1930)

'. . . angry against the people who see in war anything finer than a
supreme human disgrace.'
(*Tatler* review of Henry Williamson's *Patriot's Progress*, 18 May
1930)[1]

'On the score of courage, patriotism, sacrifice and death, we had
been deceived and with the first bullets we recognized at once the
falsity of anecdote, history, literature, art, the gossip of veterans,
and public speeches.'
(Translation of Jean Norton Cru, *Du Témoignage*, Librairie
Gillimard, Paris 1931, published as *War Books: A Study in Historical Criticism*, San Diego State University Press, 1976, p. 8)

'. . . there is nothing very new to learn about this war or the end it
was fought for; England had destroyed, as in each preceding
century, a trade rival.'
(John Maynard Keynes: *The Economic Consequences of the
Peace*, Macmillan, 1920, p. 30)[2]

Almost every part of the common mythology of the wars of the First Industrial Revolution is bad: bad professionally, bad politically, bad nationally, and ultimately bad internationally. The 'futility' myth is the worst of all, the destructive end product of all the rest. The steady repetition of the word 'futile', as I have said on p. 103, has much to answer for: it has helped to warp professional reappraisal, twist political intentions, rot national morale and confuse international relations. I have also said, elsewhere, speaking of British 'disenchantment' in the 1920s and 1930s:

'. . . disenchantment with the war bred distrust of all things military. Disarmament . . . became the great quest of the post-war years, and nowhere was it pursued more whole-heartedly than in Britain, where dread of military commitment was linked to dread of military expenditure, and both were excused by constant reference to the "futility of war".'[3]

Fundamentally, the 'futility myth' offers two arguments: that wars (especially the First World War) have been fought in a 'futile' manner, and that they have been fought for a 'futile' cause (or lack of cause). I have shown in Section VI how the failure to appreciate stern truths about the American Civil War helped to provide a basis for the futility myth of the First World War; in Section XI I have pointed out how the repeated use of the word 'futility' in association with the Battle of the Somme cast its evil shadow forward into the Second World War. These are examples of baleful mythology concerning the manner in which wars are fought, the failure to understand that it is above all the social and technological background that decides what that manner shall be. There are, of course, many other examples.

Inevitably one keeps returning to certain myth themes – the casualty theme, the generalship theme. It was the casualty theme that so excited Liddell Hart, and prompted his various theories of war, above all the theory of the 'indirect approach'. This theory had much to answer for in the Second World War. It was not a theory which made much appeal to the Germans, who generally assaulted their enemies head-on, often with excellent results, or the Russians, who always assaulted their enemies head-on and ultimately crushed them flat, or the Americans (excepting General MacArthur; but contrary to widespread belief it was not his command that was doing the hard work in the final stages of the war). The British, with or without acknowledgment to Liddell Hart, seem to have been obsessed by indirect approaches. Captain Stephen Roskill suggests a reason for this; writing of the period of

the National Government (1931–35) he says, very sensibly, that
defence failings during that period are as much due to opposition
attitudes as to Tory 'guilty men' or the Chiefs of Staff:

As to the latter it is appropriate to recall the obloquy heaped on the
soldiers and sailors of World War I – such as Kitchener, Haig and
Robertson, Fisher, Jellicoe and de Robeck – especially in Lloyd
George's and Churchill's war memoirs; and it is reasonable to suggest
that the treatment meted out to them may well have influenced, perhaps
subconsciously, the attitude and outlook of the men who, if another war
did come, were certain to be blamed for the deficiencies it would reveal
and the military defeats which would probably be suffered.[4]

To advocate preparation for another war of masses on the
European continent was not the way to professional advancement
for Service leaders in the 1930s; to advocate head-on encounters
with large enemy forces was not the way to win Churchill's esteem
between 1940 and 1945. Any kind of 'indirect approach', no matter
how expensive in skilled manpower or special equipment, seemed
better. 'Private armies' are a case in point. This was, *par eminence,*
the war of 'private armies'; they abounded in every theatre. The
result, as Field-Marshal Slim says,

was undoubtedly to lower the quality of the rest of the Army, especially of
the infantry, not only by skimming the cream off it, but by encouraging
the idea that certain of the normal operations of war were so difficult that
only specially equipped *corps d'élite* could be expected to undertake
them. Armies do not win wars by means of a few bodies of super-soldiers
but by the average quality of their standard units . . . The level of
initiative, individual training, and weapon skill required in, say, a
commando, is admirable; what is not admirable is that it should be
confined to a few small units. Any well-trained infantry battalion should
be able to do what a commando can do; in the Fourteenth Army they
could and did. This cult of special forces is as sensible as to form a Royal
Corps of Tree Climbers and say that no soldier, who does not wear its
green hat with a bunch of oak leaves stuck in it, should be expected to
climb a tree.[5]

Slim spoke with some feeling, because the biggest, most
expensive 'private army' of them all was formed at his expense:
Major-General Orde Wingate's 'Special Force', the 'Chindits'.
The first Chindit operation (LONGCLOTH) in 1943 has much to
commend it, despite its nearly 30 per cent casualties; at a time when
the morale of the British and Indian forces in the Burma theatre

was unquestionably low, Wingate's feat behind the Japanese lines showed conclusively that the enemy could be beaten in the jungle. His big operation the following year (THURSDAY), in which he lost his life, was more ambitious but less fruitful. Using, according to the latest historian of the Chindits, 'the equivalent of a small army corps',[6] his achievement nevertheless 'had no significant bearing on the main course of the war'.[7] When the remains of the élite Chindit columns were pulled out of Burma after nearly six months of gruelling warfare, it was found that 50 per cent of the survivors were unfit for further service. It was a high price to pay for an indirect approach to nowhere.

What made it the more galling for a general like Slim was that his Fourteenth Army was at the time locked in decisive battle with the Japanese Burma army's main body at Imphal and Kohima – and finding itself at critical stages desperately short of British infantry. Infantry was what the mythologists had said would not be needed, yet by 1944–45 this shortage was felt more or less acutely in every theatre. In Italy, American officers were heard to remark that the British habitually sent a boy to do a man's job; this sometimes meant that the job would have to be done all over again, with the result that already weak units would be weakened even more. In north-west Europe it was noted by the Germans that British infantry sought 'to occupy ground rather than fight over it'.[8] British commanders from Field-Marshal Montgomery downwards showed themselves reluctant to accept casualties; one reason for this, as a recent biographer of the Field-Marshal says, is that 'he was careful of his diminishing supply of British troops'.[9] Yet, as we have seen (p. 51), mobilization both in the United Kingdom and in the British Empire was substantially larger in the Second World War than in the First. What had gone wrong?

Table L (p. 219) supplies most of the answer, and I would suggest that the most significant figure in it is the peak strength of the Royal Air Force in June 1944 – 1,012,000 (to compare, say, with 1,037,600 for the entire B.E.F. in February 1916). The drop of some 50,000 by June 1945 is accounted for by a combing out – in order to reinforce the infantry, whom air and mechanized forces were supposed to replace, according to the 'experts' and mythologists. The irony is that the very preservation of the R.A.F. between the wars had at times depended on the promise that 'above all it was to be small and therefore cheap',[10] and on the fact that it developed methods of policing the wilder parts of the Empire which, says Sir Maurice Dean, 'proved far more effective and far less expensive in lives and material than the older military methods'.[11] The R.A.F., then, was supposed to be a means of avoiding both mass manpower mobilization, and mass casualties. As an American historian remarks:

One of Churchill's primary preoccupations (one might almost say obsessions) throughout the war was the avoidance of mass British casualties. The national hemorrhage of World War I, and its cost to British greatness, weighed heavily on English minds and inevitably affected strategic thinking. Churchill's addiction to peripheral operations . . . and strategic bombing was in part the product of the British past . . . 'Victory Through Air Power' seemed a cheap way to win.[12]

Churchill was not the only one. That life-saving quality which such different people as John Connell and General Guderian attributed to tanks (see pp. 156-7) was attributed by others to the air supremacy which America and Britain undoubtedly obtained; thus Sir Maurice Dean:

'The contribution of this factor to the saving of human lives, especially soldiers' lives, is beyond computation, but it was without question immense. In the First World War, 750,000 members of the Armed Forces from Britain were killed. In the Second World War this grievous total was divided by three.'[13]

And here lies the second irony. (The first being, the development of the R.A.F. into a mass Service.) One of the aspects of the First World War, especially on the Western Front, that had so appalled Lloyd George (see p. 103) and Churchill was the loss of officers, the flower of the nation, the natural leaders of the rising generation. The total number of British officers killed during the First World War, including the Royal Navy and the R.A.F., was 38,834.[14] The total of aircrew of Bomber Command, exactly the same type of men, killed during the Second World War was 55,573.[15] Soldiers' lives were indeed saved, but not by the R.A.F.; they were saved, as I have repeated before, because the Army did far less fighting than between 1914 and 1918.[16] Officers were less fortunate; yet even as we reflect on this great increase of officer mortality produced by the life-saving weapon, we must remember that our experience, sad though it was, was again far surpassed. The United States Army Air Force lost 120,000 aircrew.[17]

So we see how the deep-rooted casualty myth melded with the futility myth, together lending unhappy weight to a weaponry myth. This is not a treatise on contemporary defence problems, but before moving on I would say this: any part or combination of these myths still extant cannot fail to be damaging to the rational consideration of defence now and in the future.

I intend to return in a moment to the generalship myth, to note some further unfortunate results arising from it. First, however, it is valuable to look at its 'reverse side' – a belief which became widespread, in democracies above all, that not merely generals, but actually any officers above regimental rank are 'irrelevant' to the true consideration of war. In its purest form it is stated by M. Jean Norton Cru:

If anyone knows war, it is the lower ranks, from private to captain; what we see, what we live, 'is'; what contradicts our experience 'is not', whether it comes from the general-in-chief, from the Memoirs of Napoleon, from the theories of the War College, or from the unanimous judgment of all the historians of war. There was nothing boastful in this attitude of ours. We were none the prouder for knowing what Joffre and Foch did not know. We knew because our five senses, the flesh of our bodies repeated to us for months on end the same impressions and the same sensations. The high command could not know, for only their intelligence was in contact with the war, and war is not to be perceived by the intelligence alone . . .'[18]

This is a very remarkable expression of sentiments which have attracted many admirers, among old soldiers, naturally, each one convinced that *his* war was *the* war, and that nothing else was, and among those with a disposition to take automatically an 'underdog' view. It requires some analysis, and with all respect to its author that analysis does require some application of intelligence.

First we must consider who these lower ranks were. I find it difficult to believe that M. Jean Norton Cru, means the clerks and typists at G.H.Q. or other headquarters; I don't think he means the lower ranks of, say, the Service Corps or the Ordnance Corps at base depôts; does he even mean the gunners, bombardiers or section commanders of the Artillery? I believe M. Cru means, quite simply, the front-line infantry, war's chief sufferers. Now what is their rôle? Very frigidly, it may be put like this: to advance, with their personal weapons and such others as are permitted to them, against enemy positions when ordered to do so; to defend positions against enemy attack when ordered to do so; to submit to death or wounds in the cause of victory when ordered to do so. That is what is expected of them: all that; no more. Performing battle is their function; without them there could be no battle, no war.

Let us consider 'performing battle'. Since I have not been in one, I shall let one who has had that experience speak for me, a British ex-soldier this time, unfortunately anonymous, but clearly an infantryman. He was one of many who were prompted by the B.B.C.'s famous television series, 'The Great War' (1964), to put some serious thoughts down on paper; I was involved in making that series, and I took care to preserve my copy. Casualties are the first subject he deals with; he points to ways in which confusion has surrounded it, and continues:

Of all aspects of the war on the Western Front the prospect of death or mutilation was the one which weighed most heavily on the minds of men. It was a factor of immeasurably greater importance than the transient rigours imposed by cold, rain, mud, vermin, dirt, smell and toil. Such things afflicted men temporarily. They came and went, taking their modest toll, and there was an end to them for the time being. By the prevailing standard of the time they left men little the worse. In prospect men approached them with nothing more than the utmost distaste. In experiencing them they were moved to a greater or lesser degree of physical misery, which was stoically accepted in the knowledge that these things would not last. Such an attitude and philosophy requires no explanation, and can be fully understood by all men by reason of their common experience. But fear of death or mutilation was a different matter altogether, and this fear was always with them. It is not intended to imply that men brooded on it. Healthy young men cannot be said to brood on contingencies which have not yet arisen however speedy and certain their arrival. It is the nature of youth to be sanguine. Outwardly therefore they lived as cheerfully and hopefully as their immediate circumstances allowed, but at the back of their minds lay their apprehensions. The possibility of dying was very often an immediate possibility, often a possibility lying a week away, and, very occasionally, a possibility which approached from a distance of as much as two months. But, if it was not actually standing across a man's path, it was approaching, and its approach was inexorable.

This man belonged to one of the regular battalions which went out to France in August 1914 and remained on the Western Front throughout the War, a period of nearly fifty-two months. He tabulates this battalion's experience as follows:

1	Numbers who served with the Battalion	8,313
2	Killed and died of wounds	1,462
3	Wounded (including gassed)	3,648
4	Invalided to U.K. sick	2,066
5	Transferred to units in U.K.	227
6	Transferred to other battalions and units	896
7	Commissioned in field and transferred	11
8	Drowned	1
9	Shot by order of Field General Court Martial	2

Notes

1   The figure above under item 4, 'Invalided to U.K. sick, 2,066', is suspect. It has been extracted by me as the necessary figure to strike the balance with the total of 8,313 who passed through the Battalion.
2   I do not know if those 'Commissioned in field' (11) are also included in the heading 'Transferred to other battalions and units' (896) or not.
3   'Wounded' indicates cases of wounding. The man who joined the battalion and was wounded, recovered, rejoined it a second time, and got wounded a second time, would appear twice in the category of 'numbers served' and twice in the category of 'wounded'.
4   There is no mention in the table of Prisoners of War. I do not know under what heading they appear, nor can I find their numbers, but there is a note which states that fourteen men of the battalion died as prisoners of war. Some of these would, I presume, have died of wounds. If pushed to give an arbitrary figure of prisoners, I would put it at about 250.

There is, of course, one interesting omission from this table: the survivors. To complete our picture we need to know how many there were in the ranks of the battalion at the Armistice; since our informant was presumably one of them, it is odd that he should leave them out.

Still more interesting, however, is his statement that during the whole of the time that this unit was in France, nearly fifty-two months, 'It appears that there were, as far as I can find, about 20 days in which the whole battalion was in general and active conflict with the enemy.'[19] What this means is that while, as he says, the apprehension of death or mutilation in battle was permanent, the actual experience of battle itself was spasmodic. The War, however, was continuous, not spasmodic, so clearly 'knowing' battle is not the same as 'knowing' war. By M. Cru's definition of 'knowing war', we would have to accept that this, if confined to the lower ranks as he says, would mean that war could only be known by inert portions of sentient matter, but not by human soldiers. These portions of matter would be capable of dying, of experiencing the pain of mutilation, and the terrors of the spasmodic battles, but they would not require to eat or drink, to be clothed, sheltered, equipped or armed; they would need no ammunition, no medicine, no surgery, no dentistry, no transportation, no wash-houses, no spiritual or creature comforts. Yet the human soldier needs all these, and more, not spasmodically, but *all the time*. Without these things there is no such thing as an army, only a crowd of starving, naked, unarmed

men, bound soon to die of hunger, exposure or disease. Surely it is
an integral part of 'knowing' war – war as it is, day in, day out,
battle or no battle – to ensure that such things do not happen. This
is one of the functions – some would say, the chief function – of
the higher ranks. That, by and large, they carried it out with very
considerable skill is shown by the fact that in most armies the
human soldiers who depended on it took it so much for granted that
they did not even notice.[20]

So we return to the generals, and their myth. One form of it is the
widely held belief that the British generals of the Second World
War were, quite simply, 'better' than those of the First. (It is to be
noted that the question is hardly ever raised in terms of the generals
of other nations.) Before making any detailed comment on this
belief, I should like to remark that, in general, historical
comparisons of this kind are unrewarding, because of the difficulty
of comparing like with like. Once technological change began to
accelerate – e.g. in the Industrial Revolution – this difficulty
intensified. Before the Industrial Revolution the pace of change
was much statelier: the Tower musket ('Brown Bess') was
introduced in the reign of William III and remained the basic
British infantry weapon until the Indian Mutiny some 160 years
later; H.M.S. *Victory* was forty years old when she sailed into the
Battle of Trafalgar – and so on. Even so, I wonder whether there is
any real profit to be had from asking whether Nelson was 'better'
than, say, Lord Hawke or Admiral Blake,[21] whether Wellington
was 'better' than Marlborough, or vice versa. With even more
widely separated persons there is even less to be gained: all one can
usefully say is that, for example, Julius Caesar and Gustavus
Adolphus were both highly skilful commanders of their day.
Comparing Genghiz Khan and Marshal Murat does not help at all;
comparing Murat with General J. E. B. Stuart does not help much;
comparing Stuart with General Philip Sheridan helps a great deal.

That said, let us look again at the two generations of British
generals. I have already pointed out the immense quantity of
technological innovation which the First World War generation
had to face; it need only be said here that land warfare in the
Second World War produced no new problems, only new answers
to old problems. The next thing that needs to be said is that it is just
not possible to compare any British field commander of the Second
World War with the Western Front generals of 1916–18. To give
but one example of what I mean: on 21 March 1918, General Sir
Julian Byng, commanding the Third Army, and General Sir
Hubert Gough, commanding the Fifth Army, found themselves in

action against fifty different German divisions, identified on that day by British Intelligence, with more to come. No British general of the Second World War ever faced such an onset, or anything remotely like it. Indeed, the only British commanding general who was even involved in a large action against the main body of the main enemy during the whole war was Field-Marshal Lord Gort in 1940. But, as Table G (p. 129) shows, the absolute maximum that his small expeditionary force faced was sixteen German divisions. When the British Army returned to north-west Europe in 1944, it very quickly became the decidedly junior partner in a campaign which itself was only engaging a fragment of the main enemy. So comparisons with the Western Front generals are impossible; there was no Haig in the Second World War, no one in that war ever had such a job to do. On the other hand, I would suggest that there does exist a useful comparison for Haig, both in his capacity as commander of a group of armies and as a national Commander-in-Chief: General Ulysses Grant in 1864–65. Much can be learned by studying them together.

We lack, then, the requisite knowledge of the real capacities of the Second World War generals; we simply don't know how they would have measured up in the 'big league'. With some, the indications are that they would have measured up very well, but we don't *know*. The only real comparisons that we can make are with such men as General Sir Ian Hamilton, Commander-in-Chief at Gallipoli, Generals Sir John Maxwell, Sir Archibald Murray and Sir Edmund Allenby, successive Commanders-in-Chief in Egypt and Palestine, Generals Sir J. E. Nixon, Sir P. Lake and Sir Stanley Maude in Mesopotamia, and General Sir George Milne at Salonika. All except the last were engaged against a very tough secondary enemy, Turkey. The Turks were hard to beat despite their grave material shortages; beyond saying that I think they were harder to beat than the secondary enemy of the Second World War, Italy, I see no advantage in detailed comparison with Lord Wavell, General Cunningham, Sir Claude Auchinleck, Lord Alexander, General Anderson or General Maitland Wilson. Both generations had a mixed record of failure and success; both were ultimately successful, which is what finally counts.

War in the Far East, 1941–44, endorses this picture. When the claim is made for the 'superiority' of the second generation, it does not usually embrace such names as General Percival, who surrendered in Singapore, General Hutton, the first C.-in-C. to face the Japanese in Burma, or General Irwin, who unsuccessfully attempted a counter-offensive in that theatre in 1943. If Field-

Marshal Lord Alexander were judged only by the outcome of his tenure of command in Burma (a continuous retreat with no Corunna or Marne at the end of it) his reputation, except among a handful of professionals, would not be great. Lieutenant-General W. J. (later Field-Marshal Lord) Slim took part in that retreat and might have found his way to an early scrap-heap on that account. Instead, however, he remained to command the Fourteenth Army in its magnificent advance from Imphal back to Rangoon in 1944–45. This was unquestionably one of the finest feats of the British (and Indian) Army in that war. Yet even here the historian wryly notes that the Japanese forces in Burma in 1945 amounted only to some 9 divisions out of an order of battle containing 174 divisions.[22]

It is Slim, who as well as being a fine soldier was also a fine writer, who gives us the yardstick by which the maligned generation of the First World War should be judged. Writing of 1942 and that horrible retreat to India, he says:

'Defeat is bitter. Bitter to the common soldier, but trebly bitter to his general. The soldier may comfort himself with the thought that, whatever the result, he has done his duty faithfully and steadfastly, but the commander has failed in *his* duty if he has not won victory – for that *is* his duty. He has no other comparable to it.'[23]

This is surely the truth; it is his estimated capacity to obtain victory that entitles a general to his badges of rank, his quarters, his A.D.C.s, the salutes of the Quarter-Guard, and the salary he receives. The careers of unvictorious generals are apt (though not bound) to come to sudden, ignominious halts. Now, in this fundamental requirement, it is a simple historical fact that the British generals of the First World War, whatever their faults, did not fail in their duty.

It was not a British delegation that crossed the lines with a white flag in November 1918.

No German Army of Occupation was stationed on the Thames, the Humber or the Tees.

No British Government was forced to sign a humiliating peace treaty.

The British generals had done their duty; their army and their country were on the winning side. That is the only proper, the only *sensible* starting point for an examination of their quality.

Unfortunately, Churchill for one did not see it that way – unfortunately for the next generation. Steeped in a mythology about First World War generals which he had himself done much to manufacture, Churchill approached those of the Second World War with profound reservations. Some of these were in due course overcome, others led to much harassment and discord; Wavell and Auchinleck were the chief recipients of the latter (the former, with more justification than the mythology of that War generally allows). Sir Alan Brooke, as Chief of the Imperial General Staff, had to expend much energy defending these officers against the Prime Minister's hostility, in addition to the time he had to spend (at all hours of the day or night) combating Churchill's strategic vagaries.

The post of C.I.G.S. is one of the two areas where a direct comparison can be made between the incumbents of the two wars. Sir William Robertson, between 1916 and 1918, had similar problems; he and his assistant, Major-General Sir Frederick Maurice (Director of Military Operations), were, in the words of General Spears, 'daily on the track of Mr Lloyd George's strategic conceptions'.[24] Colonel Repington said to Maurice in September 1917

'that after the war it would be found that 50 per cent. of the time and energy of soldiers had been expended in fighting their own politicians. M. thought that my percentage was much too low.'[25]

Here again, all that one can say is that the country was well served by the two officers who occupied what was a very 'hot seat' in both wars. Robertson and Brooke both fought the good fight for the principles of war; neither ever compromised on a principle. Robertson was forced out of office by Lloyd George in February 1918; Brooke lasted the course and in the end was accepted by Churchill as a friend. But Churchill was a much nicer man than Lloyd George – and Brooke did have a support that Robertson never had: the Chiefs of Staff Committee (see p. 81). It must have made a great difference, not to be a lone voice.

The other important post where a comparison can profitably be made is that of Commander-in-Chief, India. Here again the British Empire had the good fortune to be served by two most able officers at the critical time – though again neither found much favour in Churchill's eyes. General Sir Charles Monro arrived in India to take up the post of C.-in-C. on 1 November 1916. Prior to that he had been commanding the First Army in France; in 1915 he was sent to the Dardanelles to report on the advisability or otherwise of evacuation. He recommended (with the virtually unanimous support of senior officers on the spot) that the Peninsula should be evacuated. This aroused Churchill's deep wrath; he fixed a cruel label on Monro. In *The World Crisis* he called him

'an officer of swift decision. He came, he saw, he capitulated.'[26]

Nor did Churchill think fit to amend that wounding judgment in the light of Monro's later career; yet that career was remarkable.

At the outbreak of war in 1914 the strength of the Indian Army was 159,134. By the time of Monro's arrival, over two years later, astonishing though it may seem, only three new battalions had been added to its strength. C. T. Atkinson tells us:

It is from the autumn of 1916, when General Sir Charles Monro arrived in India, that the development of a new system of recruiting, the consequent expansion of the Indian Army, and the great increase in India's share of the Empire's burden should be dated . . . As a result of these new methods the supply of recruits increased enormously. In 1917 nearly as many recruits were taken as had come in up to the end of 1916, and in consequence the number of additional battalions rose to over 50 before the end of the year . . . The expansion of the Indian Army by another 50 battalions between March and May 1918 allowed of the 'Indianization' of the bulk of the Egyptian Expeditionary Force . . . When the difficulties not only of recruiting, raising and equipping so largely augmented an army, but of providing it with British officers, are taken into consideration, the expansion of the Indian Army in the years 1917 and 1918 will be seen to rank high among great administrative achievements . . .[27]

By the end of the War, India had raised 1,440,437 men, and 'was the one portion of the British Empire whose effective man-power was still increasing'. Small wonder that Sir William Robertson was heard to remark: 'No C.-in-C. in India, not even Bobs,[28] did as much as Monro.'[29]

He had a worthy follower. When General Sir Claude Auchinleck returned to resume his old position as C.-in-C., India, in June 1943, he found potentially disastrous administrative chaos in the supply department, just as a new South East Asia Command was about to be set up with the mission of passing once and for all to the offensive in Burma. Auchinleck had to make that offensive possible – and this against a background of political disturbance far more serious than anything during the First World War, as well as catastrophic flood and famine in Bengal. How well he succeeded is expressed by the man who knew best, Field-Marshal Slim:

'It was a good day for us when he took command of India, our main base, recruiting area, and training ground. The Fourteenth Army, from its birth to its final victory, owed much to his unselfish support and never-failing understanding. Without him and what he and the Army in India did for us we could not have existed, let alone conquered.'[30]

Churchill, however, was never persuaded of Auchinleck's merits; he never even admitted that Auchinleck was the first British general of that war to beat a German general in battle (see p. 66). No doubt it was all part of that fatal mythology about generals which had formed in his mind during the previous war; he had a ready disposition to blame them for almost anything. As Minister of Munitions, 1917–18, he, better than anyone, should have known and understood the curious difficulties of tank production. Yet this fact was never properly grasped during the Second World War; it was easier to blame the generals for mishandling the tanks (and it must be admitted that they *were* often mishandled – the fruit of more mythology) than to produce the right tanks for the job. As a dismal consequence, from beginning to almost the very end Britain was unable to produce a good, sound 'work-horse' tank like the Panzer IV, the Sherman or the T-34. The really good British tanks only began to appear late in 1944 and in 1945. The rôle of anti-tank guns, which the Germans were already beginning to grasp in 1918, was never appreciated.

It was Churchill who uttered the famous phrase, 'their finest hour', in 1940. The demeanour of the British people in that year, under great trial, was certainly superior to that of the civilian population between 1914 and 1918. It is a pity, however, that Churchill, with his mastery of inspiring words, was never able to see that the 'finest hour' of the British Army was undoubtedly its great defensive and offensive victories in 1918; had he perceived this, he might have gone on to ask himself why, with profitable results. He would have understood better the true nature of war in his time. A mythology which caused praise to be withheld from deserving men in one generation led to serious difficulties for other deserving men in the next – and to a new mythology of over-praise, potentially just as damaging. Will we never learn?

---

1   All these excerpts are culled from pp. 434–5 of Corelli Barnett's *The Collapse of British Power*, Eyre Methuen, 1972. Pp. 424–35 of that book contain a masterly statement on the 'disenchantment' of the 1930s.
2   Quoted by Major-General J. F. C. Fuller, *The Conduct of War 1789–1961*, Eyre and Spottiswoode, 1961, p. 144.

3   John Terraine, *The Mighty Continent*, B.B.C. and Hutchinson, 1974.
4   Captain Stephen Roskill, *Hankey: Man of Secrets*, Collins, 1974, iii, p. 176.
5   Field-Marshal Lord Slim, *Defeat into Victory*, Cassell, 1956, pp. 546–7.
6   Shelford Bidwell, *The Chindit War: The Campaign in Burma 1944*, Hodder and Stoughton, 1979, p. 74.
7   *Daily Telegraph*, 13 September 1979: review of *The Chindit War* by Ronald Lewin.
8   Chester Wilmot, *The Struggle for Europe*, Collins, 1952, p. 519.
9   Alun Chalfont, *Montgomery of Alamein*, Weidenfeld and Nicolson, 1976, p. 243.
10 Sir Maurice Dean, *The Royal Air Force and Two World Wars*, Cassell, 1979, p. 37.
11 Ibid., p. 35.
12 Hanson W. Baldwin, *The Crucial Years 1939–41*, Weidenfeld and Nicolson, 1976, p. 192.
13 Dean, op. cit., p. 237. 750,000 is a 'round figure'.
14 O.H., *1918*, v, p. 597.
15 Peter Young, *World War 1939–1945*, Arthur Barker, 1966, p. 265.
16 See Table G (p. 129).
17 Young, op. cit., p. 265.
18 Jean Norton Cru, *War Books*, pp. 8–9.
19 These are 'days of battle', when the battalion 'went over the bags', or defended itself aganst heavy attack. Of course, far more time than this was spent in front-line contact with the enemy, which might be a quiet experience or quite the reverse. The French liked to keep their 'quiet fronts' quiet, the British were more active. My anonymous informant estimates that in his battalion, 'from every 100 men among the companies there was, each month, an average casualty toll ᴄ‘6 killed, 14 wounded, 10 evacuated sick or transferred to other units, and 70 who survived unhurt.'
       In October 1917 General Maurice (D.M.O.) informed the War Cabinet that 'the normal average monthly casualties, when there was no severe fighting, was 35,000' for the whole B.E.F. (War Cabinet No. 263, 2 Nov.; CAB 23/4).
20 The ordinary soldier's experience of battle seems to me to be a constant. I know no better description (out of hundreds) of that private world of mysterious movement, incomprehensible behaviour, abrupt outrage and devouring fear than Stephen Crane's *The Red Badge of Courage*, a story of the American Civil War which first appeared in 1895.
21 It could be argued that the French and Spanish (and Danish) fleets which Nelson encountered had none of the tough professional seamanship of the Dutch in Blake's day.
22 Major-General S. Woodburn Kirby, *The War Against Japan*, H.M.S.O. 1969, v, Appendix 10 (pp. 461–4). This shows that the main body of the Japanese Army, sixty-four divisions, was in Japan itself (June 1945) and the Kurile Islands, awaiting the assault of Admiral Nimitz's Central Pacific Command, and possibly the Russians. There were a further nineteen divisions in Manchuria and Korea; there were thirty-two in China; twenty-seven in General Douglas MacArthur's South-West Pacific Command area (part of which was about to be transferred to S.E.A.C) and six in Indo-China and Siam.
23 Slim, op. cit., p. 121.
24 Sir Edward Spears, *Prelude to Victory*, Jonathan Cape, 1939, p. 36.
25 Colonel Repington, *The First World War*, Constable, 1920, ii, p. 58.
26 Odham's Ed., 1938, ii, p. 908.
27 In *The Empire at War*, ed. Sir Charles Lucas, O.U.P., 1926, vol. v.
28 Field-Marshal Lord Roberts of Kandahar.
29 General Sir George Barrow, *The Life of Sir Charles Carmichael Monro*, Hutchinson, 1931, p. 249.
30 Slim, op. cit., p. 176. N.B. Total voluntary recruitment to the Indian Forces, 1939–45, was about 2 million.

XXIII

Table L

Anti-Myth: 'A Matter of Flesh and Blood'*

Strength of the Armed Forces of the United Kingdom

	Royal Navy	*Army*	*Royal Air Force*
November 1918	407,316	3,563,466	293,532
August 1939	161,000	402,000	118,000
June 1940	276,000	1,656,000	291,000
June 1941	405,000	2,221,000	665,000
June 1942	507,000	2,468,000	840,000
June 1943	671,000	2,692,000	969,000
June 1944	790,000	2,742,000	1,012,000
June 1945	789,000	2,931,000	963,000

*See p. 59

The Women's Auxiliary Services (including Nursing Services) reached a maximum strength of 446,000 in June 1944. The Home Guard reached a peak of 1,784,000 by the middle of 1943, dropping away to about 1¾ million thereafter.

All Second World War figures from Cmd. 6832, H.M.S.O. 1946.

XXIV

THE FUTILE MYTH:
'Futility' (2)

' "But what good came of it at last?"
Quoth little Peterkin.
"Why, that I cannot tell," said he,
But 'twas a famous victory".'
(Robert Southey, 'The Battle of Blenheim')

There appears to be a deep-seated, perhaps ineradicable, instinct of self-denigration among the 'Anglo-Saxon' peoples. Each of their wars in the period of the First Industrial Revolution has its accompaniment of disparagement mounting at times to absolute vilification. 'Futility' is the tag-word of much of this. Clearly, a civil war, offering the spectacle of actual families, as well as the great national 'family', divided among themselves, lends itself readily to such a tag; the American Civil War was no exception. It was all very well for Lord Morley, for example (a man of pacific principles which caused him to resign from the British government in August 1914), to call America's struggle

'the only war in modern times as to which we can be sure, first, that no skill or patience of diplomacy could have avoided it, and second, that preservation of the American Union and abolition of Negro slavery were two vast triumphs of good by which even the inferno of war was justified.'[1]

Morley could remember that war; he could remember its profound impact on British Liberals; its justifications were untarnished in his mind. Not so with the revisionists, who multiplied, and put forward a multiplicity of arguments, arriving at the harsh conclusion that

'The men of 1860–61 allowed an academic argument about "an imaginary Negro in an impossible place" to end in a bloody Civil War'.[2]

Exactly the same process of standing beliefs on their heads began to take place with the First World War even before it ended, composing a mythology of futility that would fill volumes by itself. The British version contributed handsomely to the moral and material weakening of the nation between the wars and to international impotence later in the face of the threat from the Dictators. Thanks to the demoniac qualities of one of these, Adolf Hitler, it is less easy to say bluntly that the Second World War was 'futile'; the erosion of virtue has to be more subtle. One form of it, superficially possessing considerable plausibility and proferred with varying degrees of sarcasm, is the comment that the painful overthrow of one form of dictatorship merely left the democracies to face another, equally deplorable, in a much weaker state. Erosion is also achieved by stressing that the motives with which people and nations entered the war have no connection with what they achieved in the course of it, and by asserting that some of the methods employed by the victors (e.g. area bombing) placed them in the same moral category as their enemies.

It seems to me that this curious tendency, which is particularly evident among the British and Americans, may have at its root a very simple fact. England has not been successfully invaded by a foreign army since the Norman Conquest in 1066; the Spanish Armada came to grief in 1588; Napoleon could only bluster and threaten – his 'Army of England' ended up in Austria; the reality of Hitler's Operation Sealion in 1940 remains in doubt. America has not even been menaced by foreign attack since the conquest of Canada removed the French threat to the Thirteen Colonies in 1759–60. This is a very significant immunity; it deprives the populations of both countries of a powerful war motive. Consequently, in order to rally them behind a prolonged effort, appeal has to be made elsewhere – to idealism, to the idea of 'progress', to 'a better world after the war'. Whatever jars against this idea, at the time or later, contributes to the notion of 'futility'. In the two World Wars, both British and Americans had to be *for* a great cause; it was not enough to be *against*.

In the American Civil War, of course, it *was* enough. To fight for the Union, or for States' Rights, was a powerful motive indeed and there were others; but fighting against slavery was something else entirely. As Mr Peter Parish says:

'Slavery was at the root of the argument between North and South, slavery was the obvious difference between the two sections, slavery aroused conflicting passions, principles and interests. It presented a moral issue, a political issue, an economic issue, a racial issue, an ideological issue and a highly emotional issue.'[3]

The revisionists, however valuable much of their work is in bringing forward important new facts, chip in vain at this massive bed-rock of actuality. Contemporary awareness of racial tension in America also beats vainly on it; the low standard of living of many American Negroes today, the lack of opportunity which faces so many of them, the racial prejudice which persists against them more than a century after the end of the Civil War, do not make that war 'futile'. The matter can be put to a simple test: would anyone, anyone at all, outside a lunatic asylum, be found in America now who would regard a programme to 'bring back Slavery' as anything but grotesque? That matter was settled in the Civil War; whatever the reasoning or motivation of individual Americans, America had declared herself decisively *against* the institution of slavery, and that was enough to justify that war.

The First World War did not touch America in anything like the same degree, for obvious reasons: a remote theatre, a shorter duration, much less fighting, much less loss. The foreign place-names never became 'household' words, like Manassas, Vicksburg, Antietam, Chancellorsville, Gettysburg and the rest. When it was over, the temptations to return at once to an isolationism which promised not only escape from the price of such distant aberrations, but also virtually limitless material prosperity for a surprisingly large number of people, proved overwhelming; for a long time America was frankly bored by the First World War, and to this day many Americans find it a lump of quite indigestible matter.

For Britain it was altogether different; the First World War was a national trauma which has not yet been exorcised. The British people found themselves involved in the War to an unprecedented and unique degree. It was not merely that it cost them a lot of money, put them to a great deal of inconvenience and caused them much sorrow; it violated their sense of history as well as their human feelings. Accustomed during a century of sensational growth to wars of 'limited liability' (even South Africa cost only 22,000 British lives in two and a half years of war, of whom less than 6,000 died in battle), once the British began to appreciate what the War was doing to them a deep sense of 'wrongness' began to take hold. To keep them going they needed idealistic aims; this shocking experience needed to be justified by the creation of a 'land fit for heroes to live in'; above all it had to be 'the war to end wars'.

Such beliefs were much fortified by the insularity and ignorance of foreign situations which were common not merely in the uneducated classes, but among Britons of all degrees and persuasions. Thus Professor Fussell quotes, without comment, Siegfried Sassoon; in *Memoirs of an Infantry Officer* the latter's soldier-hero George Sherston reaches the point where he 'learns "the truth about the war"; that it is ruining England and has no reason for continuing'.[4] That would be at some point in 1916 or 1917. Ruin, of course, means different things to different men; we have already seen (p. 204) that to John Maynard Keynes the only significant thing about the War was that 'England had destroyed a trade rival'. President Woodrow Wilson, who never relinquished a fine command of fatuity, was of similar opinion and told his fellow countrymen in 1919: 'This war, in its inception, was a commercial and industrial war. It was not a political war.'[5] Major-General J. F. C. Fuller still believed this in 1961. All these assertions – and their ten thousand echoes – are reflections only of endemic insularity, of the inability of even very talented and in some ways very perceptive men to grasp that the First World War was indeed a *world* war, not a private contest between the English middle class (or the American Expeditionary Force) and the German Empire.

Did Sassoon (writing in 1930) really believe that Gavrilo Princip and his associates would have responded favourably if 'George Sherston' or some other had said to them in Sarajevo on that fatal 28 June 1914:

'Stay your hands! Do you not realise that this deed which you intend to commit will ruin England?'

Would the Imperial Government in Vienna have withheld its ultimatum to Serbia on 23 July, if Keynes or another prognosticator had warned them:

'What you are about to do will merely bring about the trade defeat of your German allies'?

Did the Poles (who had not possessed a country since 1795), the Finns, the Balts, the Czechs, the Yugoslavs and the Arabs (all of whom obtained independence through it) agree with Woodrow Wilson that 'it was not a political war'?

It would, of course, be ridiculous to say that the liberation of
Eastern and Central European people or Arabs in the Middle East
from the more or less oppressive régimes of the Tsar, the Emperor
and the Sultan was a conscious British war aim (any more than it
was a conscious aim of any significant number of British men in
uniform to emancipate their women-folk).[6] Yet a great surge of
national liberation and female emancipation were unquestionably
among the products of the war – for many a quite sufficient 'reason
for continuing'. Even so, although these certainly were causes for
which it was not despicable to fight,[7] what really mattered was,
once more, what was being fought *against*. This was displayed with
perfect clarity in 1918. It was in that year that the nature of a
German peace was seen: the Treaty of Brest-Litovsk, between
defeated Russia and the victorious Central Powers, was signed on 3
March. The Bolshevik Government had come to power in 1917 on
the slogan: 'Down with the War!' Now it fulfilled its pledge to the
Russian people – to their cost. By the terms of this Treaty,

Russia lost a territory (301,000 square miles) nearly as large as Austria-
Hungary and Turkey combined; fifty-six million inhabitants, or 32 per
cent. of the whole population of the country; a third of her railway
mileages; 73 per cent. of her total iron and 89 per cent. of her total coal
production; and over 5,000 factories, mills, distilleries, and refineries. By
a supplementary agreement signed in August she paid to Germany an
indemnity of 6,000,000,000 marks.[8]

A Bolshevik delegate, G. I. Sokolnikov, understandably called
Brest-Litovsk 'a peace which Russia, grinding its teeth, is forced to
accept'. To make certain that everyone understood that this was
how Germany interpreted victory in war, the demonstration was
shortly repeated, by the Treaty of Bucharest with defeated
Romania on 7 May. The German High Command actually found
this rather disappointing:

The Dobrudja question was left unsettled . . . Constanta did not become a
German port as the O.H.L. wished, but became a free port, although the
distinction between the two was somewhat academic. Germany was able
to make a profit of about 2½ billion marks by insisting that money to
cover the new currency – the 'German lei' – be deposited in Berlin
banks. Germans had the right of veto over every Romanian ministry, and
control over the railways, telegraph and post. Romanian oilfields were to
be controlled by a consortium of the '3 D-banks' – the Deutsche Bank,
Discontogesellschaft and the Dresdner Bank. All 'surplus' agricultural
produce was to be delivered to the Central Powers. Up until the very last
moment the O.H.L. tried to torpedo the negotiations on the grounds that
this peace was too weak . . .[9]

These two draconian treaties show us what the War was really about: it was *against* the imposition of such terms on France, Belgium – or Britain. Surely that was enough? One is left baffled and appalled at the apparent 'invisibility' of these transactions, and the complete neglect of them by so many writers on the War. Progressives and backwoodsmen alike, the British disregarded foreign experience, ('a faraway country . . . people of whom we know nothing'[10]), shrugged off the Treaties of Brest-Litovsk and Bucharest once the War was over, and dismissed the question of what price they might themselves have had to pay if the German March-April offensive had succeeded. And soon they began to mouth that empty word 'futility', which contributed so handsomely to their further misfortune in the 1930s and later when idealism collapsed in the face of naked power.

As I have said, Hitler's régime was such that even the devotees of disparagement have difficulty in finding ultimate 'futility' in the Second World War. Like certain horrifying scenes which have followed it, in Vietnam and Cambodia for example, the spectacles presented by the Second World War are unanswerable. Here again, of course, it would be absurd to suggest that, say, the British or the American people went to war to abolish concentration camps. Quite the contrary; being generally unimaginative about other people's ills, although they technically 'knew' what was going on, they were largely unimpressed until their own armies actually reached the camps, and direct eyewitness accounts came to them by radio, by newsreel and in the Press. Yet whenever I encounter such compilations as that of M. Cru, and take in its passionate anti-war drift, when I consider the surge of pacifism of the 1930s, the notorious Oxford Union motion of February 1933 – that 'this House will in no circumstances fight for its King and Country' – the Peace Pledge Union founded by Canon 'Dick' Sheppard in October 1934 and the extraordinary 'Peace Ballot' held in that year (as well as more recent similar manifestations), I can think of nothing but those unforgettable faces with the wide, almost disbelieving eyes, pressed against the perimeter wire of the concentration camps in 1945. What those eyes were trying to take in was the arrival of the Allied soldiers. Their owners knew – none better – that if those soldiers had not appeared (in many cases, if they had been only one day later) then these scarcely believing watchers would have joined the literally millions who had already been done to death in the camps. That was what *that* war was against – and without the war those soldiers would never have come.

Preparations for war – the parades, the uniforms, the bands, the fleet exercises, the fly-pasts – can be a pretty sight; war itself is not a pretty thing. Its more appalling aspects move men differently. The painter Paul Nash, observing the landscapes of the First World War, wrote to his wife in November 1917: 'Evil and the incarnate fiend alone can be master of this war, and no glimmer of God's hand is seen anywhere.' He then paints a word-picture of his surroundings even more striking than those that he put on canvas; it is not difficult to understand his conclusion: 'I am no longer an artist interested and curious, I am a messenger who will bring back word from the men who are fighting to those who want the war to go on for ever. Feeble, inarticulate, will be my message, but it will have a bitter truth, and may it burn their lousy souls.'[11]
An officer of the Grenadier Guards writing to his mother in the same year, saw the landscape with exactly the same eye as Nash:

. . . this country stinks of corruption. As far as the eye can reach is that brown and torn sea of desolation and every yard there is a grave, some marked with rifles others with crosses, some with white skulls, some with beckoning hands. But everything is dead: the trees, the corn, the church, even the prayers of those that went there in their Sunday clothes with their sweaty pennies for the plate: it is all dead and God has utterly forsaken it.

But the Guards officer concludes on a different note from the artist's: 'The Irish Guards pipers – a new institution – with saffron kilts and green streamers, very jaunty, performed . . . the pipes and the saffron kilts brought us back to life and the warm red blood of youth and laughter, and we walked among the dead and thought only of the spring and its awakening.'[12] For another officer the message of the hideous battlefield was different again:

One cannot see these ragged and putrid bundles of what once were men without thinking of what they were – their cheerfulness, their courage, their idealism, their love for their dear ones at home. Man is such a marvellous, incredible mixture of soul and nerves and intellect, of bravery and heroism and love – it *cannot* be that it all ends in a bundle of rags covered with flies. These parcels of matter seem to me proof of immortality. This cannot be the end of so much.[13]

No, it is not difficult to understand those who, out of deep and serious feeling and consideration, cannot bear the thought of war. Yet these wars of the First Industrial Revolution, in whose shadow we all live, when all their mythologies are put aside, seem to me to display one thing: that though war is undoubtedly dreadful, it is not the worst evil. It is possible to take up a personal position against it – an allergy, as it were, to war, as one takes up personal positions towards certain forms of food, styles of art or fashion, or modes of behaviour – but it is difficult to take up a truly moral position against it. This proposition has been put with what I consider to be definitive lucidity; I can do no better than end by quoting the text:

The real difficulty which besets the philanthropist in his endeavour to exorcise the spirit of war is caused, not by the vices of this spirit, but by its virtues. In so far as it springs from vainglory or cupidity, it is comparatively easy to deal with. In so far as it is base, there is room for a bargain. It can be compounded with or bought off, as we have seen before now, with some kind of material currency. It will not stand out for very long against promises of prosperity and threats of dearth. But where, as at most crises, this spirit is not base, where its impulse is not less noble, but more noble than those which influence men day by day in the conduct of their worldly affairs, where the contrast which presents itself to their imagination is between duty on the one hand and gain on the other, between self-sacrifice and self-interest, between their country's need and their own ease, it is not possible to quench the fires by appeals proceeding from a lower plane. The philanthropist, if he is to succeed, must take still higher ground, and higher ground than this it is not a very simple matter to discover.[14]

---

1   Quoted by John T. Winterich in his introduction to *The Red Badge of Courage* by Stephen Crane, Folio Society, 1951, p. 7.
2   Peter J. Parish, *The American Civil War*, Eyre Methuen, 1975, p. 89.
3   Ibid., p. 88.
4   Paul Fussell, *The Great War and Modern Memory*, O.U.P., 1975, p. 97.
5   Major-General J. F. C. Fuller, *The Conduct of War 1789–1961*, Eyre and Spottiswoode, 1961, p. 144.
6   In Robert Blake (ed.), *The Private Papers of Douglas Haig*, (Eyre and Spottiswoode, 1952, p. 334), we find the following interesting exchange at a War Cabinet discussion of Armistice terms which Haig attended on 19 October 1918:'Mr Balfour (Foreign Secretary) spoke about deserting the Poles and the people of Eastern Europe, but the P.M. gave the opinion that we cannot expect the British to go on sacrificing their lives for the Poles.'
7   The suffragette movement fought to the tune of no less than 107 buildings set on fire in the first seven months of 1914; see George Dangerfield, *The Strange Death of Liberal England*, Paladin edition, 1970, p. 324.
8   Sir John Wheeler-Bennett, *Hindenburg: The Wooden Titan*, Macmillan, 1967, pp. 132–3, f.n.
9   Martin Kitchen, *A Military History of Germany*, Weidenfeld and Nicolson, 1975, pp. 225–6.
10 Neville Chamberlain, broadcast on 28 September 1938.
11 Quoted by Arthur Marwick, *The Deluge*, Bodley Head, 1965, p. 221.
12 Viscount Chandos, *From Peace to War: A Study in Contrast 1857–1918*, Bodley Head, 1968, p. 182.
13 Sir John Glubb, *Into Battle*, Cassell, 1977, p. 68.
14 F. S. Oliver, *Ordeal by Battle*, Macmillan, 1915, pp. 11–12. This is not a book about the morality of war, but about preparation for it.

Works Referred to in the Text

ATTERIDGE, A. H. *The British Army of Today*, T. C. and E. C. Jack (The People's Books), 1915.

BAKER-CARR, Brigadier-General C. D., *From Chauffeur to Brigadier*, Ernest Benn, 1930.

BALDWIN, Hanson W., *The Crucial Years 1939–41*, Weidenfeld and Nicolson, 1976.

BARCLAY, Brigadier C. N., *Armistice 1918*, Dent, 1968.

BARNETT, Correlli, *The Swordbearers*, Eyre and Spottiswoode, 1963. *The Collapse of British Power*, Eyre Methuen, 1972.

BARROW, General Sir George, *The Life of Sir Charles Carmichael Monro*, Hutchinson, 1931.

BEAN, Dr C. E. W., *Official History of Australia in the Great War 1914–18*, Angus and Robertson (vol. vi, 1942).

BEAVERBROOK, Lord, *Men and Power*, Hutchinson, 1956.

BIDWELL, Shelford, in *Encyclopedia of Land Warfare in the 20th Century* (part 3), Spring Books, 1977. *The Chindit War: The Campaign in Burma 1944*, Hodder and Stoughton, 1979.

BLAKE, Robert (ed.), *The Private Papers of Douglas Haig 1914–1919*, Eyre and Spottiswoode, 1952.

BLAXLAND, Gregory, *Destination Dunkirk*, William Kimber, 1973.

BLOEM, Walter, *The Advance from Mons, 1914*, Peter Davies, 1930.

BOND, Brian, *Liddell Hart: A Study of His Military Thought*, Cassell, 1977.

BORASTON, Lieutenant-Colonel J. H. (ed.), *Despatches of Field-Marshal Earl Haig*, Dent, 1919 and 1979.

BRIDGES, Lieutenant-General Sir Tom, *Alarms and Excursions*, Longmans Green and Co., 1938.

BRYANT, Arthur, *The Turn of the Tide*, Collins, 1957.

BUCKER, Georg, *In the Line*.

CAMPBELL, P. J., *In the Cannon's Mouth*, Hamish Hamilton, 1979.

CARRINGTON, C. E., *Soldier from the Wars Returning*, Hutchinson, 1965.

CARVER, Field-Marshal Lord (ed.), *The War Lords*, Weidenfeld and Nicolson, 1976.

CATTON, Bruce, *Grant Takes Command*, Dent, 1968.

CHALFONT, Alun, *Montgomery of Alamein*, Weidenfeld and Nicolson, 1976.

CHANDOS, Viscount, *From Peace to War: A Study in Contrast 1857–1918*, Bodley Head, 1968.

CHARTERIS, Brigadier-General John, *At G.H.Q.*, Cassell, 1931.

CHURCHILL, Sir Winston, *The World Crisis*, Odham's Ed., 1938. *The Second World War*, Cassell, 1950.

CONNELL, John, *Auchinleck,* Cassell, 1959.

CORBETT-SMITH, Major A., *The Retreat from Mons, By One Who Shared In It,* Cassell, 1916.

CRAIG, Gordon A., *Germany 1866–1945,* O.U.P., 1978

CRANE, Stephen, *The Red Badge of Courage,* Folio Society, 1951.

CROZIER, Brigadier-General F. P., *A Brass Hat in No Man's Land,* Jonathan Cape, 1930.

CRU, Jean Norton, *War Books: A Study in Historical Criticism,* San Diego University Press, 1976.

CRUTWELL, C. R. M. F., *A History of the Great War 1914–1918,* O.U.P., 1934.

DANGERFIELD, George, *The Strange Death of Liberal England,* Paladin ed., 1970.

DEAN, Sir Maurice, *The Royal Air Force and Two World Wars,* Cassell, 1979.

DUFF COOPER, *Haig,* Faber, 1935.

DUPUY, R. E. and DUPUY, T. N., *The Compact History of the Civil War,* Hawthorn Books (N.Y.), 1960.

EATON, Clement, *A History of the Southern Confederacy,* The Free Press (N.Y.), 1954.

EDMONDS, Charles (C. E. Carrington), *A Subaltern's War,* Peter Davies, 1929.

EDMONDS, Sir J. E., *Military Operations, France and Belgium,* Macmillan, H.M.S.O.(Official History). *A Short History of World War I,* O.U.P., 1951.

ELIOT, T. S., *Poems 1909–1925,* Faber, 1925.

ELLIS, L. F. and WARHURST, A. E., *Victory in the West,* H.M.S.O., 1968 (Official History).

ESHER, Lord, *Journals and Letters* (4 vols.), Nicolson and Watson, 1934.

FALLS, Cyril, *The First World War,* Longmans, 1960. *Armageddon 1918,* Weidenfeld and Nicolson, 1964.

FERGUSSON, Bernard, *Wavell; Portrait of a Soldier,* Collins, 1961.

FOCH, Marshal, *Memoirs* (trans. Colonel T. Bentley Mott), Heinemann, 1931.

FULLER, Major-General, J. F. C. *The Generalship of Ulysses S. Grant,* John Murray, 1929. *The Conduct of War, 1789–1961,* Eyre and Spottiswoode, 1961. *The Decisive Battles of the Western World* (3 vols.), Eyre and Spottiswoode, 1954–56.

FUSSELL, Paul, *The Great War and Modern Memory,* Oxford University Press, 1975.

GARDNER, Brian, *The Big Push,* Cassell, 1961.

GAULLE, General de, *France and Her Army,* Hutchinson, 1944.

GIBBS, Philip, *Realities of War,* Heinemann, 1920. *The Battles of the Somme,* Heinemann, 1917.

GILBERT, Martin, *Winston S. Churchill,* vol. iv, Companion Part I, Heinemann, 1977.

GILLON, Stair, *The Story of the 29th Division,* Nelson, 1925.

GLUBB, Sir John, *Into Battle,* Cassell, 1977.

GORCE, Paul-Marie de la, *The French Army,* Weidenfeld and Nicolson, 1963.

GOUGH, General Sir Hubert, *The Fifth Army,* Hodder and Stoughton, 1931.

GRAVES, Robert, *Goodbye to All That,* Penguin ed., 1960

GREENWELL, Graham H., *An Infant in Arms,* Allen Lane, The Penguin Press, 1972.

'G.S.O.', *G.H.Q. (Montreuil-sur-Mer),* Philip Allan, 1920.

GUDERIAN, Heinz, *Panzer Leader,* Michael Joseph, 1952.

HALDANE, Lord, *Autobiography,* Hodder and Stoughton, 1919.

HANKEY, Lord, *The Supreme Command 1914–1918* (2 vols.), Allen and Unwin, 1961.

HASTINGS, Max, *Bomber Command,* Michael Joseph, 1979.

HEADLAM, C., *The Guards Division in the Great War,* John Murray, 1924.

HEDIN, Sven, *With the German Armies in the West,* John Lane, The Bodley Head, 1915.

HINDENBURG, Field-Marshal von, *Out of My Life,* Cassell, 1920.

HORN, Daniel (ed.), *The Private War of Seaman Stump,* Leslie Frewin, 1969.

HORNE, Alistair, *To Lose a Battle,* Macmillan, 1969.

HOWARD, Michael, *The Franco-Prussian War,* Rupert Hart-Davis, 1961.

HUMBLE, Richard, *Tanks,* Weidenfeld and Nicolson, 1977.

JACOBSEN, H. A. and ROHWER, J. (eds.), *Decisive Battles of World War II: The German View,* André Deutsch, 1965.

JOFFRE, Marshal, *Memoirs* (trans. Colonel T. Bentley Mott), Geoffrey Bles, 1932.

JONES, David, *In Parenthesis,* Faber, 1937.

KIRBY, Major-General S. Woodburn, *The War Against Japan* (Official History), H.M.S.O., 1969.

KITCHEN, Martin, *A Military History of Germany,* Weidenfeld and Nicolson, 1975.

LAQUEUR, Walter, *Guerilla: A Historical and Critical Study,* Weidenfeld and Nicolson, 1977.

LASH, Joseph P., *Roosevelt and Churchill, 1939–1941,* André Deutsch, 1977.

LIDDELL HART, Sir Basil, *The Way to Win Wars (The Strategy of Indirect Approach),* Faber Q Books, 1942. *The Tanks* (2 vols.), Cassell, 1959. *Memoirs* (2 vols.), Cassell, 1965–66. *History of the First World War,* Cassell, 1970. *History of the Second World War,* Cassell, 1970.

LLOYD GEORGE, *War Memoirs* (2 vols.), Odham's, 1936.

LUCAS, Sir Charles (ed.), *The Empire at War* (6 vols.), O.U.P., 1926.

LUCAS, James, *Panzer Army Africa,* Macdonald and Jane's, 1977.

LUDENDORFF, General Erich, *My War Memories 1914–1918*, Hutchinson, 1919.

LYTTON, Neville, *The Press and the General Staff*, Collins, 1920.

MACDONAGH, Michael, *In London during the Great War*, Eyre and Spottiswoode, 1935.

MACDONALD, Charles B., *The Mighty Endeavour*, O.U.P., 1969.

MACLEOD, Colonel Roderick (ed.), *The Ironside Diaries*, Constable, 1972.

McGUFFIE, T. H., *Rank and File: The Common Soldier at Peace and War 1642–1914*, Hutchinson, 1964.

MAJDALANY, Fred, *Cassino: Portrait of a Battle*, Longmans, Green and Co., 1957.

MANCHESTER, William, *American Caesar: Douglas MacArthur 1880–1964*, Hutchinson, 1979.

MANGIN, General Charles, *Lettres de Guerre 1914–1918*, Librairie Arthème Fayard, 1950.

MANNING, Frederick, *The Middle Parts of Fortune*, Peter Davies, 1977.

MARWICK, Arthur, *The Deluge*, Bodley Head, 1965.

MASTERS, John, *The Road Past Mandalay*, Michael Joseph, 1961.

MAURICE, Major-General Sir F., *Forty Days in 1914*, Constable, 1919.

MONASH, Lieutenant-General Sir John, *War Letters*, Angus and Robertson, 1925. *The Australian Victories in France in 1918*, Angus and Robertson, 1936.

MORDAL, Jacques, 'Les Pertes Humaines dans les Guerres Mondiales', *Miroir de l'Histoire*, September 1961.

OLIVER, F. S., *Ordeal by Battle*, Macmillan, 1915. *The Anvil of War*, Macmillan, 1936.

OMAN, Sir Charles, 'German Losses on the Somme', *The Nineteenth Century and After*, May 1927.

PANICHAS, George A. (ed.), *Promise of Greatness*, Cassell, 1968.

PARISH, Peter J., *The American Civil War*, Eyre Methuen, 1975.

POGUE, Forrest C., *George C. Marshall: Ordeal and Hope*, Macgibbon and Kee, 1966.

PONSONBY of Shoulbrede, Lord, *Falsehood in War-time*, Allen and Unwin, 1928.

PRENDERGAST, Brigadier John, *Prender's Progress*, Cassell, 1979.

REPINGTON, Colonel, *The First World War*, Constable, 1920.

RICHARDS, Frank, *Old Soldiers Never Die*, Faber Paperback, 1964.

ROBERTSON, Field-Marshal Sir William, *Soldiers and Statesmen 1914–1918* (2 vols.), Cassell, 1926.

ROGERS, Colonel H. C. B., *Tanks in Battle*, Seeley Service, 1965.

ROGERSON, Sidney, *Twelve Days*, Arthur Barker, 1933. *The Last of the Ebb*, Arthur Barker, 1937.

ROSKILL, Captain Stephen, *Hankey: Man of Secrets*, Collins, 1970.

SALISBURY, Harrison E. (ed.), *Marshal Zhukov's Greatest Battles*, MacDonald, 1969.

SASSOON, Siegfried, *Selected Poems*, Heinemann, 1925.

232

SHEPPERD, G. A., *The Italian Campaign 1943–45*, Arthur Barker, 1968.

SIXSMITH, General E. K. G., *Douglas Haig*, Weidenfeld and Nicolson, 1976.

SLACK, Cecil M., *Grandfather's Adventures in the Great War 1914–1918*, Arthur H. Stockwell, 1977.

SLIM, Field-Marshal Lord, *Defeat into Victory*, Cassell, 1956.

SPEARS, Sir Edward, *Prelude to Victory*, Jonathan Cape, 1939.
Statistics of the Military Effort of the British Empire, H.M.S.O., 1922.

STONE, Norman, *The Eastern Front 1914–1917*, Hodder and Stoughton, 1975.

SWINTON, Major-General Sir Ernest, *Eyewitness*, Hodder and Stoughton, 1932.

TAYLOR, A. J. P., *The First World War*, Hamish Hamilton, 1963. *The Course of German History*, Hamish Hamilton, 1945; Methuen University Paperback, 1961.

TERRAINE, John, *Douglas Haig: The Educated Soldier*, Hutchinson, 1963. *The Western Front*, Hutchinson, 1964. *The Mighty Continent*, B.B.C. and Hutchinson, 1974. *The Road to Passchendaele*, Leo Cooper, 1977. *To Win a War*, Sidgwick and Jackson, 1978.

TRYTHALL, Anthony John, *'Boney' Fuller: The Intellectual General*, Cassell, 1977.

TUCHMAN, Barbara W., *The Guns of August*, Macmillan (N.Y.), 1962.

TUCKER, John F., *Johnny Get Your Gun: A Personal Narrative of the Somme, Ypres and Arras*, William Kimber, 1978.

WARNER, Philip, *Panzer*, Weidenfeld and Nicolson, 1977.

WATT, D. C., *A History of the World in the Twentieth Century*, Hodder and Stoughton, 1967.

WATT, Richard M., *Dare Call it Treason*, Chatto and Windus, 1964.

WERTH, Alexander, *Russia at War 1941–1945*, Barrie and Rockliff, 1964.

WHEELER-BENNETT, Sir John, *Hindenburg: The Wooden Titan*, Macmillan, 1967.

WILLIAMS, T. H., *Lincoln and His Generals*, Hamish Hamilton, 1952.

WILLIAMS–ELLIS, C. and A., *The Tank Corps*, George Newnes, 1919.

WILMOT, Chester, *The Struggle for Europe*, Collins, 1952.

WILSON, H. W. and HAMMERTON, J. A., *The Great War: The Standard History of the All-Europe Conflict* (13 vols.), Amalgamated Press, 1914–18.

WOOD, Herbert Fairlie, *Vimy!*, Macdonald, 1967.

WOODWARD, David, *Armies of the World 1854–1918*, Sidgwick and Jackson, 1978.

WOODWARD, Sir Llewellyn, *Great Britain and the War of 1914–1918*, Methuen, 1967.

YOUNG, Peter, *World War 1939–1945*, Arthur Barker, 1966.

GENERAL INDEX

INDEX OF
MILITARY FORMATIONS